DEVELOPING AND VALIDATING MULTIPLE-CHOICE TEST ITEMS

Thomas M. Haladyna

Arizona State University West

 LAWRENCE ERLBAUM ASSOCIATES, PUBLISHERS

1994   Hillsdale, New Jersey   Hove, UK

Lawrence Erlbaum Associates, Inc., Publishers
365 Broadway
Hillsdale, New Jersey 07642

Cover design by Kate Dusza

Library of Congress Cataloging-in-Publication Data

Haladyna, Thomas M.
      Developing and validating multiple-choice test items /
   Thomas M. Haladyna.
          p.   cm.
      Includes bibliographical references and index.
      ISBN 0-8058-1206-7
      1. Multiple-choice examinations—Design and construction.
   2. Multiple-choice examinations—Validity. I. Title.
   LB3060.32.M85H35   1994
   371.2'61—dc20   93-45543
                                              CIP

Books published by Lawrence Erlbaum Associates are printed on
acid-free paper, and their bindings are chosen for strength and dura-
bility.

Printed in the United States of America
10 9 8 7 6 5 4 3 2 1

DEVELOPING AND VALIDATING MULTIPLE-CHOICE TEST ITEMS

CONTENTS

INTRODUCTION

Simply stated, this book addresses the related topics of multiple-choice test item development and validation of responses to these test items, which are two critical steps in the development of many cognitive tests.

Several factors contributed to the writing of this book. The first is that although statistical theories of test scores are very well developed and understood, item writing and validation are the least developed among those involved in test development. Textbooks on testing provide information on item writing and item analysis, but typically these sections are brief and not linked to existing theory or research. Volumes devoted solely to item writing and validation are very rare. Several writers have commented about the lack of research on item writing (e.g., Cronbach, 1971; Haladyna & Downing, 1989a, 1989b; Nitko, 1984). Thus, we seem to have very little information to guide our item writing practices.

Another reason for writing this book is that over the past 20 years, I have been fortunate to have been involved in a variety of test development activities and research on testing in a variety of settings that include large-scale educational assessments in reading, writing, and mathematics, as well as licensing or certification tests in accountancy, dietetics, emergency medicine technology, medical specialties (such as facial plastic surgery, hand surgery, cosmetic surgery, ophthalmology, otolaryngology), nursing, pharmacy, and denture technology. During this period I also had the opportunity to assist the U. S. Army in the evaluation of their Skill Qualification Tests used in their various training programs, including military police, military intelligence, aerial reconnaissance, chemical warfare, and rocket launch systems. To add to these experiences, teaching graduate students and undergraduate students in teacher training has enriched my perspective about the need for more effective item writing and validation. This book draws from these experiences and the extant theory, research, and technology available.

This book is intended for those persons who are seriously involved and interested in educational ability or achievement testing. Students in a graduate-level course in educational measurement or testing may find this book helpful for understanding these two critical phases of test development better. Persons directly involved in testing programs may find much of this material useful either as a reference or as new material to enhance their present understanding and their item development and validation practices.

Earlier similar treatments of multiple-choice item development and validation exist, and it would be remiss not to mention and recognize these contributions and state how this book stands relative to its predecessors.

With respect to item development, the chapter on multiple-choice testing in the first edition of *Educational Measurement* by Robert Ebel (1951) represents a major milestone in multiple-choice item writing. The chapter in the second edition of *Educational Measurement* by Wesman (1971) is another important contribution. Interestingly, both writers noted the paucity of theory and research on item writing, but their pleas for more serious study were largely ignored in the 1960s and 1970s. In Europe, monographs by Brown (1966) and MacIntosh and Morrison (1969) gave way to Woods (1977), whose monograph on multiple-choice testing was current to that date. Bormuth (1970) formulated a theory of item writing that attempted to make this process more objective and less under the idiosyncratic control of individuals. He attacked traditional ways of writing items as "unscientific." His item-generating algorithms and the work of other theorists is chronicled in a book by Roid and Haladyna (1982). Recently, Osterlind (1989) produced a book devoted to the topic of constructing test items. Millman and Greene (1989) provided a brief treatment of item development in the third edition of *Educational Measurement*. In that same volume, Nitko (1989) discussed the important concept of integrating teaching and testing. He provided us with important emerging concepts about many processes involved in pre-item-writing activities in the realm of achievement testing. But his chapter did not provide precise advice about the actual writing of test items.

With respect to item validation, we have witnessed an evolution in understanding that began with primitive ideas about item difficulty and item discrimination in the 1930s. Item analysis has been a standard feature of virtually any type of multiple-choice testing program. But as Wainer (1989) stated, item analysis is becoming necessarily more complicated. Item response theory has expanded our understanding of the nature of the item response. Chapters in successive editions of *Educational Measurement* by Henrysson (1971) and Millman and Greene (1989) have provided many insights about this evolution, but many basic theoretical papers have provided a greater foundation for the concept of item validation as presented in this volume.

Limitations of This Book

Although this book intends to provide a comprehensive treatment of multiple-choice item development and validation, it is limited in several ways.

First and foremost, although we have extensive statistical theories for test scores, we currently lack comparable validated theories of item writing. Hence, the section of this book on item development offers a technology that is not supported by theoretical development. On the other hand, some research has been reported that supports some practices and repudiates other practices.

Second, renewed interest in measuring higher level cognitive behavior has spurred educators to consider new ways to measure this elusive entity. Although, the Bloom taxonomy has continued to be considered by many practitioners, scientific evidence supporting its use is lacking (Seddon, 1976). We do not have a suitable taxonomy or typology of higher level thinking upon which to base our item-writing practices. In this volume a chapter is devoted to writing items to reflect higher level thinking, but, again, the advice is merely prescriptive and not grounded in theoretical analysis or research that validates this analysis. Although they are not validated by research, prescriptions have proven helpful to item writers in phrasing items that putatively reflect their intent, higher level thinking.

Third, we are facing paradigm shifts in the definition and measurement of both ability and achievement. This change appears to be a natural outgrowth of theory building, but school reform also may have something to do with these changes. Learners are being asked to do more than memorize responses to questions. They are being asked to think, reason, and create. Therefore testing must meet this challenge. Ability testing has been dominated by general factor theorists dating back to the beginning of this century and before with the Binet Intelligence Test and the Terman/Stanford revision. Nearly a century later and after literally thousands of validity studies, Gardner (1985) and Sternberg (1977) renewed our interest in multifactor intelligence with theories that replace the ideas of multifactor advocates Thurstone and Guilford in past generations. To say that we have a well-established paradigm for either position with respect to ability would be misleading. Nonetheless, a continuous, active debate has been sustained over most of this century over the complexity of human thought, and this debate promises to continue into the next century.

Achievement testing is also undergoing significant change. Richard Anderson (1972) claimed that we usually fail to define what we test, and, more recently, Cole (1991) described some of the problems we face in educational achievement measurement, also calling for clearer definition. Shepard (1991) revealed the ambiguity felt by practitioners who are trying to understand and adjust to this change. Some practitioners take a more behavioral view of learning, viewing it as existing in "chunks" of knowledge to be learned one chunk at a time; a more current view might view learning as a mosaic, where the whole crystallizes through a series of planned experiences. Cognitive psychologists and statistical test theorists are beginning to work in partnerships to link abstract cognitive processes with its measurement.

It is unlikely that any of these shortcomings will be corrected very soon. Item development and validation are still neonatal and dynamic processes, greatly in need of more theorizing and validating research.

Attacks and Reform in Testing

Multiple-choice testing has experienced many attacks in the past, some justified and some not. In the 1960s, harsh criticism of the "evils" of multiple-choice testing was leveled from such well known critics as Banesh Hoffman (1964), who wrote *Tyranny of Testing*. David Owen (1985) in his book *None of the Above* continued to assail the dangers of multiple-choice testing. The specific focus of his criticism was the multiple-choice *Scholastic Aptitude Test*, which is given to 1 million students annually. The well-known consumer activist, Ralph Nader, was quoted as saying that with standardized testing "60 years of idiocy is enough" (The FairTest Examiner, 1987, p. 1). Nader criticized the failure of the multiple-choice format to measure the more important outcomes of schooling and human enterprises such as determination, idealism, wisdom, strategic reasoning, judgment, experience, persistence, stamina, creativity, and writing skill. Although it is true that the multiple-choice format is not useful for measuring many highly prized human traits, responsible test makers have never claimed this ability on behalf of the multiple-choice format. The purpose of a multiple-choice test is to measure some aspects of abilities or achievement. Most test specialists still promote the multiple-choice format as the best tool among those available.

The attacks on multiple-choice testing have come more recently from other directions. For instance, Shepard (1993) contended that multiple-choice testing lends itself to multiple-choice teaching. Shepard further argued that such teaching and testing is harmful to learners. Although comments like these are not substantiated by research, cognitive psychologists are exploring format differences in mental behavior and in instances are drawing conclusions that the use of a particular format, multiple-choice or constructed response, does make a difference in the type of behavior being elicited. However, a more moderate view was expressed by Snow (1993), a leader in the testing reform movement and a reputable cognitive psychologist. He seeks a research agenda for better understanding the nuances of format in testing various types of cognitive behavior.

Despite the attacks on the multiple-choice format, multiple-choice testing has actually thrived in recent years. The need to inform policy makers and evaluators is great enough to continue to support testing programs. Little doubt should exist that testing is a major enterprise that directly or indirectly affects virtually everyone in the United States. With more than 1,400 published tests and over 400 test publishers, clearly testing is a big business (Osterlind, 1989). Not only are test companies growing in terms of multiple-choice standardized testing, but classroom testing is a firm fixture in public and private elementary and secondary schools, graduate education, professional training, and industry. Multiple-choice tests are used in many ways: placement, selection, awards, certification, licensure, course credit (proficiency), grades, diagnosis of what has and has not been learned, and even employment. According to Yeh, Herman, and Rudner (1981), more than 90% of schools and school districts use some form of standardized testing. State-mandated testing occurs in 42 of 50 states (*FairTest Examiner*, 1988). Of the approximately 40 million students in elementary and secondary schools, about 17 million take state-mandated tests each year (*FairTest Examiner*, 1988). More than 100 million persons in the United States are estimated to take some form of a standardized, multiple-choice test each year (*Fair Test Examiner*, 1988). When one considers that most classrooms and training centers in the nation also use the multiple-choice for nonstandardized testing, the actual number of persons taking multiple-choice tests must be even larger.

Recently, a noticeable shift in thinking has occurred in education regarding test formats. This shift is a byproduct of educational reform efforts (Toch, 1991), as well as a concerted effort from theorists representing cognitive psychology and testing. *Authentic assessment* is ballyhooed as a more meaningful, richer, and more appropriate way to measure educational achievement (Wiggins, 1989). This type of testing, more accurately performance- or product-based testing, essentially requires students to construct responses to complex test items. Makers and users of these items purport to reflect such characteristics as problem solving, reasoning, and critical thinking. Evaluators of student work use rating scales, called *scoring rubrics,* to judge the performance on these items. Although there are many good qualities of these performance/product-centered tests, many unsolved technical problems exist, and the validity of interpretations and uses of performance test results has not yet been resolved. Also these tests are very expensive to design and administer, and their integration with classroom teaching is a technology that is not well developed. Despite these limitations, performance/product-centered tests, which have always been a feature of sound instruction, will continue to evolve to higher forms, and their use will increase in large-scale testing programs.

In spite of these attacks on multiple-choice testing and the multiple-choice format, a major premise of this book is that there is, indeed, a place for multiple-choice testing for many legitimate purposes. Admittedly, many things are wrong with the way multiple-choice test results are presently interpreted and used. Clearly the public and many test developers and users need to be more cognizant of the *Standards for Educational and Psychological Testing* (1985). Once test users are clear about how test results should and should not be used, the quality of tests can be increased through the use of sensible and effective item development and item response validation procedures as found in this book.

Organization of the Book

The book is organized into four sections.

The first section provides a foundation for using multiple-choice items. Chapter 1 discusses the problems faced in measuring ability and achievement and the basis for using test items of various formats and tests in the framework of construct validation. Chapter 2 provides a rationale for the multiple-choice format over the constructed-response format for some kinds of cognitive behavior. Research bearing on this important issue is reviewed and synthesized. Chapter 3 discusses strengths and weaknesses of various multiple-choice formats based on several current reviews of research.

The second section contains three chapters that provide advice on how to write various types of multiple-choice test items. Many examples are provided from various sources. Chapter 4 provides a typology of item writing rules and many examples of well and poorly written items in various formats. This typology is based on two sources, the collective wisdom of various textbook writers and extant research. Chapter 5 provides a structure for writing and organizing items into various categories of higher level thinking. Chapter 6 describes the role of item shells in the creation of test items. Item shells are an item writer's aid to unblock "writer's block."

The third section addresses the complex concept of item response validation. Chapter 7 reports on the rationale and procedures involved in a coordinated series of item reviews intended to improve each test item. Chapter 8 deals with the statistical analysis of item responses to study and improve test items. A theoretical perspective is offered that accommodates working within the frameworks of both classical and item response theories. Chapter 9 offers information about how the study of item responses can be used to treat specific problems encountered in testing.

The fourth section contains a single chapter 10 which deals with the future of these two intertwined topics, item writing and item response validation. Unlike what we experience today, cognitive theorists are working on better defining what we teach and measure, and test theorists are developing item response models that are more appropriate to measuring some forms of complex behavior. This chapter reviews these emerging theories and the existing context in which they must be nurtured. The fruition of many of these theories will change the face of U. S. education in very profound ways.

In closing, development and validation of test items still remain as two critical steps in test development. This book intends to help readers understand the concepts, principles, and procedures available to construct better test items that will lead to better tests of ability and achievement.

Thomas M. Haladyna

A FOUNDATION FOR
MULTIPLE-CHOICE TESTING

1

A CONTEXT FOR MULTIPLE-CHOICE TESTING

Overview

This chapter provides a basis for the use of the multiple-choice test item format for measuring many types of ability and educational achievement. The constructs of ability and achievement are each undergoing serious attempts at redefinition. First, these two constructs are reviewed in light of these paradigmatic changes, then construct validation is discussed as the appropriate process for defining and developing measures of these constructs and for validating test score interpretations and uses. Finally, the chapter defines the roles of item development and item response validation in the contexts of changes in ability and achievement and in the context of construct validation. The essential view expressed here is that all cognitive behavior can be observed, and the measuring device may call for recognizing answers or constructing answers. Within this view, multiple-choice has a vital function.

Two Aspects of Cognitive Behavior

Two important cognitive constructs are ability and educational achievement. Messick (1984) defined abilities as "general reasoning and comprehension skills important in formal schooling that develop through learning and transfer from nonschool as well as school experiences" (p. 221). Educational achievement refers to cognitive behavior that is changeable—more subject to life's experiences. Within the education context, the main life experience is school and the teaching/learning encounters that students face in school. Although the two constructs are highly correlated, abilities are viewed as more slowly developed over a lifetime and predictors of the rate of achievement, whereas achievement is viewed as more dynamic. The next two sections of this chapter describe the status of these two constructs and how the proposed changes may affect the way we design test items and use item responses.

The Construct of Ability

The term *intelligence* has served for most of this century to describe this principal factor of cognitive behavior. The term has fallen into disfavor due to unfortunate historical misuses of intelligence test scores. Arthur Jensen's controversial research provoked significant reactions for and against his ideas about determinants of intelligence (Jensen, 1980) that may have contributed to the further unpopularity of this term. Another term used synonymously with intelligence is *scholastic aptitude*. No differentiation among these terms is intended throughout this book.

For most of this century, theory and research have favored a one-factor view of ability. The Spearman one-factor theory of intelligence has been well supported by research, including the famous Terman longitudinal studies of giftedness (Terman & Oden, 1959). However, the one-factor view of intelligence has been periodically challenged. In the 1930s, Thurstone formulated his primary mental abilities (Thurstone, 1938), and his test was widely used. In the 1960s and 1970s, Guilford's Structure of the Intellect model was supported by research (Guilford, 1967), but interest in this model has waned considerably since his passing. Gardner (1986) posited a theory of multiple intelligences and Sternberg (1977) introduced a componential theory of human abilities, both of which have generated considerable interest. Although enthusiasm for these multiple intelligence ideas has been renewed, this century-long history of the study of human intelligence in the United States has shown that scientific revolutions of this kind are hard to sustain. The cumulative body of evidence continues to support one-factor theory. However, the work of cognitive psychologists (Snow & Lohman, 1989) and reform initiatives (Toch, 1991) may fuel the efforts of persons involved in the present multifactor movement. But much remains to be achieved.

The Construct of Educational Achievement

R. Anderson (1972) has been a vehement critic of achievement measurement, stating bluntly "that educational research workers have not yet learned how to development achievement tests that meet the primitive first requirement for a system of measurement, namely that there is a clear and consistent definition of the things being counted" (p. 245).

Nearly 20 years later, this lament was echoed by Cole (1990) in her American Educational Research Association presidential address, and more recently by Glaser (1993) in a retrospective essay about achievement testing. According to

Cole, some of the conditions contributing to this problem of defining educational achievement are (a) the need for a theoretical framework for thinking about achievement, (b) implications for instructional practices from achievement test results, and (c) recognition of the need for long-term goals, as opposed to what current policy and national, state, and school district testing require with short-term goals.

Shepard (1991) reported on how this problem of definition is manifested among measurement practitioners. One group views educational achievement as the acquisition of basic skills. Learning is unitary, linear, and sequential. Complex learning follows the learning at low cognitive levels, such as recall of facts and comprehension of concepts and principles. This historical view of educational achievement is reflected in Bloom's mastery learning (Bloom, 1968), the personalized system of instruction (Keller, 1968), and competency-based instruction (Spady, 1977), among others. These methods appear to derive from behaviorism, because of the strong influence of a stimulus–response framework based on extrinsic reinforcement schedules with student outcomes being operationally defined via behavioral objectives.

An alternative view of educational achievement comes from cognitive learning theory. Rather than viewing learning as the aggregate of knowledge and skills, Shepard (1991) pointed out that learning may be represented as a mosaic, where complex cognitive behavior crystallizes in a developmental manner that is more patchwork than linear and sequential. Messick (1984) also observed that educational achievement has this developmental nature. Indeed, Snow and Lohman (1989) have synthesized the extensive and current work of cognitive psychologists toward the objective of crystallizing complex thinking and the observing how it happens. Test theorists are actively working on appropriate item response models (Frederiksen, Mislevy, & Bejar, 1993).

Another important distinction Messick (1984) made is between educational achievement and *competence*. Educational achievement consists of knowledge and skills that arise directly from a course of study, whereas educational competence is a broader concept that encompasses a course or program of study as well as other life experiences. Based on this definition, competency tests differ from achievement tests in their scope.

Although abilities are slow to develop, they appear to influence achievement. What is traditionally called "transfer of learning" or "generalizability" involves the use of developed abilities to enable complex types of achievement. This important connection between ability and achievement demonstrates how important ability is to achievement. Because ability is slowly developed, the implication is that it can be taught, but testing for accountability can be troublesome, because ability is slow to emerge and is not captured well with a single test item or test.

The reconceptualization of achievement will likely follow two complementary traditional dimensions: content and cognitive operations.

Content Dimension

David Merrill and his colleagues have described the content of educational achievement as consisting of facts, concepts, principles, and procedures (Merrill, Reigeluth, & Faust, 1979). Content can be viewed as the basic stock of learning, that all learner outcome statements and measures in some way may be classified according to one of these four essential types of content. Chapter 5 provides a more thorough discussion of this typology for content.

Cognitive Behavior Dimension

The Bloom taxonomy has served as a device for organizing cognitive behavior into six categories: memory, translation, interpretation, application, analysis, synthesis, and evaluation. Despite decades of use, research has not been very supportive (e.g., Miller, Snowman, & O'Hara, 1979; Seddon, 1978). An elementary distinction of cognitive behaviors is that between *knowledge* and *skills*. The former refers to the organization, storage, and retrieval of facts, concepts, principles, and procedures. Many types of higher level thinking can be viewed as complex entities involving these four types of content. Skills refer to the use of this content in simple or complex chains. Some skills, such as musical or artistic performance, are directly assessed, directly visible, and easily observed. Other skills, such as problem solving or reasoning, are indirectly assessed, inferred from some responses but not palpably or tangibly observed.

An emerging conceptualization that likely will replace the primitive knowledge–skill distinction is *declarative knowledge* versus *procedural knowledge* (Snow & Lohman, 1989). Declarative knowledge involves facts, concepts, principles, and procedures that we store in an organizational framework and retrieve when needed. Procedural knowledge is the use of declarative knowledge to accomplish an end.

Declarative knowledge can be characterized as many related semantic networks. The organization of these networks is critical to their use. Context-bound organizations are more difficult to construct but are more easily retrieved, while semantic memory is easy to construct but offers only short-term benefits (Snow & Lohman, 1989). From this analysis, we see that meaningful learning is more likely to be retained and used while meaningless learning is easy to acquire and measure, but difficult to retain over time. For the purpose of educational accountability, it may be easy to demonstrate that a class, school, or school district can demonstrate a high level of meaningless learning, but long-term effects may be negligible. On the other hand, meaningful learning may be harder to acquire and measure, but should have more pronounced long-term effects.

As stated earlier, procedural knowledge involves the use of declarative knowledge. Various theorists have described the developmental nature of declarative knowledge in stages. In the first stage, students know what to do but do not know how to do it. In the second stage, they develop primitive sequences of behavior to perform the complex procedure. In the final stage they have automated their behavior by condensing these steps into a single routine. A simple example of this might be hitting a golf ball. Seeing a person hit a ball may provide declarative knowledge. Taking golf lessons may formalize this declarative knowledge. Wanting to hit the ball represents motivation. Learning the steps in hitting the ball is the first stage of procedural knowledge, while hitting the ball mechanically is the second stage. The third stage manifests itself in a smooth, graceful swing that produces a consistent result. Procedural knowledge applies to physical as well as mental performance.

A more important and rare type of behavior is *strategic knowledge* (Greeno, 1980). Strategic knowledge involves the development of goals and strategies for attaining certain objectives. Traditional schooling clearly emphasizes the easy-to-measure declarative knowledge, whereas what practitioners call *authentic assessment* appears to emphasize procedural knowledge set in a meaningful context. But the teaching and measurement of strategic knowledge will be more problematic. Nevertheless, several item-writing technologies reported in several chapters in this book, including the *context-dependent item set* (Haladyna, 1992), appear suitable for measuring some types of strategic knowledge.

Ample evidence exists to suggest a crisis in the measurement of higher level outcomes for achievement tests (Crooks, 1988; Green, Halpin, & Halpin, 1990; Stiggins, Griswold, & Stikelund, 1989). Teachers at all levels, including college and graduate education, seldom adequately define, teach, and test higher level outcomes. At the same time concern is widely expressed that we need to test for these higher level outcomes (Nickerson, 1989). The failure to do so may be attributed to inexperience, lack of useful cognitive theory for school learning, lack of item writing theories and technology (Roid & Haladyna, 1982), or accountability (Shepard, 1991).

The reconceptualization of achievement will likely include strategic knowledge and emphasize procedural and declarative knowledge. Traditional multiple-choice achievement tests are viewed as effective ways to measure declarative knowledge, whereas newer forms of performance/product-centered tests may be more effective measures of procedural knowledge (Shavelson, Baxter, & Pine, 1992; Wiggins, 1989). The exclusive use of multiple-choice test formats in cognitive tests will end, as more attention is paid to using the format that most efficiently and appropriately measures what we intend to measure.

This next section deals with a process of construct validation, as applied to the contexts of ability and achievement measurement. The necessity for this treatment is to not only describe this process, but illustrate through the validation of ability or achievement test scores, that item development and item response validation are integral to the validation of test scores.

Construct Validation

The validity of any test score interpretation or use is dependent upon the evidence collected to support that interpretation or use. Validation is a necessary step in any testing program. In fact, the *Standards for Educational and Psychological Testing* (American Psychological Association, 1985) are very explicit about the need for validation in its first standard:

> Evidence of validity should be presented for the major types of infer-
> ences for which the use of a test is recommended. A rationale should be
> provided to support the particular mix of evidence presented for the
> intended uses. (p.13)

Messick (1975, 1984, 1989) consistently and effectively argued that all educational measures should be construct referenced, that the traditional trinity of validities including construct, content, and criterion related is really a matter of construct validity.

Messick (1989) also pointed out that specific interpretations and uses of test results are subject to a context made up of value implications and social conse-quences. Thus, it is insufficient to think that construct validation is merely the systematic collection of evidence to support a specific test interpretation or use. We must also think of the context that may underlie and influence this interpretation or use.

A good example of this point comes from the condition in schools where standardized test scores are used as a criterion for educational accountability. Because of external pressure to raise test scores to show educational improvement, some school personnel will take extreme measures to increase test scores. Studies like that of Nolen, Haladyna, and Haas (1992) show the variety of techniques used to raise scores. Haladyna, Nolen, and Haas (1991) and Mehrens and Kaminski (1989) questioned the ethics of many of these practices. McGill-Franzen and Allington (1993) further questioned whether the issue is one of validation at all or more importantly a "child advocacy issue." Paris, Lawton, Turner, and Roth (1991) reported on the pejorative effects of this pressure for accountability on children, whereas Mary Lee Smith (1991) spoke of the demeaning of the profession of teaching due to this quest for accountability. Thus, the value of Messick's idea about context of social values and consequences is vividly illustrated by this industry for raising test scores without considering the real costs for those who are targeted in this educational reformation—the children. Indeed the context is part of construct validation.

The Process of Construct Validation

Three essential phases in construct validation are formulation, explication, and validation (Cronbach, 1971). The first two steps are part of the process of theorizing leading to variable creation, whereas the third step is the empirical verification of predictions made or hypotheses drawn as a result of our theorizing. Figure 1.1 abstractly shows the logical connectedness among these three phases.

In formulation, theoretical constructs are named and defined, and their interrelationships are described in a causal network. The failure to adequately define such terms as problem solving, reasoning, abstract thinking, critical thinking, and the like may be one of the primary reasons we have so much difficulty measuring higher level thinking.

Through this process of formulation, the definition and connectedness of constructs must be clear enough for researchers to construct variables that behave according to the lawfulness of our hypothetical constructs, as Fig. 1.1 illustrates. In Fig. 1.1, constructs A, B, and C are defined, and their relationships are described, as A has a causal influence on B and B has, in turn, a causal influence on C.

In explication, measures of each construct are created or identified. Generally, multiple measures are used to more adequately tap all the aspects of each construct. In Fig. 1.1, variable a is a measure of construct A; variable b is a measure of construct B; variable c is a measure of construct C. The process of explication encompasses all of those activities we know as *test development*, including development of content specifications and test specifications, item writing, test design, test construction, test production, and test administration.

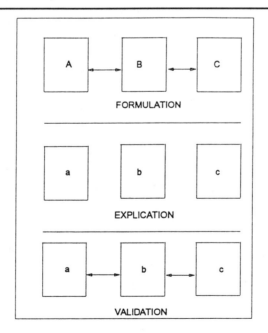

Fig. 1.1. The logic of construct validation.

In validation, empirical observations are collected with the objective of proving or disproving the reasoning used in the formulation stage. Some of the important specific studies involved in validation include (a) reliability of test scores, (b) group differences, (c) trends over time, and (d) relationships. In each of these studies, implicit standards or objectives exist, and empirical verification is a desirable quality if an interpretation or use of a test score is construct valid. Validity, however, is a matter of degrees, not absolutes. This evidence is taken collectively as supporting or not supporting interpretations or uses to some degree. The caution or aura of doubt about each interpretation or use is always present, because the process of construct validation seldom provides complete evidence of validity. In summary, we must recognize that validity exists in degrees and is a property of test interpretations or uses, not of tests.

For the abstract example shown in Fig. 1.1, validation involves the use of a causal modeling procedure, such as LISREL or path analysis, to explore the credibility of the theoretical formulation that A influences B, and B influences C.

The interpretation or use of a measure of a familiar construct, such as ability or achievement, can be undermined by any of three types of problems:

1. failure to define constructs adequately (inadequate formulation),
2. failure to identify or create measures of the aspects of each construct (inadequate explication), or
3. failure to assemble adequate evidence supporting interpretations and uses of test scores (inadequate validation).

The next section examines the construct validation of achievement test scores in the current environment of educational accountability and reform.

Construct Validation of Achievement Test Scores

As noted earlier in this chapter, the initial consideration in construct validation is identifying the interpretation or use intended for the test scores. Haladyna et al. (1991) provided a convenient list of 29 possible interpretations or uses of educational achievement measures, shown in Table 1.1. This list is further complicated by the fact that for each interpretation or use, we may use different units of analysis, and for each of these units of analysis, interpretations or uses are likely to be different (Sirotnik, 1979). Because of this, construct validity evidence is needed for each unit of analysis. Millman and Greene (1989) describe two kinds of inferences we might wish to make, curricular and instructional. Most achievement tests are designed with these inferences in mind, for the purpose of evaluating a curriculum innovation or instructional effectiveness. However, other interpretations or uses are often made without any supporting evidence (Haertel, 1986; Haladyna et al., 1991; Mehrens & Kaminski, 1989).

Formulation

In this initial stage of construct validation, the construct we wish to measure is defined. Unfortunately, as with the item writing, no well established technique exists yet for defining constructs.

Unfortunately, we have no well accepted theory of school learning that clearly defines school achievement, and the construct of ability has continually been under scrutiny as a one-dimensional versus a multidimensional entity. Thus, we are faced with the practical necessity of measuring constructs that are not well established in the methodology of construct validity. This confirms Anderson's and Cole's criticisms about our general failure to define educational achievement and to adequately measure it, which was discussed earlier in this chapter.

Further, a technique for taking abstract definitions of content and clarifying these as an enabling process is sorely needed. Millman and Green (1989) provided a brief discussion of content in test design and raised important issues such as (a) sources of content, (b) dimensionality, (c) bandwidth-fidelity, (d) domain and norm-referenced interpretations, and (e) content distribution. The procedures for resolving these issues do not yet exist in a well documented testing technology.

Nonetheless, we variously have used goals, objectives, topic outlines, and textbooks to define content. Some theoretical work was reported using domain specifications as methods to operationalize constructs (see Roid & Haladyna, 1982). With these approaches, item-generating algorithms operationally define the content domain through the use of rules for developing test items. But none of this work is recent or has developed into common practice. For certification and licensing tests, which by Messick's definition measure competency (Messick, 1984), professional organizations conduct job analyses, task analyses, practice analyses, or role delineation studies that carefully document what a practicing professional does, how often they do it, and how important they think each task is to their profession.

In summary, construct formulation for educational achievement has not yet been successfully completed, as critics Anderson (1972) and Cole (1990) have stated. An urgent need exists to define educational achievement in a universal way that permits the clear delineation of various forms of higher level thinking desired.

Explication

The information defining the construct is transformed into test specifications, which normally specify the percentages of content areas in one dimension and the percentages of differentiated cognitive behavior in another dimension. Other terms often used instead of test specification are *two-way grid* or *test blueprint*. Like the problem with formulation, the process of explication does not have a well known technique for transforming the abstract content of a construct into test specifications. Although most textbooks on testing provide examples of test specifications,

Table 1.1
Consumers and Uses of
Standardized Achievement Test Information

Consumer: National Level	Units of Analysis
Allocation of Resources to Programs and Priorities	Nations, States
Federal Program Evaluation (e.g., Chapter I)	States, Programs

Consumer: State Legislature/State Department of Education	
Evaluate State's Status and Progress Relevant to Standards	State
State Program Evaluation	State, Program
Allocation of Resources	Districts, Schools

Consumer: Public (Lay persons, Press, School Board Members, Parents)	
Evaluate State's Status and Progress Relevant to Standards	Districts
Diagnose Achievement Deficits	Individual, Schools
Develop Expectations for Future Success in School	Individuals

Consumer: School Districts—Central Administrators	
Evaluate Districts	Districts
Evaluate Schools	Schools
Evaluate Teachers	Classrooms
Evaluate Curriculum	District
Evaluate Instructional Programs	Programs
Determine Areas for Revision of Curriculum and Instruction	District

Consumer: School Districts—Building Administrators	
Evaluate School	School
Evaluate Teacher	Classrooms
Grouping Students for Instruction	Individuals
Placement into Special Programs	Programs

Consumer: School Districts—Teachers	
Grouping Students for Instruction	Individuals
Evaluating and Planning the Curriculum	Classroom
Evaluating and Planning Instruction	Classroom
Evaluating Teaching	Classroom
Diagnosing Achievement Deficits	Classroom, Individuals
Promotion and Graduation	Individuals
Placement into Special Programs (e.g., Gifted, Handicapped)	Individuals

Table 1.1 (cont.)

Consumer: Educational Laboratories, Centers, Universities

Policy Analysis	All units
Evaluation Studies	All units
Other Applied Research	All units
Basic Research	All units

we again are working in a nebulous area of test development. The way this problem is addressed in many testing programs is through consensus obtained from a panel of experts convened for the purpose of developing test specifications. But as experience has shown, such consensus is often hard to reach.

An important step or decision to be reached in this stage of construct validation is test design, which includes a myriad of decisions. Millman and Greene (1989) provided a useful description of these activities in test development. Nitko (1989) addressed some of these important considerations in the context of achievement testing that is intimately linked to curriculum and instruction.

Validation

Validation follows test administration and includes a variety of activities designed to collect evidence to support our intended purpose. As noted earlier in this chapter, these studies may include any of the following:

1.   Studies of the reliability of test scores.
2.   Studies of the comparability or uniqueness of these scores to other measures in ways that are predictable or meaningful, or studies that reveal the intended complexity of a set of test items administered as a single test, also in ways that are predictable or meaningful.
3.   Studies of trends over time that confirm theoretical analysis.
4.   Studies of group differences that also confirm theoretical analysis.

For example, the State of Arizona initiated a state testing program to inform legislators and the public regarding the achievement of its students. The Essential Skills, approved by teachers and curriculum directors and enacted as law, became the state's curriculum. These essential skills were linked to national standards of professional organizations, such as those of the National Council of Teachers of Mathematics. A study of a standardized achievement test revealed roughly a 26% overlap with these essential skills, thus the standardized test was rejected as a measure of these intended constructs (Noggle, 1987). The state developed tests expressly to measure these essential skills. Subsequent field testing provided some information about the reliability of test scores, the comparability of scores to standardized achievement tests, studies of performance over grades, and studies of group differences that we might predict. For example, performance by groups of children classified as second language learners of English and children with low economic resources was substantially lower than other groups of children. Data reported from the field test tended to confirm the use of the scores as a basis for judging how the state was doing overall with respect to these essential skills.

In summary, the construct validation of achievement test scores is a process that begins with a stated purpose and ends with the reporting evidence that a specific interpretation or use of a test score is valid. Although construct validity of interpretations or uses of test scores is an explicit objective, the connection between items and tests is not always so explicit in this framework of construct validation. The next sections make these connections explicit and attempt to show that the validation of item responses is a critical aspect of construct validation.

The Role of Item Development in Construct Validation

Defining the Test Item

The *test item* is the basic unit in constructing any test. The test item is either a command or question that states in clear, unequivocal terms the cognitive task required of the examinee. As defined in this book, the test item is intended to measure some aspect of ability or achievement generally related to school learning or training. However, this definition of a test item is not limited necessarily to these applications. The test item may contain a series of potential right responses, hence the term *selected-response*, or it may require the examinee to construct his/her own answer, hence the term *constructed-response*. The term *multiple-choice* is used instead of selected-response because of its familiarity to readers.

Chapter 2 addresses the issue of what is measured by multiple-choice and constructed-response formats. Chapter 3 presents a variety of multiple-choice formats, two of which are not recommended for use.

Thorndike (1967) described the test item as a type of "mini" test, with the response being a molecular test score. Unfortunately, few tests would stand on the basis of a single item, and because of the complexity of our measures and the fallabilities of test items, we use aggregates of item responses, called *test scores*, instead of the individual responses. Yet, we may subject the item response to the same standards and criteria that we subject test scores, if we expect our test scores to be valid for the purposes intended. It is easy to show both in the framework of classical or item response theory, that a causal relationship exists between the discriminating ability of items and the reliability of test scores. Furthermore, the existence of nondiscriminating items will detract from the assignment of items from test specifications, because these nondiscriminating items do not contribute information to the test score. In other words, if a 100-item test is planned, and these items are chosen mainly on the basis of fulfilling the test specifications, and 20 items are faulty in some way, the test specifications are not being satisfied and the interpretation or use of the test scores is weakened.

Formulation

The process of formulating a construct deals with the abstraction of cognitive behavior, which, we have indicated in the area of achievement, will likely focus on types of higher level thinking, such as reasoning and problem solving. There is no formulation step for item development, because the basis for defining content is an abstract process that applies equally to the test (as the sample of behavior from the construct domain) and the item (the basic unit of the test). There is, however, a great need for a formulation step in item writing that essentially develops the basis for the content of the item in a way that is more systematic than the familiar test specifications (two-way grid or test blueprint) found in most textbooks on educational measurement and evaluation. This issue is discussed more completely in chapter 10.

Explication

Earlier in this chapter, two constructs, ability and achievement, were presented and discussed as focal ideas in educational testing. A subtle difference exists between measures of ability and measures of achievement. As pointed out earlier, the former is a slowly developed cognitive trait. Cognitive psychologists have emphasized the importance of ability in learning, which is why in the educational reform movement, the development of ability is more intentional than accidental. Achievement is dynamically affected by teaching. The test item written for a measure of ability is not instructionally targeted, but is often intended to represent a cognitive behavior that is more generalized. The test item written for a measure of achievement is instructionally targeted. Therefore it is more specific. This distinction is also important at the test score level. For example, the *Scholastic Aptitude Test* is supposed to be a measure of scholastic aptitude, which is slowly developed over a lifetime and augmented by high quality educational experiences. This test is often misused as a measure of achievement by policy makers and the press. Elementary and public high schools do not create curricula that promote high scores on the SAT, but over a long period, high quality schools may develop scholastic aptitude that directly affects these scores. Some profit-making organizations teach students how to take this test, in effect, tampering with the validity of test score interpretation and uses. On the other hand, achievement tests are interpreted and used as if teaching the test's content were part of the process. Thus, any deliberate attempt to raise scores on an achievement test may be legitimately viewed as a valid activity, that is, not leading to a misuse or misinterpretation of test scores, but leading to an inference about the success of educational endeavors.

Ideally, in this second phase of construct validation, we would like to use an item-writing theory, such as that proposed by Bormuth, Hively, or Guttman (Roid & Haladyna, 1982). These theories automate item writing and operationalize the content to be tested. By achieving this, an important step in explication is done by regulating the way items are written to represent an achievement or ability domain. Unfortunately, theories of item writing have not evolved to the level where any can be effectively applied. Instead we are limited to using a developing technology of item writing that is theoretical but supported by wisdom, experience, and some research (Haladyna & Downing, 1989a, 1989b). Chapters 4, 5, and 6 provide more complete descriptions of this item-writing technology.

Item writing must necessarily be aligned with test specifications. As Millman and Green (1989) observed, a set of decisions must be made about each item. These include (a) the format of the item must be determined, and (b) the number of items needed must be determined.

Once items are written, a series of reviews are needed to polish these items. These reviews are described in chapter 7, and include:

1. Connection of each item to the test specifications.
2. Correctness of the correct answer for each item.
3. Analysis of each item according to validated item-writing rules.
4. Editorial review of each item that addresses style, clarity, and grammatical concerns.
5. Bias review to identify and remove or rephrase test items that may offend test-taking subgroups.

The explication process is not empirical. It mainly involves expert judgment and activities performed by competent test developers. These activities are vital to the construct validation of item responses, because if items are misclassified by content, the key is incorrect, item-writing rules have not been followed, the editorial process has failed, or the item contains some form of bias, then the response to that item might not be as expected, and inferences we make from test results are weakened. This is the very fabric of validity.

In summary, item development is viewed as an integral part of construct validation, residing mainly in the second phase, explication, which involves the development of the variable we use to measure the construct. Despite the lack of extant theories for construct specification and the immature item-writing theories, the necessity of developing measures forces us to work with an existing technology that has its basis in collective wisdom, experience, and limited research.

The Role of Item Response Validation in Construct Validation

As with test scores, item responses are subject to the same standards and criteria as test scores in construct validation. This section briefly outlines some of the concepts, problems, issues, and activities faced in item validation and characterizes item validation as an emerging concept, encompassing a broader range of activities. Item validation also necessarily focuses on the whole item instead of treating all distractors as equal.

The Nature of an Item Response

In the explication phase of construct validation, the multiple-choice test score is the sum of correct answers, subject to linear transformations to other scales. In item response theories, transformations are made to logarithmic scales with different scalar properties than raw scores. In general, the degree of difference in these transformations is inconsequential as the correlations among raw and transformed scores is typically in the high .90s.

The correct multiple-choice answer has a typical monotonically increasing option characteristic curve, hence referred to as a *trace line*. Figure 1.2 provides a trace line for the right answer. The trace line for all wrong answers is a mirror image of the trace line for the right answer, that is, monotonically decreasing. In dichotomous scoring, the assumption is made that all distractors are equally informative; therefore, no attempt is made to discern the discriminating ability of each distractor. Indeed, authoritative sources and textbooks give scant treatment to the evaluation of distractors in item development and validation (Henrysson, 1971; Millman & Greene, 1989).

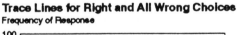

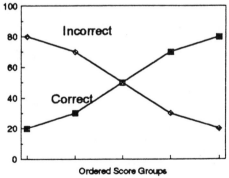

Fig. 1.2. Trace lines for correct and collectively incorrect option responses.

Theory and Research on the Role of Distractors in Test Scoring

In the 1930s, Paul Horst developed the method of reciprocal averages for rating scales (Nishisato, 1980), but it was Louis Guttman (1941) who first proposed this method for multiple-choice tests. This method purifies the construct through iterative scoring of options. Lord (1958) demonstrated that reciprocal averages maximize coefficient alpha. Thus, reciprocal averages has the curious property of making a variable as internally consistent as possible.

Bock (1972) introduced an item response theory that dealt with the differential nature of distractors. Other theorists such as Samejima (1979), Thissen and Steinberg (1984), Masters (1982) and Sympson (1983, 1986) proposed item response theories for scoring options that deal with the differential information contained in distractors.

Haladyna and Sympson (1988) reviewed the breadth of research in this area and concluded that studies consistently have shown small advantages for polytomous scoring over dichotomous scoring in terms of internal consistency reliability. Numerous studies have established that a patterned relationship exists between item responses and test scores (e.g., Bock, 1972; Changas & Samejima, 1984; Haladyna & Downing, in press; Jacobs & Vandeventer, 1970; Levine & Drasgow, 1983; Sympson, 1983, 1986; Thissen, 1976). Without any doubt, this research points to the fact that even though we do not intend to write items with differential distractor effectiveness, reliable information exists in the distractor responses that can be productively used to score tests.

Traditional Item Analysis

Wainer (1989) stated that the purpose of item analysis is to improve test items, which, in turn, improves tests and the results of test scores. Thus, the attention given to item analysis is directly related to the quality of our test score interpretations and uses. Therefore, the process of item analysis is part of the construct validation of test scores.

Traditional item analysis provides a measure of item difficulty and discrimination and the frequency of response for each option. Test score characteristics, including descriptive statistics and reliability are standard features. Distractor information is rare, and at best may provide a crude type trace line representation by dividing the examinee pool into three score groups and then calculating the mean of each group. Some computer programs will correlate distractor responses to total test scores, a procedure with many flaws, one being that the responses to distractors are too few to justify using the product-moment correlation.

Traditional item analysis has been made inexpensive and routine due to the existence of powerful, high speed personal computers and an abundance of inexpensive item analysis computer programs. However, traditional item analysis does not consider the differential nature of distractor responses in any productive way.

With the advent of item response theory, item analysis has become more sophisticated. But dichotomous item response theories also ignore the information contained in distractor responses. Moreover, Wainer (1989) has submitted that this kind of item analysis is often beyond the scope of understanding of many test practitioners.

The Future of Item Analysis

Wainer (1989) warned that item analysis will become increasing complex, probably because of the realization that distractors are an important part of the test item. Thissen, Steinberg, and Fitzpatrick (1989) provided useful insights into the values of distractor, and prior research has more than demonstrated that information from distractors can be used to study the item, improve the item, and score the item response. The trace line is viewed as a graphical means to help test developers better understand the effectiveness of distractors in item development and item validation.

Chapter 8 provides more comprehensive treatment of the process of item validation.

Summary

This section has briefly introduced the idea of item validation as a broader concept than item analysis and as an integral part of the construct validation process. Both theory and research point conclusively to studying item responses that involve the systematic differential nature of responses to distractors. This state of affairs points to a significant change in the way items need to be evaluated and the way item responses are aggregated to form test scores. Because we already know that these polytomous scoring methods produce more reliable test scores than dichotomous methods, validity is positively affected through the use of polytomous scoring. Therefore, the attention paid to distractors will have two positive benefits to validation: (a) to improve the way we develop and improve test items, and (b) to improve the way we score test results.

Conclusions

This chapter was intended to provide a context for using multiple-choice test items for measuring many important abilities and types of educational achievement. The redefinition of both ability or achievement is also part of this context. Construct validation is viewed as an appropriate process for (a) defining constructs, like ability and achievement, (b) creating or identifying measures of these constructs, and (c) using empirical studies to confirm or disconfirm our beliefs about how these constructs interrelate in a causal framework.

2

SELECTED- AND CONSTRUCTED-RESPONSE
TEST ITEM FORMATS

Overview

Robert Thorndike (1967) once said that the test item is the basic building block of a good test. The more effort we put into building better test items, the better the test will be. Toward that end, test items can be designed to represent a number of different types of content and cognitive behaviors.

Two types of test item formats exist: one where we select the correct answer among several choices, hence the term *selected-response*, and one where the answer is constructed, hence the term *constructed-response*. Does it matter whether the test item requires the test taker to choose an answer instead of writing out the answer? In some circumstances it does, and in other circumstances it does not seem to matter.

This chapter begins with a distinction between knowledge and skill and then illustrates how selected-response and constructed-response formats may be used. Then research is reviewed bearing on the similarity or difference of information obtained via these two formats for certain kinds of content and cognitive behavior. Finally, recommendations are made for the use of appropriate test formats that focus on (a) the kind of content to be tested, and (b) the cognitive behavior that is intended to be elicited when answering the question or responding to the item's command.

The Distinction Between Knowledge or Skill

Knowledge refers to any cognitive behavior of an abstract nature, typically involv-

21

ing such content as facts, concepts, principles, or procedures. The act of knowing a fact, concept, principle, or procedure is a private, personal event. We infer knowledge in the human mind through the use of a response to either a selected-response or a constructed-response test item. A term commonly used for the constructed-response test item is *essay*.

Skill refers to the actual performance or the result of a performance, namely a product. If a student learning outcome (instructional objective) involves hitting a baseball, this is clearly performance. If the student learning outcome is baseball hitting effectiveness, it is measured by computing the batting average. The batting average is the result of performance, so, in a sense, it is a product. Skill involves many products, for example, a skilled surgeon repairs a facial injury or an accomplished artist completes a painting.

Confusion often arises with the act of writing. Does the written product demonstrate a student's knowledge or skill? The answer involves a consideration of what the stimulus for obtaining the writing was. If the intent of obtaining the writing sample is to measure what a person knows about some topic, then the measurement of knowledge is our objective. If the intent is to demonstrate how well a person can write, then this intent requires the measurement of a skill, a constructed-response. Some examples of the use of written products to demonstrate skills are a(n):

1.   Critique of a play, or any critique for that matter.
2.   Plan for the development of some land in a township.
3.   Writing sample to exhibit penmanship.
4.   Essay arguing for or against an issue.
5.   Poem or story.
6.   Solution to a complex problem.

We might rightfully argue that all writing involves knowledge, but the real distinguishing feature is the intent or outcome. A play critic must have extensive knowledge of plays and considerable experience in criticism, but the act of writing a review of a play demonstrates a complex thought process of evaluation that rightfully falls under the category of skill not knowledge. In fact, all six activities above represent some form of skill where a constructed-response format seems appropriate.

A Taxonomy of Test Item Formats

Table 2.1 provides a listing of test formats that might be considered when addressing the problem of measuring knowledge or a skill. As shown there, knowledge can be measured by either selected-response or constructed-response formats. The measurement of any skill can be determined by viewing a process or performance or an outcome or product. We have a rich and growing array of activities in schools, in training, and in professions that represent skills. Whether the activity is solving a complex problem, performing surgery, operating equipment, planning a business, buying a car, or disciplining a child, we can measure this behavior through the use of familiar response formats, such as instrument-aided observation, visual observation, rating scales, or checklists. However, this book and the subsequent sections of this chapter are not devoted to skill measurement but rather to knowledge measurement. In the context of measuring knowledge, an important issue is addressed: Should one use selected-response or constructed-response items?

The Distinction Between
Selected-Response and Constructed-Response Formats

Generally speaking, selected-response formats are recommended for measuring knowledge and constructed-response formats are recommended for measuring skill. However, complex mental acts such as reasoning, critical thinking, and problem solving may be effectively measured with either format. For example, Bridgeman and Rock (1992) reported their study where they compared selected- and constructed-response versions of analytical reasoning and found that the two measures were indeed equivalent, but when they devised a measure of a different

---

Table 2.1
A Taxonomy of Item Formats for Measuring Knowledge and Skill

Knowledge

Selected-Response Formats   Constructed-Response Formats
    Conventional Multiple-Choice   Completion
    Matching   Short-answer essay
    Alternate-Choice   Extended-answer essay
    Complex Multiple-Choice   Oral essay
    Multiple True-False   Take-home essay
    True-False
    Context-Dependent Item Set

Skill

Selected-Response Formats   Constructed-Response Formats[1]
    Context-dependent Item Sets   Performance Item
        Product Item

[1]These formats are used to provide test data regarding problem solving, creative production, performance (e.g., musical, speech, motor), exhibits of work, portfolios (an exhibit of written work to demonstrate writing skill or creative work), and other written products.

---

mental skill, they found the new test unique from the selected- and constructed-response versions of analytical reasoning. These kinds of high quality studies consistently illustrate that format does not make a difference when the intent is to measure a common trait. But in some instances, one format may be more appropriate to measure that trait than another.

As indicated in Table 1.1, seven selected-response formats and three constructed-response formats exist for measuring knowledge. Chapter 3 describes and illustrates these selected-response formats. The three constructed-response formats are extended-answer essay, short-answer essay, and completion. This topic is well treated in standard textbooks about educational testing and by Coffman (1971).

This chapter presents the advantages and disadvantages of selected-response testing versus constructed-response testing when the objective is to measure knowledge, not skill. It is recognized that when measuring skill, the most direct way is through a constructed-response test item.

Discussion of the advantages and disadvantages of selected-response and constructed-response testing will follow along major areas of concern, such as ease of item and test construction, administration, scoring, analysis and evaluation of test items, guessing, reliability, and validity.

For the purpose of achieving greater clarity, let us use the term *multiple-choice* for selected-response testing and *essay* for constructed-response testing in this context of measuring knowledge.

Ease of Item Construction

In most general textbooks on educational measurement, essay test items are generally thought to be easy to write. We can consider the student learning outcome upon which the essay item is based and write the item. The item is usually in the form of a question that has greater generality than a multiple-choice item. There is often a striking resemblance between a learning outcome and an appropriately written essay item. Essay items usually are not reused because, since so few are administered in a typical achievement test, these items can be easily remembered by students for future reference.

Multiple-choice items are generally regarded by testing specialists to be more difficult to prepare than essay items. The wording of the stem, the identification of a single correct answer, and the writing of several wrong but plausible choices is a challenging task. Because 50–60 multiple-choice items can be administered in an hour, these items are more difficult to remember. Therefore, items can be reused. The fact that these items can be reused is a major advantage of the multiple-choice format over the essay format. However, in some high stakes testing programs, such as any licensing test, security may be an issue, and reuse may be limited. In some states, truth-in-testing legislation requires the release of many test items, thus making reuse of items less likely.

Ease of Test Construction

Once the essay test items are written, it is very easy to prepare a test. It is strongly recommended that model answers be prepared for scoring essays. Answer preparation can be a significant activity, as model answers are typically recommended in standard textbooks on this subject (e.g., Ebel & Frisbie, 1991).

With the advent of word processing, laser printers, and item banking systems, the storage and retrieval of multiple-choice items are routine. Preparing the key for a multiple-choice test is somewhat easy.

All things considered, it is easier to construct the essay test than the multiple-choice test. However, modern technology is making it easier to construct multiple-choice test items once the items are stored in a computer. Indeed, some forms of automated item writing and item banking may make multiple-choice item writing even easier in the future. Chapter 10 addresses some of the trends for the future of multiple-choice testing.

Administration

For the mainstream of classroom educational achievement testing, a class period (50 minutes) is allocated for a test. For special tests, this period of time may be 2 hours. In formal testing programs, it is common to allocate 2 to 4 hours for a test of knowledge, or even two 4-hour sessions in one day for some licensing and certification tests.

Essay tests require more time because each test-taker has to write the response. A 1-hour essay test is a physically demanding exercise, while selecting answers in a 1-hour multiple-choice test is far less demanding. Students generally prefer a multiple-choice format for this reason, among others provided in this chapter.

Scoring

An essay test is judgmentally scored, usually with a rating scale or a checklist. The ideal procedures for scoring are highly involved and laborious (Coffman, 1971). A number of biases exist in scoring essays. Chase (1979) established evidence for an expectation effect on essay test scores, as well as the influence of handwriting, a finding which Hughes, Keeling, and Tuck (1983) replicated. The relation of sentence length to test score and the influence of penmanship on the test score are well documented (Coffman, 1971). In a more recent review, Chase (1986) indicated several studies showing the existence of racial and gender bias in scoring essays. Such biases are very serious threats to the validity of interpretations and uses of essay test scores. Some work has reported that attempts have been made to solve these scoring problems (Braun, 1988), but these problems are large indeed.

A multiple-choice test is objectively scored. One can use a key, a scoring template (overlay) which identifies the right answer on a multiple-choice answer sheet, or an optical scanning machine, which provides a total score for each test taker with a high degree of accuracy. The scanner also provides an electronic file that can be used to analyze characteristics of the total test scores and the items.

Analysis and Evaluation of Test Items

Essay test items are not easily analyzed and evaluated. The ambiguous essay test item is difficult to detect; the difficulty of an essay test is hard to determine. What constitutes effective and ineffective essays is not clearly discernible. A curious oddity in educational measurement textbooks in general is the lack of attention paid to item analysis and evaluation of essay test items.

With multiple-choice tests, there are many standard computerized item analysis programs that provide complete summaries of item and test characteristics. Chapters 8 and 9 provide methods for using these results to improve future tests and understand the dynamics that may explain test results. In addition to these statistical summaries, there are many activities that go into evaluating and improving test items.

Guessing

With essay tests, there is little chance that a student can guess the right answer. However, students will often confess the temptation or boast about how to bluff an essay answer.

With multiple-choice tests, guessing is a nuisance because there is a chance that students will guess a right answer. This is a very weak criticism of the multiple-choice format. First, the effects of guessing are greatly overrated. The probability of guessing a right answer is the ratio of one to the number of options in the multiple-choice item. For any four-option item, the probability of guessing a right answer is one-fourth or 25%. The probability of guessing correctly on 10 items is about .000000009! The risk of student guessing producing an artificially high score is very remote with tests of 50 items or more. Further, if a student scores in the range of 20% to 30%, we would likely interpret that result as due to random guessing and that the student does not possess any or much knowledge of what the test is supposed to measure.

Reliability

Reliability is an important concept to test makers and test takers. Reliability is a necessary condition in test validation. Reliability has to do with the degree of measurement error in a set of test scores. A reliability coefficient is generally regarded as the ratio of true score variance to test score variance. One minus the reliability coefficient provides us with an estimate of the proportion of test score variance that is measurement error. With regard to measurement error associated with a test score, it can be large or small, positive or negative. Principles derived from the theory of reliability help us control and reduce measurement error. Although we never really know whether a measurement error is positive or negative, we can shrink the overall extent of error by increasing reliability. Two important ways to increase reliability are to make tests longer and improve the discriminating ability of the items appearing in the test.

For comparable administration times, the essay test yields a lower reliability than the comparable multiple-choice version (Lukhele, Thissen, & Wainer, 1992). This is due in part to the subjective system of scoring. In fact, Wainer (1993) briefly reviewed the history of subjective scoring of essays, showing that even as early as 1911, it was noted that variation among judges exceeded variability among grades. Indeed, this problem has persisted throughout this century. Because fewer items are administered with the essay, and even though rating scales or checklists are used, the variability of scores is too limited to really differentiate among different levels of performance. However, progress has been made in the scoring of essay test results, and there is continued hope that this format might produce high reliability (Braun, 1988).

The multiple-choice format generally produces higher reliability than the essay format, particularly if the administration time is 1 hour or more. Generally, you can administer about one multiple-choice item per minute. A 50-item test can produce highly reliable scores. With an essay test, writing for 1 hour or more can be exhausting, and the quality of measurable information may be less dependable than desired.

Validity

The most important consideration in testing is validity. As described in chapter 1, Messick (1989), among others, proposed a unified concept of validity that incorporates thinking that traditionally was identified as the triad of content, construct, and criterion-related validities.

The analysis of multiple-choice and essay formats in relation to this unified construct validity approach takes on three parts: (a) the sampling of content, (b) the measurement of higher level thinking, and (c) the differentiating of test scores when the response format involves recognition versus production. These three parts represent very crucial issues in relation to validity and the debate over the meaningfulness of test scores as a function of test item format.

The essential question to be answered is: Does item format elicit a difference in performance to the extent that it affects the meaningfulness of test score interpretations and uses? The answer is addressed through a discussion of three ideas: content sampling, higher level thinking, and recognition versus production.

Content Sampling

A key concern in test design is that the test is a fair and representative sample of the domain of knowledge intended for the course or unit of instruction or training. This concern also applies to other areas, such as job analysis, task analysis, practice analysis, and other methods of content specifications, such as assessment models, objectives, or topic outlines. Often test specifications are used that instruct the test designer about the relative proportions of items that are chosen on the basis of content categories for the test.

For a 1-hour achievement test, the extended-answer essay format cannot provide a very good sample of a content domain, unless that domain is very limited. The short-answer essay format improves on the degree of sampling, and the completion format provides a very high degree of sampling of this domain, very comparable to the multiple-choice format. However, the completion format presents a scoring problem due to variations of the correct answer, since there is more than one form of a correct answer for each completion item. This factor may decrease reliability.

The multiple-choice format permits from 50 to 60 items to be administered in that comparable 1-hour test. Therefore, the sampling of content is generally greater than with the use of the essay format.

Higher Level Thinking

The essay format is easily adaptable for measuring various types of higher level thinking. Few would disagree with this statement. A common and long standing misconception used by critics of multiple-choice is that this format is restricted to trivial learning, such as the recall of useless facts (Clavner, 1985; Technical Staff, 1933, 1937). As most authors of textbooks on educational measurement can attest, higher level thinking can be measured by the multiple-choice format (Haladyna & Downing, 1989a). In fact, most of these authors provide sections in their books on how to measure higher level cognitive behavior with the various multiple-choice formats. Although such item writing is difficult, there is some technology present to show item writers how to write such items (see Haladyna, 1991, 1992a, 1992b; Roid & Haladyna, 1982). Chapters 4 and 5 in this book also provide such information.

Badger (1990) offered a related argument in the context of instructionally based testing. Even though it can be shown that an essay and equivalent multiple-choice test are highly correlated and that the multiple-choice test is more reliable, the responses to essay items in mathematics and science can reveal the nature of learning difficulty more certainly than choosing a wrong multiple-choice option.

This involves judgment from someone who is intimate with the instructional setting and who also designs, administers, and scores the essay test. This may also explain why so many teachers use essay tests despite these well-known limitations. Martinez (1990) completed a study where the item stems were identical but the response options were either multiple-choice or open-ended. He, too, detected student misunderstanding of the items from the essay test, information which is not normally available from multiple-choice formats. Thus, it would seem that some forms of essay testing provide insights into common student misunderstanding and failure to learn. This potential for essay testing is only at an experimental stage.

Although these studies point to some benefits of essay testing, several questions remain. If multiple-choice and essay scores based on the same content knowledge are highly correlated, which they invariably are, why not use the more efficient and reliable format? Also unconventional multiple-choice formats presented in chapters 4 and 5 provide insights into measuring higher level thinking that fulfill the need for measuring higher level thinking. Thus, the implication that essay format is best for measuring higher level thinking and that the multiple-choice is best for measuring recall is simply not supported by current and past research, experience, and current technology.

Recognition Versus Production

Critics of multiple-choice contend that the essay measures something different than what the multiple-choice measures (Fiske, 1990; Nickerson, 1989). In short, picking the right answer from a list of possible answers is believed to be different than writing the right answer. Therefore, the essay format may represent a cognitive behavior that is different than what is measured with the multiple-choice format. The persistent use of the essay test is justified with this line of reasoning.

Cognitive psychologists have hypothesized that recognition and recall test formats belie different thought processes (Anderson & Bower, 1972; Kintsch, 1970). Because the essay is capable of detecting steps in multistage thinking, it is preferable to multiple-choice. This line of reasoning would favor using essay formats. On the other hand, the distinction described here may be more of a performance of a problem-solving skill, and would, on the basis of definitions offered in this chapter, not apply to the essay format. Nonetheless, increasing attention has been paid to designing multiple-choice test items that measure complex achievement. A fundamental premise in this book is that many types of multiple-choice items can be used to measure complex cognitive behavior.

The fundamental question is: Do results produced from an essay test of some specific knowledge differ from results produced from a comparable multiple-choice test? The answer to that question appears to be a resounding NO.

Research on this topic is complicated by the fact that some researchers examine the comparability of testing for knowledge with an essay test with testing for skill by using a written product (Hogan & Mishler, 1980). For example, Moss, Cole, and

Khampalikit (1982) compared scores on a multiple-choice test of language errors with actual writing samples. This kind of research examines the use of multiple-choice as a substitute for a performance test—the direct measurement of writing skill.

In a similar and related line of research, Oosterhof and Coats (1984) found similarities in the results of comparable multiple-choice and completion formats for measuring mathematical problem solving, which is a mental skill. In other words, is the multiple-choice mathematical problem solving item a good proxy for a straightforward mathematical problem solving exercise?

Bridgeman (1990), Bridgeman and Lewis (1991), and Bridgeman and Rock (1993) examined this issue in the context of college admissions testing, where prediction is the objective of the test. Bridgeman's (1990) review of research reported little or no contribution from essay test results above objectively scorable test results and high school grades . These studies revealed that the multiple-choice is a better predictor in some circumstances and about as effective as essay in other circumstances. Another important finding was that gender differences existed with multiple-choice in some circumstances, but not with essay. This result suggests that either real performance differences or bias exist. Bridgeman and Rock (1992) found no material difference between multiple-choice and constructed-response versions of the same measure of analytical reasoning.

The intents of measurement as discussed above are, in a subtle way, different. As a result, the research appears to distinguish between (a) multiple-choice compared to essays in the measurement of knowledge, and (b) multiple-choice compared to written performance test for the measurement of writing skills (Ackerman & Smith, 1988). Another complicating factor is that some researchers use achievement tests, whereas others use ability tests (e.g., Ward, Frederiksen, & Carlson, 1980). Finally, the quality of research studies varies considerably, and the credibility of results has been questioned by some authors (e.g., Gay, 1980).

In high quality studies, where achievement tests were used and comparisons between essay and multiple-choice tests were done as well as in reviews of these studies, the results consistently showed a high correlation between comparable essay and multiple-choice tests, as high as the reliability of the respective tests permits (Bennett, Rock, & Wang, 1990; Bennett, Sebrechts, & Rock, 1991; Bracht & Hopkins, 1970; Bridgeman & Rock, 1993; Gay, 1980; Hancock, 1992; Heim & Watts, 1967; Joorabchi & Chawhan, 1975; Lukhele, Thissen, & Wainer, 1992; Patterson, 1926; Smith & Smith, 1984; Thiede, Klockars, & Hancock, 1991; Traub & Fisher, 1977; Traub, 1993; Ward, 1982).

Smith and Smith (1984) argued that performance differences between multiple-choice and essay might occur due to general verbal ability, amount of testwiseness, and reading ability. Their studies failed to support this idea. Another possibility they studied was that differences in difficulty may be produced by using an essay format versus a multiple-choice format. But this is not a serious problem, because we can correct for the inherent difficulty produced by various formats using statistical methods (Frisbie, 1981), or by standard test score equating methods using item response theory. Wainer and Thissen (1993) shed more light on this topic. With newer extensions of item response theory, the mechanisms for scaling tests with different formats is becoming more and more automated and theoretically defensible. Readers interested in this technical issue might consult the Wainer/ Thissen paper as well as the manual for the computer program *PARSCALE* created by Muraki and Bock (1993).

Levine and McGuire (1971) studied the similarity between oral performance and multiple-choice in medical specialty board examinations. Although the assessment system was complex, high correlations were observed between multiple-choice scores and oral essay ratings. A subsequent study showed that in this setting, the measurement of clinical skill via various techniques is generally unreliable and highly correlated with multiple-choice performance, suggesting that the performance-type measures are different from the content of the multiple-choice (Levine, McGuire, & Natress, 1970). Studies examining the use of problem-based, patient-management problems were neither reliable nor more valid than multiple-choice (Norcini, Swanson, Grosso, & Webster, undated). They concluded that multiple-choice testing of knowledge can be reliably done and that it complements other types of measures needed to measure medical competence in a specialty. Studies like these form the basis for the continued use of multiple-choice tests in medicine and other health professions.

This research stemming from elementary, secondary, college, and medical education has consistently shown that reliability of the essay tests is lower than multiple-choice tests, and that correlations with like measures based on differing formats is typically as high as reliability permits. The scoring of essay tests is riddled with biases that undermine the validity of test score interpretations and uses. After an extensive review of this literature and after completing their study, Bennett, Rock, and Wang (1990) concluded that "the evidence presented offers little support for the stereotype of multiple-choice and free-response formats as measuring substantially different constructs (i.e., trivial factual recognition vs. higher-order processes" (p. 89).

Multiple-Choice as a Proxy for Measuring Writing Skill

Multiple-choice is generally preferred over essay tests for various reasons discussed in this chapter. If one wants to measure writing skill, the direct method is to obtain a writing sample and perform a primary trait or holistic analysis, which normally involves trained judges, exemplars for each level of performance, and rating scales or checklists.

Multiple-choice items may be used as a relatively objective, efficient proxy for the costly process of measuring writing with a written performance test involving trained judges and the traditionally unreliable rating scale. In one significant study,

Benton and Kiewra (1986) showed that two sets of multiple-choice measures, the Test of Standard Written English and a battery of tests of organizational ability, were highly correlated with a holistically scored measure of writing ability. These results were further theoretically validated against a theory of writing behavior, explaining the potential validity of multiple-choice formatted tests as proxies for measures of writing skill.

If this research can be replicated in other contexts, then the multiple-choice format may even provide an efficient substitute for the more expensive writing performance test. On the other hand, the face validity of using proxy measures is always questioned. If writing skill measures are desired, a performance test is surely the best choice. Under extreme circumstances, proxy multiple-choice measures might provide useful information to instructors and students regarding micro writing skills, but this has to be viewed as indirectly related to writing.

Multiple-Choice as a Proxy for Measuring Some Types of Higher Level Thinking

Although a widely accepted typology for defining and measuring higher level thinking is lacking, the many attempts to measure problem solving, critical thinking, reasoning, and other complex forms of higher level thinking can be labeled as *prescriptive*, just like the approach offered in chapter 5.

Much work on this has emanated from the Educational Testing Service. Ward et al. (1980) observed that multiple-choice and constructed-response versions of a test for formulating hypotheses may tap different skills. But other research, (e.g., Bridgeman & Rock, 1993) suggested that multiple-choice and constructed-response versions of a similar higher level trait were equivalent.

Bennett (1993) provided a taxonomy for organizing various types of constructed-response item formats, including the essay offered in this chapter. Although the six types of item formats he proposes convey a sense of the variety of cognitive behavior, the formats do not capture the full array of constructed-response items that comprise the authentic assessment movement, including portfolios, performances, problems, inventions, proposals, projects, and other creative endeavors of a complex nature.

When we face a problem such as those typically encountered in consumer mathematics, both multiple-choice and completion exercises seem appropriate. Although the completion exercise is inarguably the most direct measure of such problem solving ability, proxy multiple-choice measures have been successfully used because of their many good qualities, as described earlier.

One example is the use of problem-based scenarios (Haladyna, 1991, 1992a). This format is extensively used in licensing testing to provide realistic problems with a set of multiple-choice test items that reflect steps in a problem solving set. Methods of scoring have been devised by various theoreticians to enhance the use of these problem-based scenarios (e.g., Thissen, Steinberg, & Mooney, 1989; Wainer & Kiely, 1987). Thus, this work seems to offer hope that some forms of complex thinking that quite naturally might be tested in a performance format might be more efficiently tested with this proxy technique. Chapter 3 presents more information about this format.

Format Bias

It would be remiss not to discuss the possibility that format is a factor in determining test scores of various subgroups. If, indeed, males outperform females in one type of test format but not in the other, then bias may account for group differences. Burkam and Burkam (1993) reviewed gender differences in cognitive performance and, in particular, focused on the potential that some of the gender difference observed in many studies may be attributed to item format, specifically multiple-choice and essay. One speculation offered in this review was that females are believed to have better expressive writing skills and are, therefore, at a disadvantage when taking selected-response tests. This argument would favor using multiple-choice where expressive writing skill is not a factor. Another speculation is that males have better test-taking skills, thus they gain an advantage with multiple-choice. If this is true, then all test takers should be equally trained in test-taking skills to reduce this bias. From this review it, would appear that, although gender differences exist, these differences cannot be attributed to formats used in testing but to other factors residing with the use of multiple-choice tests, such as writing skill, test-taking skills, calculating ability, and problem-solving ability.

Burkam and Burkam (1993) examined statewide assessment data at three grade levels in four subject matters. The results showed effect size differences ranging from .04 to .36 with a median of .155 in favor of females. They point out that these results do not take into account differential experience, test-taking skills, and other factors, which prior research indicates should be controlled in such studies. When statistically controlled using variables of prior experience, their findings were complex. Generally, gender differences were of a small magnitude, less than one tenth of a standard deviation. They reported that the use of calculators favored females. Their study demonstrates a need for more research into format differences, but also the potential for the interaction with other factors such as classroom experiences, interest, motivation, test-taking skills, to mention a few of the more potential variables.

Thus, the threat of format as a determinant of test scores does not yet seem borne out by these studies. At best, a small difference has been observed; the causal attribution of this difference is not purely item format but seems to be related to other variables in complex ways.

Summary

When the content involves a procedure or when the type of cognitive behavior is process- or product-oriented, a performance test is appropriate, with the caveat that using rating scales invites various kinds of bias. When the content involves knowledge, one can choose between essay and multiple-choice formats. This chapter has pointed out that the multiple-choice is desirable from many standpoints and that the essay format is undesirable. The factors considered in this evaluation included: (a) ease of item and test construction, (b) administration, (c) scoring, (d) analysis and evaluation of test items, (e) guessing, (f) reliability, and (g) validity. The issue of validity is the most complex, and the evidence gathered in favor of using multiple-choice over essay is very convincing. In his review of this basic issue, Traub (1993) did not give a definitive answer but stated that if differences did exist, they were very small in terms of total test variance. Traub made the excellent point that a theory about why test formats make a difference is much needed, and that future research should concentrate on the equivalence issue with respect to this theory. When one considers such factors as content domain, type of cognitive behavior (knowledge or skill), type of higher level thinking, among other factors, differences may exist that may cause one to choose one type of format over another. Not surprising, it is concluded that under most circumstances the multiple-choice format is more effective than the essay format for measuring knowledge. In some instances, the multiple-choice format might be as effective or even more effective for measuring some mental skills, such as problem solving or clinical judgment in a profession like medicine.

However, a disclaimer offered here is that there is some value to reading the responses to essay test questions. Someone close to the instructional setting, such as the teacher, is likely to derive a better understanding of learner difficulties and weaknesses in teaching from an analysis of written student responses. But such analysis is strictly judgmental and hardly a science. Also, responses to multiple-choice items can be put to the same kind of scrutiny as essay answers. In fact, recent research by Kikumi Tatsuoka examined the diagnostic value of multiple-choice distractors (Tatsuoka, 1990). Finally, some research has been reported that actually supports multiple-choice testing as an inexpensive and efficient way to measure writing skill. Although direct measurement via the writing performance test is currently very popular, this evidence suggests that, in some circumstances, multiple-choice items can serve as a proxy. Finally, when we address the problems of measuring various types of higher level thinking, direct assessment using constructed-response formats may be more appropriate with respect to the validity of interpretations, but the multiple-choice proxies often provide a less expensive and more reliable basis for measuring many forms of cognitive behavior.

3

MULTIPLE-CHOICE FORMATS

Overview

This chapter illustrates a variety of multiple-choice formats. Most of the formats presented in this chapter are traditional, whereas several others are somewhat new. Two of these formats are not recommended. With all of these formats, relevant research is reviewed.

Conventional Multiple-Choice

The most common variety of multiple-choice is the *conventional* format, shown in the following example. It has three parts: (1) a *stem*, (2) the *correct answer*, and (3) several wrong answers, called *foils* or *distractors*.

```
Who is John Galt?  <————————————————stem
A.   A rock star  <————————————————foil or distractor
B.   A movie actor  <———————————————foil or distractor
C.*  A character in a book  <——————————correct choice
```

Stem

The stem is the stimulus for the response. The stem should provide a complete idea of the problem to be solved in selecting the right answer. For example, the next stem is written in a *question* format:

> Which test format is likely to provide the best sampling of
> content for an achievement test?

The stem also can also be phrased in a partial-sentence format, called the *incomplete-sentence* format:

> The test format most likely to provide the highest degree of
> sampling of content is the:

Whether the stem appears as a question or a partial sentence, it also can present a problem that has several right answers with one option clearly being the best of the right answers. This is the *"best answer"* format:

> Among the advantages of multiple-choice testing, which stands
> out as most important?

A list of options can all be correct in the sense that each is an advantage, but one of these is the best.

Correct Answer

The *correct answer* is undeniably the one and only right answer. In the question format, the correct choice can be a word, phrase, or sentence. In some rare circumstances, it can be a paragraph or even a drawing or photograph (if the distractors are also paragraphs, drawings, or photographs). Here is an example:

> Which term below means the same as the word <u>egregious</u>?
> A.   Friendly
> B.* Outrageous
> C.   Quizzical
> D.   Intelligent

Distractors

Distractors are the most difficult part of the test item to write. Distractors are unquestionably wrong answers. Each distractor must be plausible to test takers who have not yet learned the knowledge that the test item is supposed to measure. To those who possess the knowledge asked for in the item, the distractors are clearly wrong choices.

Distractors should resemble the correct choice in grammatical form, style, and length. Subtle or blatant clues that give away the correct choice should always be avoided.

The conventional multiple-choice is the most frequently used multiple-choice format. It is the standard of the testing industry. Because of its familiarity to millions of test makers and test takers and its many fine qualities, it is highly recommended.

Matching

A popular variation of the conventional multiple-choice is the matching format. This format has two or more options presented first followed by the item stems. The instructions that precede the options and stems tell the test taker how to respond and where to mark answers. A traditional matching item looks like this:

Mark your answer on the answer sheet. For each item select from options provided.

A. Minnesota
B. Illinois
C. Wisconsin
D. Nebraska
E. Iowa

1. Home state of the Hawkeyes
2. Known for its cheese
3. Land of a thousand lakes
4. Cornhuskers
5. The largest of these states
6. Contains Cook County

There are many advantages to the matching format:

1. The format lends itself nicely to testing associations, definitions, or characteristics or examples of concepts.
2. The format is efficient based on the amount of student testing time consumed and space. The example just provided could be expanded to produce as many as 30 items on a single page.
3. The options do not have to be repeated. If this were reformatted into the conventional multiple-choice, then it would require the repeating of the five options for each stem.

Among the few limitations of this format are:

1.   A tendency exists to write as many items as there are options, so that the test takers matches up five items to five options. This problem can be avoided by making the number of options unequal to the number of items.

2.   A tendency exists to mix the options–have several choices be people and several choices be places. The problem is "nonhomogeneous options," and it can be solved by ensuring that the options are part of a set of things, like all people, or all places. In the example provided on the previous page, the options were all states.

Because this format is very similar to the conventional multiple-choice, there is no research to report on its unique features. It is often recommended by textbook authors, and often used in formal and informal testing programs.

An unusual example, adapted from Technical Staff (1937) is a complex matching item, and it appears in Table 3.1. The matching format should continue to be used. As a variation of the conventional multiple-choice, it is efficient to

Table 3.1
Unconventional Matching Exercise

Choice	Personality Type	Type Characteristic
A. Kretschmer	_1. hypokinetic	_2. intellectual
B. Berman	_3. rationalistic	_4. indifferent, hedonic
C. James	_5. extrovert	_6. pleasantly toned
D. Morgan	_7. knowing	_8. unpleasantly toned
E. Jung	_9. mercurial	_10. immature, docile
F. Thompson	_11. aesthetic	_12. objective, social
G. Warren	_13. sanguine	_14. short, obese

Note. From *Manual of examination methods* (2nd ed.) (p. 73) by the Technical Staff, 1937, Chicago: University of Chicago. Adapted with permission.

construct and administer, and it can be used to test understanding of concepts and principles.

Alternate-Choice

This format is nothing more than a two-option multiple-choice.

> What is the most effective way to motivate a student?
> A. Punishment
> B.* Praise

Ebel (1981, 1982) has been the staunchest advocate of this format. He argued that many items in educational achievement testing are "either/or," lending themselves nicely to the alternate-choice format. Downing (1992) reviewed the research on this format and also concluded that the format is very viable.

Although alternate-choice is a downsized multiple-choice version, it is NOT a true-false item. Alternate-choice offers a comparison between two choices, whereas the true-false format does not provide an explicit comparison. With the true-false format, the test taker must mentally create the counter example and choose accordingly.

The alternate-choice has several attractive characteristics and some limitations:

1. The most obvious advantage is that it is easy to write. One only has to think of a right answer and one plausible distractor.

2. The efficiency of the use of this format with respect to printing costs, ease of test construction, layout, and storage and retrieval is high.

3. Another advantage is that if the item has only two options, one can ask more questions per testing period than with conventional multiple-choice. Consequently, the alternate-choice format will provide better coverage of content.

4. Alternate-choice items are not limited to low-level thinking and can be written to measure higher level thinking (Ebel, 1982).

5. Ebel (1981, 1982) argues that alternate-choice is more reliable than multiple-choice because more alternate-choice items can be asked in a fixed time period. Research on alternate-choice supports Ebel's contention (Burmester & Olson, 1966; Ebel, 1981, 1982; Ebel & Williams, 1957; Hancock, Thiede, & Sax, 1992; Maihoff & Mehrens, 1985; Sax & Reiter, undated). Also, alternate-choice items have a history of exhibiting satisfactory discrimination (Ruch & Stoddard, 1925; Ruch & Charles, 1928; Williams & Ebel, 1957).

6. Lord (1977) suggested another advantage: a two-option format is probably most effective for high-achieving students because of the tendency to eliminate other options as implausible distractors. Levine and Drasgow (1982) and Haladyna

and Downing (in press) provided further support for such an idea. When analyzing several standardized tests, they found that most items contained only one or two plausible distractors. Many of these items could easily have been simplified to the alternate-choice. If this is true, then two options should not only be sufficient in many testing situations but a natural consequence when we remove useless distractors from an item containing four or five options.

The most obvious limitation of the alternate-choice format is that guessing is a factor– the test takers may possibly choose the correct answer even if they do not know the answer. The chance of randomly guessing the right answer is 50% for one item. By recognizing the floor and ceiling of a test score scale consisting of alternate-choice items, we overcome this limitation. For instance, the lowest probable score for a 30-item alternate-choice test is 50%, if random guessing happens. The ceiling of the test is, of course, 100%. A score of 55% on such a test is very low, whereas a score of 75% is in the middle of this scale. Given that guessing is a larger factor in alternate-choice items when compared to conventional multiple-choice, you only have to make an interpretation in keeping with the idea that 50% is about as low a score as you can expect. Any passing standard or other evaluative criteria you use should be consistent with the effective range of the alternate-choice test score scale, which is from 50% to 100%.

Table 3.2 contains a set of alternate-choice items designed to measure word meaning in sentences. The distinctions are subtle, and the two choices offered are both plausible, one being right. Table 3.2 contains only several items, but the original source offered 36 items like these on a single page.

Table 3.2
Example of Alternate-Choice Items
for Testing Word Meaning

For each sentences, select the most appropriate (for formal English) of the two words given, and write its letter in the space provided.

___1.   (A-Providing, B-Provided) that all is quiet, you may go up.

___2.   The (A-exact, B-meticulous) calculation of votes...

___3.   I make (A-less, B-fewer) mistakes now than previously.

___4.   All orders should be written, not (A-verbal, B-oral).

___5.   The climate of Arizona is said be very (A-healthful, B-healthy).

Note. From *Manual of examination methods* (2nd ed.) (p. 73) by the Technical Staff, 1937, Chicago: University of Chicago. Adapted by permission.

This format may be useful for classroom testing. Downing (1992) recommended it for formal testing programs, because alternate-choice has been found to be comparable to three- or four-option items, if properly constructed (Burmester & Olson, 1966; Maihoff & Phillips, 1988). The added advantage for alternate-choice is that more items can be used per time period. Also, the construction of alternate-choice items is easy and gives good feedback for most testing situations.

True-False

This format has been well established for informal testing but seldom used in standardized testing programs. There has been significant, increasing evidence to warrant its use with caution or not at all (Downing, 1992; Haladyna, 1992b). Like other multiple-choice formats, it is subject to many abuses. The most common abuse may be a tendency to test trivial knowledge. The example shows the more effective use of this format:

Mark A on your answer sheet if true and B if false.

1. The first thing to do with an automatic transmission that does not work is to check the transmission fluid. (A)
2. The major cause of tire wear is poor wheel balance. (B)
3. The usual cause of clutch "chatter" is in the clutch pedal linkage. (A)
4. The distributor rotates at one-half the speed of the engine crankshaft. (B)

Table 3.3 presents a very effective, although unconventional, use of this format. The items in Table 3.3 occupy a small space but provide for complete analysis of plant anatomy.

There are more subtle and serious problems with the true-false format. For example, Peterson and Peterson (1976) investigated the error patterns of positively and negatively worded true-false questions that were either true or false. Errors were not evenly distributed among the four possible types of true-false items.

Table 3.3

Example of an Innovative True-False Format

Place an "X" beneath each structure for which each statement is true?

	Root	Stem	Leaf
Growing point protected by a cap	____	____	____
May possess a pithy center	____	____	____
Epidermal cells hair-like	____	____	____
Growing region at tip	____	____	____

Although this research is not damning, it does warn item writers that the difficulty of the item can be controlled by its design.

Hsu (1980) pointed out a characteristic of true-false items when they are presented as a group using the generic stem:

Which of the following statements are true?

Such a format is likely to interact with the ability of the group being tested in a complex way. Both the design of the item and the format for presentation are likely to cause differential results. Ebel (1978), a proponent of true-false items, opposed the grouping of items in this manner.

Grosse and Wright (1985) described a more serious threat to the usefulness of true-false. They argued that true-false has a large error component due to guessing, which other research supports (Frisbie, 1973; Haladyna & Downing, 1989b; Oosterhof & Glasnapp, 1974). Grosse and Wright claimed that if a test taker's response style favors true instead of false answers in the face of ignorance, the reliability of the test score may be seriously undermined.

As with alternate-choice, Ebel (1970) advocated the use of true-false items. The chapter on true-false testing by Ebel and Frisbie (1991) remains a major authoritative work. Ebel's arguments (1970) are simply that the command of useful knowledge is important, that all verbal knowledge can be stated in terms of propositions, and each proposition can be truly or falsely stated. We can measure student knowledge by determining the degree to which each student can judge the truth or falsity of knowledge. Frisbie and Becker (1991) synthesized the advice of 17 textbook sources on true-false testing. The advantages of true-false items can be summarized in the following way:

1. True-false items are easy to write.
2. True-false items can measure important content areas.
3. True-false items can measure higher thought processes.
4. More true-false items can be given per testing period than multiple-choice items.
5. True-false items are easy to score.
6. True-false items occupy less space on the page, therefore minimizing the cost of production.
7. The judgment of a proposition as true of false is realistic.
8. We can minimize reading time.
9. Reliability of test scores is adequate.

The disadvantages are as follows:

1. Items tend to reflect trivial information.
2. True-false items tend to promote rote learning.

3. Guessing is too influential.
4. The format is resistant to detecting degrees of truth or falsity.
5. True-false tests tend to be slightly less reliable than comparable multiple-choice tests.
6. There are differences between true true-false items and false true-false items, which have caused some concern.
7. True-false items are not as good as alternate-choice items (Hancock, Thiede, & Sax, 1992).

Some of these criticisms can be defended. The reputation for testing trivial content is probably deserved, but only because item writers write trivial items. Trivial content can be tested with any format. The more important issue is: Can true-false items be written to measure nontrivial content? A reading of the chapter on true-false testing in the book by Ebel and Frisbie (1991) provided an unequivocal "yes" to this question. The issue of testing higher level thought processes is also answered by better item-writing techniques.

The criticism about rote learning is similar to the criticism about test content. Testing for recall is a chronic problem in American education, and is not limited solely to true-false testing. Again, Ebel and Frisbie (1991) provided examples of true-false items that measure higher level thinking.

Guessing is not much of a factor in a true-false test, as with alternate-choice, for the same reasons offered in the previous section. If one keeps in mind that the floor of the scale for a true-false test is 50% and the ceiling is 100%, then our interpretations can be made in that light. And it is very difficult for a random guesser to exceed 60% on these tests when the test length is substantial, say 50 to 100 items. This is the same argument that applies to alternate-choice.

Despite Ebel's persistent support of true-false, this format does not measure up very well to the alternate-choice or the conventional multiple-choice. In conclusion, this format is not recommended for standardized testing programs but may be useful for classroom testing, and is certainly open to more definitive research.

Complex Multiple-Choice

The Educational Testing Service first introduced this format, and the National Board of Medical Examiners later adopted it for use in medical testing (Hubbard, 1978). Because many items used in medical and health professions testing programs had more than one right answer, this format proposes to accommodate those occasions where more than one choice was correct. Because items are scored either right or wrong, it seemed sensible to set out combinations of right and wrong answers in a multiple-choice format where only one choice was correct:

> Which affects test score reliability?
> 1.   Test length
> 2.   Homogeneity of the sample of examinees being tested
> 3.   Item length
>
> A.* 1 and 2
> B.   2 and 3
> C.   1 and 3
> D.   1, 2, and 3

Although this format is very popular in formal testing programs, Albanese (1992), Haladyna (1992b), and Haladyna and Downing (1989b) gave several reasons to recommend against its use:

1.   Complex multiple-choice items appear to be more difficult than comparable single-best-answer multiple-choice.
2.   Having partial knowledge, knowing that one option is absolutely correct or incorrect, helps the test taker identify the correct option by eliminating distractors. Therefore, test-taking skills have a greater influence on test performance than intended.
3.   This format produces items with lower discrimination, which, in turn, lowers test score reliability.
4.   The format is difficult to construct and edit.
5.   The format takes up more space on the page, reducing the overall efficiency of testing process.
6.   The format requires more reading time, thus reducing the number of items of this type one might put in a test. Such a reduction negatively affects the sampling of content, therefore reducing the validity of interpretations and uses of test scores.

Recent studies by Case and Downing (1989), Dawson-Saunders, Nungester, and Downing (1989), Shahabi and Yang (1990) provided additional evidence of the inferiority of the complex multiple-choice. Subhiyah and Downing (1993) provided evidence that no difference exists, that complex multiple-choice items have about the same qualities as conventional multiple-choice. Further, this format fills a need when "list-type" questioning is needed. Fortunately, multiple-true false is a viable alternative to the complex, multiple-choice format.

Multiple True-False

This alternative to complex multiple-choice is the multiple true-false (MTF), sometimes known as *Type-X*. Using the previous example, the complex multiple-choice item can be transformed to an MTF in the following way:

> For each item, mark on your answer sheet A if true or B if false.
> Which effects test score reliability?
> 1. Test length (A)
> 2. Homogeneity of variance (A)
> 3. Item length (B)

We can improve this situation by adding more items to the list:

> For each item, mark on your answer sheet A if true or B if false.
> Which affects test score reliability?
> 1. Test length (A)
> 2. Homogeneity of variance (A)
> 3. Item length (B)
> 4. Test score variability (A)
> 5. Dimensionality (B)

Table 3.4 contains a pictorial multiple-true false (MTF) item that requires an evaluation and response to each stimulus. The attractiveness of this MTF item set is that each item offers a natural dichotomy and provides 10 or more such items in a single page. One criticism of items involving pictorial material is the space it occupies in a test booklet and the yield in terms of items per page. This example shows a good yield, but this may be atypical.

Frisbie (1992) reviewed research on the MTF format and supported its use. However, he stated that one detriment to its use is a lack of familiarity by item writers. The advantages of the MTF format are as follows:

1. This format avoids the disadvantages of the complex multiple-choice format.

Table 3.4

Pictorial Multiple True-False Items

Below are five angles: a, b, c, d, and e. Mark A if acute or B if not acute in the space provided below.

1. ____

2. ____

3. ____

4. ____

5. ____

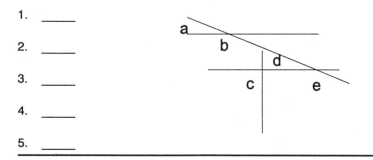

---

2.   Recent research shows that the MTF item format is very effective in terms of reliability and validity (Frisbie, 1992). Several researchers have established that the MTF format produces higher reliability estimates when compared to the conventional multiple-choice items (Albanese, Kent, & Whitney, 1977; Frisbie & Druva, 1986; Frisbie & Sweeney, 1982; Hill & Woods, 1974).

3.   Frisbie and Sweeney (1982) reported that students perceived that the MTF items are easier and preferred them to conventional multiple-choice. Oddly enough, Hill and Woods (1974) reported that the MTF items seemed harder, but several students anecdotally reported that the MTF items were better tests of their under-standing.

4.   This format is very efficient from the standpoints of item development, examinee reading time, and the number of questions that can be asked in a fixed time period. For instance, it is possible to place nearly 30 MTF items on a page and administer over 100 questions per 50-minute testing period. Given that guessing can play a strong role in such items, the effective range of scores for such a test will range from 50% to 100%. As with alternate-choice and true-false, guessing will not greatly influence scores if enough items are used.

There are some potential limitations to this format:

1.   The MTF format appears limited to testing the understanding of concepts by listing examples and nonexamples, characteristics and noncharacteristics. Al-though MTF items are further illustrated in chapters 4 and 5, the variety of content seems limited.

2.   One technical problem that might arise with the MTF format is that of estimating reliability. Generally, multiple-choice test items (including the MTF format) are assumed to be independent from one another with respect to responses. One item might cue another item. The technical term for this is *local dependence*. Dependency among items of a single MTF item set would make that set of items operate as one multiple-choice item. Frisbie and Druva (1986) and Albanese and Sabers (1988) established that no dependence existed with their test data. None-theless, local dependency will result in an overestimation of reliability and is a caution with this format.

The MTF format is an effective substitute for the complex multiple-choice. Because the MTF has inherently good characteristics for testing knowledge, it should be more widely used. Tables 3.3 and 3.4 present examples that illustrate the variety and scope of this format for testing achievement.

Multiple-Response

Somewhat related to the MTF format is the multiple-response (MR) format. Strictly speaking, this format is the conventional multiple-choice where more than one right answer exists. The underlying rationale for this is that different lines of reasoning by test takers may logically lead to the selection of other answers that are also correct. The only material difference between MR and conventional multiple-choice is that test takers are informed that they may select more than one answer, but if they choose incorrectly a penalty is assessed.

In one study of the efficacy of this format, Ryan (1993) examined the MR format in a statewide science assessment and found it to have qualities similar to conventional multiple-choice. Students reported the format to be more difficult than conventional multiple-choice.

The use of this format is not recommended, but new formats, like this one, should be studied to determine if they provide appropriate ways to observe complex mental behavior.

Context-Dependent Item Sets

Although this format has a long history, it is becoming more popular, perhaps because its scoring is improving. Terms used to describe items sets include *interpretive exercises, scenarios, vignettes, item bundles, problem sets, super-items* and *testlets*.

The item set lends itself nicely to testing a variety of types of complex thinking, such as problem solving. One can present an introductory paragraph that states a problem and then asks from five to ten questions in any format about the information presented.

Haladyna (1992a, 1992b) reviewed the research and development of this format and found that very little formal study of this format had been done, even though this format appears in many standardized achievement tests and some professional licensing and certification examinations. For example, the National Association of Boards of Pharmacy has adopted this format for its national licensing examination. Recent work by Wainer and Kiely (1987) and Thissen, Steinberg, and Mooney (1989) introduced and described testlets as bundles of items with a variety of scorable predetermined paths for responding. This is a considerably more complex idea than presented here, but the technical issues addressed by these authors offer some guidance in future research on item sets.

Like the MTF format, context effects or interitem dependence is a threat. In fact, the MTF format is a type of item set. If items are interdependent, the discriminative ability of the items, therefore, reliability of scores, will be diminished (Sireci, Thissen, & Wainer, 1991). Wainer & Kiely (1987) explored methods for scoring these *item bundles*, as applied to computerized adaptive testing, but these methods can apply to conventional fixed-length testing. They further explore hierarchical testlets, but this is futuristic, and little, if any, technology presently exists for doing this. One theoretician suspects that the problem of dependence may not be very serious if item sets are scored as minitests (testlets) (see the discussion by Rosenbaum, 1989).

Table 3.5
Comprehension Type Item Set

Our **solar system** mainly includes nine **planets**, their **moons**, and the **sun**. These nine planets **revolve** around the sun. Each planet **rotates** as it revolves. On planet Earth, each rotation takes one earth day. The path that each planet follows is an **orbit**. **Moons** are smaller bodies that revolve around planets. Earth has one moon, and other planets may have no moons or many moons. Any body that revolves around another body is called a **satellite**. All bodies have attraction for one another, which is called **gravitation**. The tendency for smaller bodies to be attracted to a larger body, such as you to the earth, is called **gravity**.

1. Which of the following describes any planet?
    A.   It rotates around the sun.
    B.   It revolves around a moon.
    C.   It has a moon.
    D.* It both rotates and revolves.

2. Which is an example of a satellite?
    A.   Earth
    B.   Its moon
    C.* Both A and B
    D.   Neither A nor B

3. What condition listed below demonstrates gravitation?
    A.* The pull between the earth and the sun
    B.   The pull between the earth and an ocean on the earth
    C.   Any body falling to earth
    D.   Any body that rotates and revolves

4. If a new body is discovered that revolves around the sun, what term best describes it?
    A.   Satellite
    B.* Planet
    C.   Moon
    D.   Gravitational body

There are several types of items sets, each intended for a certain type of cognitive activity: (a) reading comprehension, (b) problem solving, (c) interlinear, and (d) figural. Each type is briefly discussed to provide the essence of what type of content is being measured, and each is illustrated. Item sets are also illustrated in chapters 4, 5, and 6.

Reading Comprehension

The item set shown in Table 3.5 presents information about planets and other heavenly bodies for an elementary grades science unit and asks questions to measure student understanding of the introductory paragraph. The use of boldface for key concepts focuses the test taker's attention on the concepts to be tested. The test taker can show understanding of several concepts. The second page of the item set might contain more items dealing with the balance of the concepts. Typically,

Table 3.6
Problem-Solving Type Item Set

Jack and Jill were planning to go to a rock concert with their friends Hansel and Gretel. The tickets were $15.00 per person if purchased before March 1, and $16.00 if purchased after March 1. There is a group discount of 10% with purchase of four or more tickets. There is also a $2.00 handling charge per ticket regsrdless of when they were purchased.

1. What is the total cost of the four tickets if purchased on February 16?
    A.* $62.00
    B. $56.00
    C. $54.70
    D. Not given

2. What is the cost of one ticket bought on March 8?
    A. $13.50
    B. $15.00
    C. $16.00
    D. $17.00
    E.* $18.00

3. What is the total savings with the group discount if they purchase the tickets on before March 1?
    A. $1.60
    B.* $6.40
    C. Cannot determine from information given
    D. There is no savings

one can get six multiple-choice items to a page. So the two-page item set might contain as many as 10-12 items, allowing for a brief introductory passage on the first page.

Problem Solving

Table 3.6 contains an example of mathematical problem solving, a variation of the traditional story problem, except that the test items provide for a more thorough problem-solving exercise. It is important to note that each item tests a different solution process. Item 1 requires the test taker to determine the total cost by multiplying, deducting a 10% discount, and correctly adding the handling charge to arrive at the total cost. Distractors should represent common student errors in solving this very difficult and complex problem. Item 2 requires careful reading and the adding of the ticket price and the handling charge. Item 3 requires the test taker to compute the amount of the 10% discount for each ticket and multiplying by four.

Problem solving also can be done abstractly, for instance in a nursing examination. Table 3.7 provides a patient problem with a slight variation in the problem solving where the stimulus presents the problem and several questions later, a change in the scenario introduces a new problem, with new questions asked.

Table 3.7
Problem-Solving Item Set in Professional Testing

Ms. Maty Petel, 28-years-old, is seen by her physician for complaints of muscular weakness, fatigue, and a fine tremor of the hands. Hyperthyroidism is suspected and her prescriptions include a radioactive iodine uptake test.

307. The nurse should explain to Ms. Petel that the chief purpose of a radioactive iodine uptake test is to
    A. ascertain the ability of the thyroid gland to produce thyroxine.
    B. measure the activity of the thyroid gland.
    C. estimate the concentration of the thyrotropic hormone in the thyroid gland.
    D. determine the best method of treating the thyroid condition.

308. In preparing Ms. Petel for the radioactive iodine uptake test, the nurse should provide which of the following instructions?
    A. "You will have to rest quietly in bed from the time you receive the radioactive iodine until the procedure is completed."
    B. "You will have to save all your urine for 48 hours after the ingestion of the radioactive iodine."
    C. "You will have a series of X rays taken immediately after the injection of the radioactive iodine."
    D. "You will have a thyroid scan done 24 hours after taking the radioactive iodine."

The results of the diagnostic tests confirm a diagnosis of hyperthyroidism. Ms. Petel consents to surgery on a future date. Her current prescriptions include propylthiouracil.

309. The nurse should explain to Ms. Petel that the propylthiouracil initially achieves its therapeutic effect by which of the following actions?
    A. Lowering the metabolic rate
    B. Inhibiting the formation of thyroxine
    C. Depressing the activity of stored thyroid hormone
    D. Reducing the iodide concentration in the thyroid gland

Two months later, Ms. Petel is admitted to the hospital and undergoes a subtotal thyroidectomy.

310. During the immediate postoperative period, the nurse should assess Ms. Petel for laryngeal nerve damage. Which of the following findings would indicate the presence of this problem?
    A. Facial twitching
    B. Wheezing
    C. Hoarseness
    D. Hemorrhage

311. If Ms. Petel were to develop carpopedal spasms, which of the following medications should the nurse have available for administration?
    A. Calcium gluconate
    B. Potassium chloride
    C. Diazepam (Valium)
    D. Phenytoin sodium (Dilantin)

Interlinear

This format is useful for objectively testing such writing skills as grammatical usage, spelling, capitalization, or punctuation. The introductory stimulus has an annotated paragraph containing the correct and incorrect usages and identifying choices. This format comes very close to matching what a student would do in a writing class with an essay needing corrections. The major difference is that this format is objectively scorable. Table 3.8 provides an example of this format.

Pictorial

This format provides a stimulus that has verbal material and some pictorial representation such as a chart, graph, table of data, work of art, photograph, drawing, figure, map, or the like. Table 3.4 provides an example of an item set in the MTF format. Table 3.9 gives an example of an item set where a geometric drawing provides the stimulus to ask a battery of questions designed to test one's understanding of different types of angles and relationships among these types of angles.

Innovative Variations of The Item Set Format

The pictorial variation of the context-dependent item set offers considerable opportunity to ask questions in interesting and effective ways. Table 3.10 provides an example of a table showing number of participants and number of injuries for 20 sports. Test items can be written to test one's understanding of the data as well as inferences that can be made from these data. The test items reflect reading the table and evaluating data presented in the table. Some items require that a ratio of injuries-to-participants be created for each sport, to evaluate the rate of injury.

Table 3.3 presents an item set using true-false items. This item set contains a situation and a series of statements which must be derived from the situation.

The author cleverly used the true-false format to question the students about their understanding of plant photosynthesis and the biochemical reactions in plant

---

Table 3.8
Interlinear Item Set

For each numbered pair of choices, choose the letter next to the correct spelling of the word and fill in your answer sheet with that letter next to the number of the item.

There (**1. A. our or B. are**) many ways to invest money. You can earn (**2. A. intrest or B. interest**) by buying savings bonds. Or you can (**3. A. bye or B. buy or C. by**) corporate bonds. Or you can become a (**4. A. part-owner or B. partowner**) of a company by owning stock in a company. As a shareholder in a company, you can share in company (**5. A. profits or B. prophets**).

Table 3.9
Pictorial Item Set

Refer to the figure to answer the next five questions.

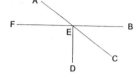

1. What is the sum of angles
    BEC and CED?
    A. less than 90 degrees
    B.* 90 degrees
    C. 180 degrees
    D. more than 180 degrees

2. Which angle is equal to
    CED?
    A. BEC
    B.* AEF
    C. AEB
    D. FED

4. Which is a right
    angle?
    A.* BED
    B. AEF
    C. CED
    D. BEC

3. Which angle is greater than
    90 degrees?
    A. BEC
    B.* AEB
    C. FED
    D. AEF

5. Which is an
    acute angle?
    A.* AEF
    B. AEB
    C. FED

growth. The format permits the presentation of an ordinary-looking problem, but the use of the true-false format enables the test maker to ask as many questions as are relevant to the subject of the test and its purpose. As many as 25 of these items could be presented on a single page.

Summary

The context-dependent item set is one of several effective ways to measure complex thinking. Constructed-response questioning has been a traditional option for such testing, but historical efforts as reported by the Technical Staff (1933, 1937) and more current efforts clearly illustrate that writing such items may be more difficult than other formats, but the results are more realistic of mental processes involved in problem solving and in other types of higher level thinking.

Calculators and Multiple-Choice

Recently, the use of inexpensive, simple electronic calculators become part of the multiple-choice testing experience. Because the National Council of Teachers of Mathematics (1989) strongly encouraged the use of calculators in instruction, it seems natural to use calculators in testing as well as in teaching. Prominent standardized testing programs have recently introduced calculators into the testing situation (for example, the recently renamed Scholastic Assessment Test and the Uniform Certified Public Accountancy Examination). However, the use of calculators may affect test results or redefine what we are trying to measure via our test items. Calculators can be used in the testing process but with the understanding that the use of calculators may change the performance characteristics of items intended for use without calculators.

Loyd (1991) made some noteworthy observations about using calculators with these item formats. Although calculation errors will likely diminish with the use of calculators, the amount of time needed for administration of a test consisting of calculator items may actually increase because the nature of the task being tested will become more complex. Actual performance changes under conditions of calculators and no calculators, depending on the type of material tested (e.g., concepts, computation, problem solving) and grade level is very complex (Lewis & Hoover, 1981). Some researchers reported that calculators have no or small effects on test performance because the construct tested is not affected by using calculators (Ansley, Spratt, & Forsyth, 1988). Loyd (1991) further reported that these studies show that, in an item-by-item analysis of the use of calculators, some items requiring calculation have improved performance because of calculators, whereas other items are impervious to the use of calculators. A study by Cohen and Kim (1992) showed that the use of calculators for college-age students actually changed the objective that the item represented. These researchers recommended that even the type of calculator used can have an untoward effect of item performance. Poe, Johnson, and Barkanic (1992) reported a study using a nationally normed standardized achievement test where calculators had been experimentally introduced several times at different grade levels. Both age and ability were found to influence test performance when calculators were permitted.

This research shows that the use of calculators should be governed by the nature of the task at hand and the role that calculators are supposed to play in answering the question. Thus, the actual format of the item (e.g., multiple-choice or true-false) is not the issue in determining whether or not a calculator should be used. Instead, we need to study the mental task required by the item in conjunction with the decision to use a calculator.

In conclusion, calculators should be used with test items if the intent is to facilitate computations as part of the response to the test items. With standardized tests, calculators should be used in such a way as to minimize the variability of experience in using calculators, and interpretations should be made cautiously in this light. This is analogous to giving a test in English to a non-English speaker and drawing the conclusion that the person cannot read. Calculators should not be used if the standardized test was normed under conditions where calculators were not used. Thus, using calculators may provide an advantage that will bias the reporting and use of test scores. If the test is classroom specific, then the use of calculators

Table 3.10
Sports and the Emergency Room

SPORT		INJURIES	PARTICIPANTS[1]
1.	Basketball	646,678	26.2
2.	Bicycle riding	600,649	54.0
3.	Baseball, softball	459,542	36.1
4.	Football	453,684	13.3
5.	Soccer	150,449	10.0
6.	Swimming	130,362	66.2
7.	Volleyball	129,839	22.6
8.	Roller skating	113,150	26.5
9.	Weightlifting	86,398	39.2
10.	Fishing	84,115	47.0
11.	Horseback riding	71,490	10.0
12.	Skateboarding	56,435	8.0
13.	Ice hockey	54,601	1.8
14.	Gymnastics	44,877	n/a
15.	Wrestling	43,894	n/a
16.	Golf	38,626	24.7
17.	Tennis	29,936	16.7
18.	Ice skating	29,047	7.9
19.	Water skiing	26,333	9.0
20.	Bowling	25,417	40.4

[1] In millions.

SOURCE: National Safety Council's Consumer Product Safety Commission, National Sporting Goods Association

Table 3.10
(continued)

1. Which sport has the greatest number of participants?
   A. Basketball
   B. Bicycle riding
   C.* Swimming
   D. Football
   E. Fishing

2. Which sport has the least number of injuries?
   A. Gymnastics
   B. Ice hockey
   C. Basketball
   D.* Bowling

3. Which of the following sports has the highest injury rate,
   considering numbers of participants?
   A. Basketball
   B. Bicycle riding
   C. Baseball
   D. Ice hockey
   E.* Football

4. What is the average number of injuries per participant for fishing?
   A. 47.0
   B.* .002
   C. 84,115
   D. Not able to determine from data given

5. Which is the safest sport of those listed?
   A.* Weightlifting
   B. Horseback riding
   C. Wrestling
   D. Water skiing

6. Which sport is the most dangerous of those listed?
   A. Soccer
   B.* Ice hockey
   C. Bicycle riding
   D. Bowling

---

can be integrated with instruction, and any novelty effect of calculator use can be avoided.

On the Value of Accompanying Graphs, Tables, Illustrations, and Photographs

Many standardized tests as well as credentialing tests use graphs, tables, illustrations, or photographs as part of the item. There are many pros and cons to consider before choosing to use accompanying material like this.

Primary among the reasons for using material is that it completes the presentation of the problem to be solved. In many testing situations, it is inconceivable that we would not find such material. Imagine certification tests in medicine for plastic surgery, ophthalmology, dermatology, orthopedic surgery, and otolaryngology that would not have items that present patient diseases, injuries, or congenital conditions in as lifelike a manner as possible. Tests in virtually any subject matter can be enhanced by visual material. But are such items better than items with no visual material? Washington and Godfrey (1974) reported a study on a single military test where the findings provided a scant margin of advantage for illustrated items. Lacking descriptive statistics, this study can hardly be taken as conclusive.

The arguments against using illustrated items is that they require more space and take more time to read. One would have to have a strong rationale for using these items. That is, the test specifications or testing policies would have to justify illustrated items. On the whole, the main advantage would appear to be face validity.

Dangerous Answers

The purpose of any licensing/certification test is to pass competent candidates and fail incompetent candidates, to protect the public from incompetent practitioners. In the health professions, one line of promising research has been the use of *dangerous answers*, distractors that if chosen would have seriously harmful effects on patients portrayed in the problem. The inference is that a physician who chooses a dangerous answer potentially endangers his or her patients. The use of dangerous distractors in such tests would assist in the identification of dangerously incompetent practitioners.

Skakun and Gartner (1990) provided a useful distinction. Dangerous answers are choices of actions that cause harm to patients, whereas deadly answers are fatal actions. Their research shows that (a) these items can be successfully written, and (b) the inclusion of such items was agreed as content relevant by appropriate content review committees of professional practitioners. The study by Slogoff and Hughes (1987), however, provided a more thorough analysis. First, they found that passing candidates chose fewer dangers answers (3.4) than failing candidates (1.6). In a follow up of 92 passing candidates who chose four or more dangerous answers, a review of their clinical practices failed to reveal any abnormalities that would raise concern over their competence. They concluded that the use of such answers was not warranted. Perhaps the best use of dangerous answers is in formative testing during medical and other professional training.

Comparability of Test Results
When Using Different Formats

A major issue in the design of test items and tests is the idea that different test formats presented in this chapter are inherently different in terms of the difficulty of test results, the actual content measured by a particular item format, or the type of mental activity. This is an important concern because the choice of any of these formats may significantly affect test results. Smith and Smith (1984) reported significant differences in difficulty as a function of formats. They also hypothesized that these differences may be attributed to verbal ability, testwiseness training, or reading ability. Although their study did not address differences among the formats presented in this chapter, it did raise important questions regarding potential differences among the conventional multiple-choice and other formats described in this chapter. Definitive research on this issue will give us more effective guidance about formats to embrace or avoid in the future.

Summary

This chapter has presented and evaluated seven types of multiple-choice item formats. The conventional multiple-choice, the matching, the alternate-choice, and the multiple true-false items are clearly useful formats for many types of cognitive behavior. The complex multiple-choice and true-false formats are not recommended. The item set is the most problematic because of our lack of experience with it and lack of research on its effectiveness. Scoring item sets presents a challenge as well. However, with significant increased interest in testing higher level thinking, the item set may be a more valued member of the family of multiple-choice formats to be used in the future.

DEVELOPING MULTIPLE-CHOICE ITEMS

4

WRITING THE TEST ITEM

Overview

John Bormuth (1970) commented that item writing is not a science but simply a collection of rules based on experience and the wisdom of mentors, often captured in textbooks. Indeed, for some time little scientific basis existed for advice on item writing, but slowly it is emerging. This chapter contains a collection of these item-writing rules. The basis for these rules draws from two studies. The first involved an analysis of 46 textbooks and other sources on how to write multiple-choice test items (Haladyna & Downing, 1989a). The result of that study was a taxonomy of 43 item-writing rules. Author consensus existed for most of these rules. But for other rules, a lack of consensus was evident. A second study involved an analysis of over 90 research studies on the validity of these item-writing rules (Haladyna & Downing (1989b). Only a few rules received extensive study, and nearly one half of these 43 rules received no study at all. Since the appearance of these two studies, other, newer studies have contributed to our understanding of how to and how not to write items.

This chapter contains mostly advice, not scientific principles or laws of item writing as Bormuth had so strongly desired to achieve in his book. All advice should be taken with the proviso that item writing is still only an emerging science. In the long term, theories of item writing, like Bormuth's algorithmic approach, are desirable. In the short term, item writers need a set of working principles and procedures from which to base their item-writing craft. Item writers might apply these rules judiciously, but not rigidly, as the authenticity of some rules appears to still be in question.

Each item-writing rule is presented and discussed, and examples exemplify a use or misuse of the rule. The rules and examples fall into several categories: (a) general procedural item-writing concerns, (b) general content item-writing concerns, (c) stem construction, (d) general option development, (e) correct answer concerns, and (f) distractor development.

General Procedural Item-Writing Concerns

Use The Best-Answer or Correct-Answer Formats. As stated in chapter 3, one can use a multiple-choice format that requires the examinee to distinguish a right answer from the wrong answer. A variation of the multiple-choice is the "best-answer" format. With this format, all options are correct, but one is the best correct answer in terms of degrees of correctness. For example:

> Which is the most effective painkiller for a migraine headache?
> A.   Tylenol
> B.   Bufferin
> C.   Ordinary aspirin
> D.* Anaprox

Although there is no research to report the effectiveness of either format, the best answer format seems well suited for testing a student's ability to evaluate. One should feel free to use either format.

Avoid Complex Multiple-Choice. Chapter 3 suggests that this format should be avoided. Research has shown conclusively that such items are more difficult, less discriminating, and lead to tests that are less reliable (Albanese, 1992). Further, these test items require more reading and occupy more space on the test page. This format also requires more effort to develop the item. Because the multiple true-false format is a viable alternative with research supporting its use, the complex multiple-choice should be avoided.

Format the Item Vertically or Horizontally. Any multiple-choice item can be formatted either way. The most conventional format is vertical as shown below:

> Which is the most desirable test format for measuring evaluating behavior?
> A.   True-false
> B.   Testlet
> C.   Multiple-true false
> D.* Best answer

This item could be reformatted horizontally:

> Which is the most desirable test format for measuring evaluating
> behavior?
>   A. True-false   B. Testlet   C. Multiple true-false
>   D. Best answer

The advantage to the latter format is that it occupies less space on a page and is therefore more efficient in terms of printing cost. On the other hand, cramped items affect the look of the test. If appearance is important, horizontal formatting should be avoided. With younger children or test anxious test takers, the horizontal format may be more difficult to read thus needlessly depressing test performance.

Allow Time for Editing and Other Types of Revisions. Depending upon the purpose of the test and the time and other resources devoted to testing, one should always allow for editorial review, review of adherence to the item-writing rules in this chapter, and constant reevaluation of items. Because chapter 7 treats this topic in greater detail, it is sufficient to say here that each test item should be free of editorial flaws or lack of clarity. The constant vigilance of editing and other types of review do not guarantee a good item. However, editing assures that lack of editing and other revisions did not contribute to poor performance. One discouraging observation by an experienced professional test builder, Steve Downing of the American Board of Internal Medicine (personal communication, June 7, 1993) is that even with expert item development, as many as 40% all new items may fail to perform as intended when first tried. Therefore, one should never overlook the opportunity to improve each item by subjecting it to reviews.

One note of caution should be made here. Cizek (1991) reviewed the research on editing test items. He reported findings that suggest that if an item is already being effectively used, editorial changes may disturb the performance characteristics of these test items. On the other hand, O'Neill (1986) and Webb & Heck (1991) reported no differences between items that had been *style* edited. Dawson-Saunders, Reshetar, Shea, Fierman, Kangilaski, and Poniatowski (1992, 1993) experimented with a variety of alterations of items. They found that reordering options with other editorial decisions may have a pronounced effect on item characteristics. A prudent strategy would be to concentrate editing on the item before instead of after its use. If editing does occur after the first use of the item, these authors suggested that one consider content editing versus statistical editing. The former suggests that content changes are needed because the information in the item needs to be improved or corrected. Statistical alteration would be dictated by information showing that a distractor did not perform and should be revised or replaced. The two kinds of alterations may lead to different performances of the same item. Expert test builders consider items that have been statistically altered as new. Such items would be subject to pretesting and greater scrutiny before being used in a test. Reordering options to effect key balancing should be done cautiously.

Avoid Errors of Grammar, Abbreviation, Punctuation, and Spelling.
There are many reasons for supporting such a rule. First, every test, despite its
purpose, is a reflection of the test maker. Errors of grammar, abbreviation,
punctuation, and spelling reflect poorly on the test maker.

As noted previously, validity is an important concept in testing. A test should
look like a test. It should be attractive. Errors of grammar, abbreviation,
punctuation, and spelling reflect an impression that the test was casually or
improperly prepared. Such errors, although superficial to some, may reflect a
deeper and more significant neglect, such as insufficient or inadequate content
definition. Some test takers might be distracted from the test-taking process by such
errors. If this is true, then these errors have another negative effect, that of causing
some students to lose concentration and fail to perform as they should. This
inattention produces a bias in test scores that undermines the valid interpretation or
use of test scores.

Minimize Examinee Reading Time. Items that require extended reading
lengthen the time needed to complete a test. Consider an important test with
alternative forms and a fixed time period. The test with wordy items requiring much
reading will provide for fewer items per fixed time period than the test with fewer
words per item.

Thus, one benefit of minimizing examinee reading time affects the number of
items one can ask in a fixed time period. Because the number of items given in a
fixed time period directly affects the reliability of test scores and the adequacy of
sampling of content, items need to be as brief as possible. Because reliability and
validity are two very important characteristics of test scores, one should make a
strong effort to minimize reading time. Unless it can be shown that lengthy reading
is necessary, such as with some complex problem-solving exercises, such items
should not be used.

Avoid Trick Items. Trick items are hard to define and illustrate. In a recent
review, Roberts (1993) reported few references in the measurement literature on
this topic. Roberts clarified the topic by distinguishing between two types of trick
items: those items deliberately intended by the item writer and those items that
accidentally trick test takers. Roberts' study revealed seven types of items that
students perceived as tricky included items:

1. where the item writer's intention appeared to be to deceive, confuse, or
    mislead test takers.
2. representing trivial content.
3. where the discrimination was too fine—referred to elsewhere in this
    chapter as overspecific items.
4. that had window dressing that was irrelevant to its answering.
5. with multiple correct answers.

6. that present principles in ways that were not learned, thus deceiving students.
7. that were so highly ambiguous that even the best students had no idea about the right answer.

Whereas Roberts encourages more work on defining trick questions, his initial research makes a much needed start on this topic.

A negative aspect of trick questions is that such questioning strategies, if frequent enough, build an attitude by the test taker characterized by distrust and potential lack of respect for the testing process. There are enough problems in testing without contributing more by using trick questions.

General Content Concerns

Base Each Item on an Important Learner Outcome (Instructional Objective). A prevailing theme in educational achievement testing for many decades has been to match the content of teaching to testing. Cohen (1987) referred to this as instructional alignment, and Nitko (1989) referred to this as integrating teaching with testing. Earlier research and theoretical discussions have evolved into a well accepted technology of teaching and training that makes the specification of learner outcomes, whether as overviews, advanced organizers, goals, objectives, learner outcome statements, and the like, essential.

The alternative is vague specification of content, often resulting in inferior achievement by students who are being instructed or trained. Also, it can be argued that if content is not well defined, the construct validity of test score interpretations and uses is undermined.

Yet, not all achievement tests reflect learner outcomes. Tests for professional licensing and certification or admissions are not designed to measure specific teachable outcomes. The method of writing and choosing items for these tests is derived from clear content definition and the selection of good items based on test specifications that identify the exact content to be included in the test. Test specifications, in turn, are derived from role delineation studies, task analysis, practice analysis, or the like. These studies usually determine the knowledge and skills needed to function in a profession, such as medicine, architecture, pharmacy, or accountancy.

Focus on a Single Problem. Every test item should be based on a single idea. The principle is that for a single fact, concept, principle, or procedure, one item represents one type of content. If a test item represents a complex, multistage thinking process to reach the correct answer, when a student misses the item, the instructor does not know what step in the process that was not learned. Complex, multistage thinking can be measured, but with a battery of items, such as found in the context-dependent item set or through a performance test with a checklist linked to these essential steps.

Keep Vocabulary Consistent with the Group of Students Being Tested.

The purpose of any achievement test is to measure accomplishment. These accomplishments are desirably linked to learner outcome statements known as objectives or goals, or to a set of test specifications. The purpose of the test is not to test one's ability to read or translate the item. Therefore, vocabulary should be simple enough for the weakest readers in the tested group. If reading is confounded with the achievement being measured, then the test score will reflect a mixture of reading ability and achievement instead of the intended outcome.

Avoid Cuing One Item With Another; Keep Items Independent of One Another.

A tendency when writing sets of items for a goal or an objective is to permit one item to provide sufficient information to answer another item. For example, consider a line of questioning focusing on main ideas of a novel just read:

1. In the story "Stones from Ybarra," who was Lupe's best friend?
   A. Kate
   B. Dolores
   C.* Roxie
   D. Mary

2. Who was quarrelling with Lupe?
   A. Kate
   B. Sara
   C. Roxie
   D.* Mary

Once a student correctly answers item 1, this testwise student will look for clues in the next item. If Roxie is correct for item 1, it must be incorrect for item 2. Kate and Roxie were mentioned in items 1 and 2, while Sara was not mentioned in item 1. Might it be the right answer?

Testwise students use these kinds of strategies to select answers to items they do not know. In writing sets of items from a common stimulus, care must be exercised to avoid this kind of cuing. Other types of trick questions can hinge from a violation of other item-writing rules that will be shown elsewhere in this chapter.

Use Others' Items as a Basis for Writing Items.

One should not knowingly use another's item, as items, like other creative efforts, are original. With a copyrighted test, plagiarism is illegal. However, there is much to be gained from modeling or imitation. There are many sources of model items, and these models should be observed, learned, and used whenever possible to develop one's own items. It is far better to work from familiar examples than to be completely creative in item writing. This is not to say that there is not a need for creative item writing. In most circumstances, there is a need to develop items that follow some content considerations expressed in a goal or objective, and to converge on an item format and item that looks as good as other items in the item pool.

The item shell technique presented in chapter 6 shows that such modeling or imitation will often result in the development of additional high quality items with less effort than is normal. Consequently, many examples are provided in chapters 4, 5, and 6.

Avoid Overspecific Knowledge. The concept of overspecific knowledge refers to a continuum of specificity that ranges from abstract to concrete:

abstract————————————————————————————concrete

The following item shows one extreme:

Which is the most serious problem in the world?
A. Hunger
B. Education
C. Disease
D. Intolerance

What is life?
A. The exchange of oxygen for carbon dioxide
B. The existence of a soul
C. Movement

Entire books cover each of these topics. There is probably no correct answer to these simplistic items, but each defies a specific answer because each is so abstract. This is clearly one type of problem in specificity/abstractness. At the other extreme:

Who is the second author of the 1968 book *Statistical Theories of Mental Test Scores*?
A. Lord
B.* Novick
C. Gulliksen
D. Jackson
E. Bock

Whereas this second item might reflect violations of other item-writing rules as well, this item reflects a tendency to ask students for information that is ultraspecific.

The judgment of specificity is a personal, subjective decision, and each item writer must decide how specific or how abstract each item must be to reflect adequately the selected learner outcome statement. Ideally, item specifications would help with the specificity of an item, but such devices are rare and difficult to construct. Chapter 10 addresses this problem as well as the need to provide more structure for item writers.

Generally, items are members of content domains, and tests consist of samples from this domain; therefore, items should have some generality to this domain and to regions in the domain.

Avoid Textbook, Verbatim Phrasing. A superficial way of writing test items and one that is not recommended is to identify important sentences from a textbook or other authoritative sources and transform the sentence into a test item. Bormuth (1970) proposed a theory of item writing that transforms such prose into multiple-choice test items. Although the theory has many sound features, it promotes undesirable rote learning of textual materials. Instructors, instructional designers, and curriculum specialists probably will want to emphasize higher level thinking such as defining, predicting, evaluating, and problem solving. Using familiar textbook materials for test questions restricts learning and testing to simple recall. Most modern educators would not support such a teaching or testing philosophy. In fact, there are strong indications that the future of educational testing will emphasize higher level thinking instead of recall that is found in many achievement tests (Nickerson, 1989).

Avoid Items Based on Opinions. This advice derives from the value that items should reflect well-known and publicly supported facts, concepts, principles, and procedures. To test a student over an opinion about any content seems unfair, unless the opinion is qualified by some logical analysis, evidence, or presentation cited in the instructional materials. For example:

Who is the best baseball player in the National League?
A.   Ryne Sandberg
B.   Barry Larkin
C.   Will Clark
D.* Bobby Bonds
E.   Bobby Bonilla

Although the answer is arguable, the criteria for judging "best" are unclear.

According to The Sporting News, who was the best player in the National League in 1990?
A.   Ryne Sandberg
B.   Barry Larkin
C.   Will Clark
D.* Bobby Bonds
E.   Bobby Bonilla

This second question has a qualifier and refers to a specific season, and there is clearly a correct answer.

Emphasize Higher Level Thinking. Although this advice borders closely on other advice, such as *avoiding overspecific knowledge*, a heavy emphasis exists in education to teach and test for outcomes reflecting more complex content and higher level thinking. There is a prevailing perception that in the past there has been too much reliance on low-level recall type teaching and testing (Stiggins, Griswold, & Wikelund, 1989). That is why there is a tendency to diminish the teaching of facts and increase the teaching of concepts and principles, and also to teach for higher level thinking processes. Chapters 5 and 6 provide methods for doing this.

Test for Important or Significant Material; Avoid Trivial Material. Much has been said about trivializing education by teaching and testing for the recall of insignificant content. This rule complements several others presented previously. The issue here is not the cognitive level (recall vs. higher level thinking). Rather the issue is what content should be tested. In other words, what is the relevance of the content of any test? The issue of relevance is one that every teacher and test maker faces. Learning does not happen in isolation. We need to be aware of causes of learning. One of those causes is the relevance of the material learned.

In the selection of content, in teaching and in testing, students are most effectively served by selecting important or significant content and avoiding trivial learning. Current initiatives in school reform and cognitive psychology point to constructivism, where meaningful learning is a necessary ingredient in learning.

Some examples of trivial questioning follow:

1. When was the Webster-Ashburton treaty signed?

2. Who wrote *Crime and Punishment*?

3. What is the Capital of Delaware?

4. How many home runs did Luke Appling hit in 1954?

Some examples of more significant questioning with complex content or higher level thought processes provide alternatives to the above:

1. What was the significance of the Webster-Ashburton to American diplomacy in the mid-1800s?

2. What was Dostoyevski's motivation in writing *Crime and Punishment*?

3. Why did Dover become the state capital of Delaware?

4. What accomplishments qualified Luke Appling for the Hall of Fame?

Stem Construction

<u>**State the Item in a Question Format Instead of a Completion Format.**</u> Chapter 3 presented two types of multiple-choice formats, the question and the completion. Research shows a preference for the question format (Haladyna & Downing, 1989b; Statman, 1988). Although the two formats offer very little difference in appearance and length, the question format is a simpler and more direct tactic for eliciting a response from a test taker. In keeping with the idea that multiple-choice questions should emphasize attainment of knowledge instead of reading, every tactic designed to make the item read more clearly should be employed. The question format appears to more effectively accomplish that end.

Statman (1988) provided a very reasoned analysis of the problem. She maintained that with the completion format, one has to retain the stem in short-term memory while completing the stem with each option, evaluating the truthfulness of each option, or if short-term memory fails, the test taker has to range back and forth from the stem to each option, making a connection and evaluating the truth of that connection. Testing is anxiety provoking, and the added stress of the completion format may contribute to test anxiety, a problem that already troubles about one in four test takers, according to research by Kennedy Hill and his colleagues (e.g., Hill & Wigfield, 1984). The mental steps involved in answering a completion item also takes more time, which is undesirable. The problem is great for the native speaker, but the learner with English as a second language has an even greater problem. From the standpoints of reading comprehension, administration time, anxiety, the quality of the test item, and efficiency, the question format is a more effective way to test for knowledge than the completion format. An example in the question format is:

> For multiple-choice items, which format is recommended?
> A.* Question
> B. Completion
> C. Complex multiple-choice
> D. Multidimensional-choice

An example in the completion format is:

> For multiple-choice testing, one should use the
> A.* question format.
> B. completion format.
> C. complex multiple-choice format.
> D. multidimensional-choice format.

Although the completion format is not recommended, it is, and will often be used, and the completion multiple-choice items may be very adequate for many purposes. The right way to write a completion format is to develop the stem so that the correct answer and all distractors complete the sentence begun in the stem, as shown on the previous page.

If a Completion Format is Used, Never Leave a Blank in the Middle or at the Beginning of the Stem. For example:

The _____ format is the best way to format a multiple-choice item.
A. completion
B.* question
C. complex multiple-choice
D. multidimensional-choice

A main benefit of _____ testing is that it supports content sampling better than other formats.
A. paper-and-pencil
B.* multiple-choice
C. essay
D. performance

These formats are difficult for students to read. Such items also require more time to administer and reduce the time spent productively answering other questions. For these reasons, the use of internal or beginning blanks in completion-type items should be avoided.

Ensure That Directions in the Stem are Clear and That Wording Lets the Examinee Know Exactly What is Being Asked. The item stem should always phrase the problem to be answered by each option in a clear and unambiguous way. The test taker should always know what is being asked in the item.

When an item fails to perform with students as intended, there are many reasons. One of these reasons may be that the stem did not present the problem in a clear enough manner to most students. This lack of clarity is difficult to detect when items are written, but the item review or item tryout will often reveal why an item did not perform.

For example:

Recitative is
A.* a form of musical expression.
B. the spoken part of an opera.
C. the introduction to a musical work.
D. synonymous with libretto.

This stem provides no direction or idea about what the item writer wants to know. A more focused stem would be:

> In opera, what is the purpose of recitative?

Avoid Window Dressing (Excessive Verbiage) in the Stem. Some items contain words, phrases, or entire sentences that have absolutely nothing to do with the item. One reason for doing this is to make the item look more lifelike or realistic, to provide some substance to it. For example:

> High temperatures and heavy rainfall characterize a humid climate. People in this kind of climate usually complain of heavy perspiration. Even moderately warm days seem uncomfortable. Which climate is described?
> A. Savanna
> B.* Tropical rainforest
> C. Tundra

A better version is:

> Which term below describes a climate with high temperatures and heavy rainfall?
> A. Savanna
> B.* Tropical rainforest
> C. Tundra

There are times when window dressing may be appropriate. For example, in problems where the test taker sorts through information and selects information to solve a problem, excessive information is necessary. (Note that the phrase *window dressing* is used exclusively for situations where useless information is embedded in the stem without any purpose or value.)

> A compact disc at the music store was specially priced at $9.99, but typically sells at $12.00. This weekend, it was marked at a 20% discount from this special price. Sales tax is 6%. Tina had $9.00 in her purse and no credit card. Does Tina have enough money to buy this compact disc?

In this item, the student needs to compute the discount, figure out the actual sales price, compute the sales tax, add the tax to the actual sale price, and compare that amount to $9.00. The $12.00 is irrelevant, and the student is supposed to ignore this fact in the problem-solving effort. This is not window dressing.

Word the Stem Positively; Avoid Negative Phrasing. The reason for this rule comes from a consensus of experts in the field of testing who feel that the use of negative words in the stem have negative words effects on students and their responses to such items. Some research on the use of negative words also suggests that students have difficulty understanding the meaning of negatively phrased items.

> Which is NOT a benefit of multiple-choice testing?
> A. Better sampling of content
> B. Greater reliability of test scores
> C.* More appropriate for measuring performance
> D. Objectivity of scoring results

A better way to phrase such an item is to remove the NOT and make the item a multiple-true false with more options:

> Which are benefits of multiple-choice testing?
> Mark A if true or B if false
> 1. Greater potential for content sampling (A)
> 2. Greater potential for high reliability (A)
> 3. More appropriate for measuring aspects of performance (B)
> 4. Objectively scored (A)
> 5. Able to measure higher level thinking (A)
> 6. Subject to guessing (A)
> 7. Free of bias (B)

Another benefit of this transformation is that because the options now become items, more items can be added, gaining more content coverage.

Another variation of this rule is that when a negative is used, it should be stressed or emphasized by placing in bold type, capitalizing it, or underlining it, or all of these. The reason is that the student often reads through the not and forgets to reverse the logic of the relationship being tested. This is why the use of **not** is not recommended for item stems.

Include the Central Idea and Most of the Phrasing in the Stem. One fault in item writing is to have a brief stem and most of the content in the options. For example:

> Corporal punishment
> A. has been outlawed in many states.
> B.* is psychologically unsound for school discipline.
> C. has many benefits to recommend its use.
> D. is commonly practiced in our schools.

The test taker does not obtain the intent of the item after reading the stem. Thus, the diffuse nature of the options makes the test item less likely to succeed. If the objective of the item is to define corporal punishment, then the item could be more effectively rephrased to include the main idea of the item in the stem, as follows:

> What is corporal punishment?
> A.* A psychologically unsound form of school discipline.
> B. A useful disciplinary technique if used sparingly.
> C. An illegal practice in the nation's schools.
> D. A widespread and proven effective discipline method.

Although the completion format is not recommended, it is widely used. When it is used, repetitious wording in the options is a common error, as the example below shows:

> Occlusion of the right coronary artery near its origin by a thrombus would most likely result in:
> A. infarction of the lateral wall of right ventricle and the right atrium.
> B. infarction of the lateral left ventricle.
> C. infarction of the anterior left ventricle.
> D. infarction of the anterior septum.

An improved version of this item, using the recommended question format would be:

> What area would suffer an infarction following occlusion of the right coronary artery near its origin by a thrombus?
> A. Lateral wall of the right ventricle and the right atrium
> B. Lateral left ventricle
> C. Anterior left ventricle
> D. Anterior septum

Option Development

Use as Many Plausible Distractors as Possible. The ideal number of options for test item is a matter of considerable debate (Haladyna & Downing, in press; Lord, 1977; Trevisan, Sax, & Michael, 1991). One issue is the way distractors perform with test takers. A good distractor should be selected by low achievers and ignored by high achievers. As chapters 8 and 9 show, a science of option response study is available.

To summarize briefly this research on the correct number of options, evidence exists to suggest a slight advantage to having more options per test item, but only if each distractor is doing its job. Haladyna and Downing (in press) found that the number of useful distractors per item on the average for a well developed standardized tests was one or two. Another implication of this research is that three options may be a natural limit for most multiple-choice items. Thus, item writers are often frustrated in finding a useful fourth or fifth option because they do not exist.

The advice given here is that one should write as many good distractors as one can, but should expect that only one or two will really work as intended. Thus, it does not matter how many distractors one produces for any given multiple-choice item, but it does matter that each distractor performs as intended. This advice runs counter to most standardized testing programs. Customarily, answer sheets are used with a predetermined number of options, such as four or five. However, research has shown that items typically have only one or two performing distractors, so the existence of nonperforming distractors is nothing more than "window dressing." Thus, test developers have the dilemma of producing unnecessary distractors, which do not operate as they should, for the appearance of the test versus producing tests with varying degrees of options.

One criticism of using fewer instead of more options for an item is that guessing plays a greater role in determining a student's score. The use of fewer distractors will increase the chances of a student guessing the right answer. However, the probability that a test taker will increase his or her score significantly over a 20-, 50- or 100-item test by pure guessing is infinitesimal. The floor of a test containing three options per item for a student who lacks knowledge and guesses randomly throughout the test is 33% correct. Therefore, administering more test items will reduce the influence of guessing on the total test score. This logic is sound for two-option items as well, because the floor of the scale is 50% and the probability of a student making 20, 50, or 100 successful randomly correct guesses is very close to zero.

Place Options in Logical or Numerical Order. In the formatting of test items for a test, the options should always appear in either logical or numerical order. Answers should always be arranged in ascending or descending numerical order.

WRONG	RIGHT
What is the cost of an item normally sells for $9.99 that is discounted 25%?	What is the cost of an item that that normally sells for $9.99 that is discounted 25%?
A. $5.00	A. $2.50
B.* $7.50	B. $5.00
C. $2.50	C. $6.66
D. $6.66	D.* $7.50

Answers should always be arranged in ascending or descending numerical order. Remember that the idea of the item is to test for knowledge in a direct fashion. If a student has to unnecessarily hunt for the correct answer, then the stress level for the test is unnecessarily increased and the test taker's time is wasted.

Logical ordering is more difficult to illustrate, but there are some examples that offer hints at what is meant by this rule. The following example illustrates illogical ordering.

What are three important concerns in achievement testing?
A.* Validity, reliability, efficiency
B. Objectivity, validity, reliability
C. Reliability, objectivity, efficiency
D. Efficiency, objectivity, validity

Although such a questioning strategy may be criticized for other reasons, this popular format is additionally and unnecessarily confusing because the four possible terms (validity, reliability, efficiency, and objectivity) are presented in an inconsistent order. A more logical ordering and presentation is:

A.* Validity, reliability, efficiency
B. Validity, reliability, objectivity
C. Validity, efficiency, objectivity
D. Reliability, efficiency, objectivity

There are instances where the logical ordering has to do with the form of the answers instead of the content:

When an item fails to perform, what is the most common cause?
A.* The item was faulty.
B. Instruction was ineffective.
C. Student effort was inadequate.
D. The objective did not match the item.

In this instance, answers should be presented in order of length, short to long.

Keep Options Independent; Options Should Not Be Overlapping. This subtle item-writing fault is very much like the advice on interitem cuing. If options are overlapping, they are unlikely to be correct. If overlapping options are correct, then the item may have two or more correct answers.

The item below illustrates this problem:

> What age range represents the physical "peak" of life?
> A. 11-15
> B. 13-19
> C. 18-25
> D.* 24-32
> E. over 32

Numerical problems that have ranges that are close make the item more difficult. More importantly in this example, options A, B, C, and D overlap slightly. If the answer is age 25, then one can argue that both C and D are correct, when the author of the item meant C. This careless error can be simply corrected by developing ranges that are distinctly different. The avoidance of overlapping options also will prevent embarrassing challenges to test items.

Keep All Options in An Item Homogeneous in Content. The use of options that are heterogeneous in content is often a cue to the student. Such cues are not inherent in the intent of the item, but an unfortunate accident. Therefore, the maintenance of homogeneous options is good advice. The following item illustrates homogeneous options:

> What will make salsa hottest?
> A. Adding red chili peppers
> B. Adding green chili peppers
> C. Adding onions and green peppers
> D.* Adding jalapeno chili peppers

Three options are similar and one is dissimilar. The student is likely to select the option that is unlike the others. Of course, if one of the homogeneous options is correct, the item may be a trick question.

Keep Option Lengths Similar. One common fault in item writing is to make the correct answer the longest. This may happen very innocently. The item writer writes the stem and the right answer, and in the rush to complete the item adds two or three hastily written wrong answers that are shorter than the right answer. For example:

> What does research tell us about assigning homework?
> A.* If the homework is relevant to learning outcomes,
>   it is an effective teaching strategy.
> B. The more homework each night, the better it is.
> C. Homework should be assigned on a daily basis, except Friday.
> D. If class is efficiently taught, homework is unnecessary.

Avoid _"all of the above."_ The use of this option has been controversial (Haladyna & Downing, 1989a). Nonetheless various text book writers recommend and use this option. One reason may be that in writing a test item, it is easy to identify one, or two, or even three right answers. The use of the option _all of the above_ is a good device for capturing this information. However, the use of this option may help testwise test takers. For instance, if a test taker has partial information (knows that two of the three options offered are correct), that information can clue the student into correctly choosing _all of the above_.

One alternative to the _all of the above_ option is the use of the multiple true-false format. Another alternative is simply avoid _all of the above_ and ensure that there is one and only one right answer.

Because the purpose of a test item is to test knowledge, using _all of the above_ seems to draw students into test-taking strategies instead of testing for knowledge. For that reason, this format should be avoided.

Avoid _"none of the above"._ Research has shown that this format has many negative characteristics leading to the conclusion that _none of the above_ should not be used (Haladyna & Downing, 1989a, 1989b). Perhaps the most obvious reason for not using this format is that a correct answer obviously exists and should be used in the item. No advantage exists for omitting the right answer from the list of choices.

One argument favoring using _none of the above_ in some circumstances is that it forces the student to solve the problem rather than choose the right answer. In these circumstances, the student may work backward, using the options to test a solution. In these instances, a constructed-response format should be used.

Avoid _"I don't know."_ The intention for using _I don't know_ as an option is to minimize the role of guessing the correct choice. Unfortunately, not all children, or adults, treat this option the same way. Sherman (1976) studied patterns of response for children answering items that had the _I don't know_ option. Differences existed for region, gender, personality variables, and ethnic background. Why would anyone want to use such an option that benefits some groups of test takers at the expense of others? In other words, the _I don't know_ option appears to have great potential for producing bias in test scores. Therefore, it should be avoided.

Phrase Options Positively. Stems should be phrased positively, and the same advice applies to options. The use of negatives such as NOT and EXCEPT should be avoided in options as well as the stem. Occasionally, the use of these words in an item stem is unavoidable. In these circumstances, these words should be highlighted, boldfaced, capitalized, or underlined, so that the test taker will not mistake the intent of the item.

Avoid Various Clues to the Right Answer. This advice pertains to a collection of common clues to item writing. These are clang associations and ridiculous options. Clang associations include phrases in the stem that are repeated in options. Such a connection is often a clue to the right answer. For example:

> Who are the "Magnificent Seven?"
> A.   A pro basketball team
> B.* A group of seven fictional, heroic Western figures
> C.   A protest group made famous during the Viet Nam War period
> D.   A vegetarian rock group known for their healthy approach to living

The second of these is simply the use of a ridiculous option, whether intended for humor or accidental. This second type of clue can be viewed as highly implausible, so much, in fact, that no test taker would choose it.

> Who is responsible for the MTV network programming concept?
> A.   Leonard Bernstein
> B.* Dick Clark
> C.   Andrew Rooney

The use of ridiculous options makes guessing easier by reducing the number of plausible distractors in a test item. Also, the use of such options may cause the examinees to question the quality of the examination, which may undermine the valid use of the test.

Avoid Grammatical Clues. It is possible to give away an answer through a grammatical error. For instance:

> The best way to increase the reliability of a test is to
> A.* increase the test length.
> B.   removing poor quality items.
> C.   Test should be readable for all test takers

Only option A grammatically completes the sentence. This is a very careless item writing error.

Avoid Specific Determiners. Specific determiners are so extreme that seldom are they correct answers. Specific determiners include such terms as ALWAYS,

NEVER, TOTALLY, ABSOLUTELY, and COMPLETELY. For instance:

> What is the most likely cause of low reliability in a classroom
> test?
> A.   Total lack of effective instruction
> B.   Completely ineffective items
> C.* Too few test items

Specific determiners may occasionally be the right answer, and, in these instances, their use is justified if the distractors also contain other specific determiners.

The Correct Option

Balance the Key. Research on the likelihood that a certain position will be randomly chosen over any other position by test takers is inconclusive (Haladyna & Downing, 1989b). Nonetheless many test makers and experts on testing recommend that the correct answer for any test be evenly balanced among the response options. For a four-option item, the correct answer should be located about 25% of the time at each option position. Any serious departure from this rule may cause higher performing students to see patterns that may clue them toward guessing right answers and performing higher than they should perform. Or, low performers may randomly select a choice position, such as C, and accidentally get a higher than deserved score by pure luck. Remember that random guessing will not be a serious factor in tests of more than 10 items. As noted earlier in this chapter, key balancing may alter the performance of the item. Thus, reordering of options should be done minimally.

Use Only One Correct Option. It seems reasonable to recommend that there be only one correct answer. Unless, of course, a scoring system will accept more than one right answer. To do so might create distress on the part of test takers. Of course, if the best answer format is used, all options are correct, but only the best of these is keyed as correct.

Given that multiple-choice test items are often imperfect, there may be occasions where more than one correct answer exists. This should not happen, but invariably it does. In these instances, the item should be double-keyed or triple-keyed to correct the problem created. Such action gives credit to any test takers choosing any of the multiple right answers. Such an item should be immediately retired or revised if it is to be used again.

In some standardized testing programs, guessing is discouraged. If the item is accidentally written to have multiple-keyed answers, the student might be induced to omit the item. In these circumstances, the item probably should be removed from the test and subsequently revised or retired.

Distractor Development

Use Plausible Distractors. Multiple-choice test items measure knowledge. Therefore, the right answer must be right, and the wrong answers must clearly be wrong. The key to developing wrong answers is plausibility.

Plausibility refers to the idea that the item should be correctly answered by those who possess a high degree of the knowledge that the test purports to measure and incorrectly answered by those who possess a low degree of this knowledge. A plausible distractor will look like a right answer to those who lack this knowledge. The effectiveness of a distractor can be statistically analyzed (see chapter 8). Writing plausible distractors comes through hard work and is the most difficult part of multiple-choice item writing.

Some advice follows concerning how to develop plausible distractors.

Use Common Errors of Students. One typical suggestion is that if completion items (open-ended items without choices) were given, students would provide the correct answer and plausible wrong answers that are actually common student errors. In item writing, the good plausible distractor comes from a thorough understanding of common errors.

```
77 + 34 =
A.   101
B.*  111
```

In this example, the distractor A is a logical, incorrect answer for someone learning simple addition.

Use Technical Phrases. The use of technical phrases tends to appeal to students who lack the knowledge and are looking for a plausible answer to guess. Therefore, the use of a technically sounding wrong answer may prove effective. Below is one example:

```
In the design of any test, what should one always do first?
A.  Determine the dimensionality of data.
B.  Ensure that domain and test specifications are grounded
    in theory.
C.* Specify the test score use or interpretation.
D.  Select the logistic item response model according to the
    number of parameters desired.
```

Although the distractors are somewhat plausible correct answers, all are technically written. Each could be written in simpler language, but they might be more obviously wrong.

Use True, Incorrect Phrases. Another strategy is to write distractors that are true statements, but do not answer the question. For example:

What is generally true about the relationship between item quality and reliability?
A.   You can't have validity without reliability.
B.* Weak items tend to increase measurement error.
C.   Item performance may be reflected in poor teaching.
D.   A restricted range in the test scores may reduce reliability estimates.

All of these statements are true, but options A, C, and D are irrelevant to the question.

Avoid the Use of Humor. Although humor is a valuable tool in teaching and learning and can do much to lessen tension and improve the learning environment, it should be avoided in testing. Items containing humor can reduce the number of plausible distractors, and, therefore, make the item artificially easier. Humor also might encourage the student to take the test less seriously. Limited research on the use of humor shows that, in theory, humor should reduce anxiety, but sometimes highly anxious test takers react in negative ways. Because the test measures knowledge, the use of humor detracts from this purpose and does little good. The safe practice is to avoid humor.

Special Rules

The preceding pages of this chapter focused on general item-writing advice. Many of these rules equally apply to the various formats presented in chapter 3, including alternate-choice, matching, multiple true-false, and item sets. However, special rules may be needed that are unique to each format. This next section provides some specific guidance to item writers for these other formats.

Rules For Matching Items

Generally, the set of options for a matching item set is homogeneous in terms of content. Because the benefit of a matching format is the measurement of under- standing of a single learner outcome, the homogeneity of content is a characteristic of a set of matching items.

Also, the number of options should NOT equal the number of items. The basis for this advice is that test takers may try to match up items to options believing in a one-to-one correspondence. If this is true, then there is interitem cuing. If this is not true, students will be confused.

Rules for Alternate-Choice Items

Because alternate-choice is a short form of conventional multiple-choice, no unique rules appear in this section.

Rules for Multiple True-False (MTF) Item Clusters

1. The number of MTF items per cluster may vary within a test.
2. Conventional multiple-choice or complex multiple-choice items convert nicely to MTF items.
3. No strict rules exist about how many true and false items appear in a cluster, but it seems reasonable to expect a balance between the number of true and false items per set.
4. The limit for the number of items in a cluster may be as few as 3 or as many as would fit on a single page (approximately 30-35).

Rules for True-False Testing Items

Although many experts currently do not recommend the true-false format, a body of knowledge exists on the writing of these items. In the interest of providing a balanced presentation of rules for various formats, this section exists.

Frisbie and Becker (1991) surveyed 17 textbooks and extracted 22 common rules for writing true-false items. Most of the rules are similar if not identical with those presented earlier in this chapter. One thing to keep in mind, however, is that most of these rules fail to reach consensus from writers of textbooks or from research. Nonetheless, Frisbie and Becker provided many excellent insights into true-false item writing that are reviewed and discussed here.

Balance the Number of True and False Statements. Key balancing is important in any kind of objectively scored test. This rule refers to the balance between true and false statements, but it also applies to negative and positive phrasing. So, it is actually key balancing as applied to true-false items.

Use Simple Declarative Sentences. A true-false item should be a simple, not complex, sentence. It should state something in a declarative way, not interrogative. It should not be an elliptical sentence.

Examples are provided on the next page.

> Desirable:
>   The principal cause of lung cancer is cigarette smoking.
>
> Undesirable:
>   The principal causes of lung cancer are cigarette smoking and smog.

Write Items in Pairs. The pairs of items offer a chance to detect ambiguity. One statement can be true and another false. One would never use a pair of items in the same test, but the mere fact that a pair of items exists offers the item writer a chance to analyze the truth and falsity of related statements. Examples are provided:

> Overinflated tires will show greater wear than underinflated tires (false).
>
> Underinflated tires will show greater wear than overinflated tires (true).

Make Use of an Internal Comparison Rather Than an Explicit Comparison. When writing the pair of items, if comparison or judging is the mental activity, write the item so that the comparison is clearly stated in the item. Examples are provided:

> Desirable:
>   In terms of durability, oil-based paint is better than latex-based paint.
>
> Undesirable:
>   Oil-based paint is better than latex-based paint.

Take the Position of an Uninformed Test taker. The pair of items contains a true statement and a common misinterpretation:

> A percentile rank of 85 means that 85% of test takers have scores lower than persons at that percentile rank (true)
>
> A percentile rank of 85 means that 85% of items were correctly answered (false).

The first item is another correct interpretation of the concept of percentile rank. The second item is a common misunderstanding among students learning about this topic.

Use Multiple-Choice Items as a Basis for Writing True-False Items.

Good advice is to take a poor functioning multiple-choice item and convert it to several true-false items. An example is provided:

> The best way to improve the reliability of test scores is to
> A.   increase the length of the test.
> B.* improve the quality of items from the test.
> C.   increase the difficulty of the test.
> D.   decrease the difficulty of the test.
> E.   increase the construct validity of the test.

The items that might be extracted from the item above are as follows:

> Which actions listed below improve the reliability of test scores?
>   Mark A if it tends to improve reliability, mark B if not.
> 1.   Increase the length of the test. (A)
> 2.   Improve the quality of the items. (A)
> 3.   Substitute with more difficult items. (B)
> 4.   Increase the construct validity of the test. (B)

Notice how the original item is expanded via the multiple true-false format to increase the breadth of testing the understanding of this principle.

Rules For Item Sets

Little research exists on the writing or effectiveness of item sets (Haladyna, 1992a), despite its existence in the testing literature for over 50 years. Nonetheless, some advice is offered regarding certain aspects of the item set.

Format the Item Set So All Items are on a Single Page or Opposing Pages of the Test Booklet. This step will ensure easy reading of the stimulus material and easy reference to the item. When limited to two pages, the total number of items ranges from 7-12. If the multiple-true false or alternate-choice formats are used with the item set, than many more items can be used.

Use Algorithms if Possible. An algorithm is a standard item set scenario with a fixed number of items. The scenario can be varied according to several dimensions producing many useful items. Haladyna (1991) presented examples for teaching statistics and art history. Chapter 6 provides illustrations and examples of these.

Use Any Format That Appears Suitable with the Item Set. With any item set, conventional multiple-choice, matching, alternate-choice, and multiple true-false item can be used. The item set encourages considerable creativity in developing the stimulus and using these various formats.

Summary

This chapter presented information about rules concerning the writing of multiple-choice test items. As mentioned at the beginning of the chapter, the basis for this advice comes from an analysis of 46 textbooks and other sources on writing multiple-choice test items and an analysis of over 90 research studies bearing on the validity of many of these rules. Unfortunately, despite the number and wide range of sources of information and the seeming abundance of research studies, insufficient studies exist that address the validity of most of these rules. Therefore, any of these rules should be treated simply as recommendations and not as laws.

5

MEASURING HIGHER LEVEL THINKING

Overview

Defining and measuring various types of higher level thinking has been a major challenge to educators. This chapter presents a typology of higher level thinking and provides examples of multiple-choice test items based on various types of higher level thinking. The typology is not limited to multiple-choice formats alone. In fact, any test format can be used. The goal of this chapter is to enable item writers to more successfully develop test items that reflect various types of higher level thinking.

The Problem With Defining Higher Level Thinking

Frisbie, Miranda, and Baker (1993) reported a study of tests that were written to reflect material in elementary social studies and science textbooks. Their findings predictably indicated that most items tested isolated facts. These findings are confirmed in other recent studies, for example, Stiggins, Griswold, and Wikelund (1989). Although recalling information may be a worthwhile educational objective, current approaches to teaching require more complex outcomes than recall (Nickerson, 1989; NCTM, 1989; Snow, 1989; Snow & Lohman, 1989; Stiggins et al., 1989). School reformers call for learning in various subject matter disciplines to deal with life's many challenges (*What Works*, 1985). Constructivists argue that all learning should be meaningful. Little doubt exists in this era of test reform that the measurement of higher level thinking is, and will continue to be, preeminent.

Cognitive Taxonomies

The best known approach to classifying educational objectives reflecting higher level thinking is the Bloom taxonomy (Bloom, Engelhart, Furst, Hill, & Kratwohl, 1956). Sanders (1966), in his book *Classroom Questions*, provided many examples of test items based on this taxonomy. Despite the widespread popularity of this cognitive taxonomy, Seddon (1978) reported in his review of research on the validity of the taxonomy that evidence neither supports nor refutes the taxonomy. A research study by Miller, Snowman, and O'Hara (1979) suggested that Bloom's taxonomy represents fluid and crystallized intelligence. Seddon's discouraging review and the few studies existing on this subject leave those interested in developing test items that measure higher level thinking in somewhat of a quandary about what system to use to define and classify examples of complex cognitive behavior.

Other methods for classifying cognitive behavior have been proposed. Gagne's hierarchy is one, but there is little evidence of its construct validation or widespread use (Gagne, 1968). Recently, Royer, Cisero, and Carlo (1993) presented a theoretical analysis of cognitive behaviors based on the learning theory of J. R. Anderson (1990). Although this promising work has a strong theoretical base and a growing amount of research supporting its use, it is not yet ready for implementation. Authors of textbooks on testing routinely offer advice on how to measure higher level thinking in achievement tests. But none of these systems is widely recognized or used. In fact, we are continually reminded of the difficulty of constructing good higher level thinking items by studies like Frisbie et al. (1993), but prescriptions for correcting the problem have been unsuccessful.

Theoretical Versus Prescriptive Methods

A distinguishing characteristic of these taxonomies is whether each is based in cognitive theory or is simply prescriptive.

Theoretically based methods for defining and measuring higher level thinking involve theoretical terms, statements of cause-effect relationships, and principles governing how various types of higher leveling thinking are developed. Cognitive learning theories provide that basis. The proposal by Royer et al. (1993) is a good example of theory-driven higher level thinking.

Prescriptive taxonomies provide simple nontheoretical descriptions of cognitive behavior that hopefully have achieved consensus among users of the taxonomy. The Bloom taxonomy is prescriptive. As observed previously in this section, prescriptive methods also have not been successful to date, as evidenced in research studies.

In the short term, prescriptive efforts like the Bloom taxonomy might prove useful, but in the long term, theory-based taxonomies should prove more enduring and useful because these will be integrated with instruction in a clear and under-standable way.

The Definition and Measurement Dilemma

Regardless of whether this taxonomy of higher level thinking is theory based or simply prescriptive, two aspects of the dilemma make the task of developing a workable framework for higher level thinking almost impossible. One aspect is the definition of categories of higher level thinking, and the other aspect is the measurement of each category. In construct validity, defining the construct is the initial step, formulation, and the measuring is the second step, explication.

In chapter 1, the problem of defining ability and achievement was described. With respect to complex forms of ability and achievement, the same problem exists. Such terms as critical thinking, abstract thinking, reasoning, problem solving, strategic knowledge, metacognition, among others, are used to characterize desir-able forms of cognitive behavior. But these terms are seldom described in ways that are easy to teach and to measure.

A test item may be designed to measure a specific form of complex behavior. A student responds to a set of items representing that behavior. No one really knows what actual mental processes were used in making the correct choices in this multiple-choice test item or answering the constructed-response questions. For any test item, the test taker may appear to be thinking at a higher level thinking, but in actuality may be remembering identical statements or ideas presented before, perhaps verbatim in the textbook or stated in class and carefully copied into the student's notes. Mislevy (1993b) provided an excellent example of a nuclear medicine physician who at one point in a career might detect a cancerous growth in a CT (computerized-tomography) scan using reasoning, but at a latter time in his or her career would simply view the scan and recall the patient problem. In fact, the change from a high cognitive demand to less cognitive demand for the same complex task is a distinguishing characteristic between experts and novices in an area. The expert simply uses a well organized knowledge network to easily respond to a complex problem, whereas the novice has to employ a number of higher level thought processes to arrive at the same answer. This is the ultimate dilemma with any test item. Although a consensus of content experts may agree that an item appears to measure one type of behavior, it may measure an entirely different type of behavior simply because the test taker has a different set of experiences than the other test takers. This may also explain our failure to isolate measures of higher level thinking, because the items intended to reflect loftier modes of thinking are often just recall to a highly experienced test taker. Therefore, no empirical or statistical technique will ever be completely satisfactory. Whatever measures we develop will only approximate what we think the examinee is thinking when answering the test item.

With this disclaimer being given about higher level thinking, this chapter describes a typology for writing and classifying multiple-choice items for five types of cognitive behavior, including simple recall. Referring to an earlier distinction drawn in this chapter, this typology is descriptive. It does not derive from any theory of cognitive development. This typology has a set of propositions that appear to enable conveniently the writing and classification of test items that measure something more complex than simple recall. It is a heuristic device, intended for item writers who want to develop items beyond recall. The typology to be introduced here derives from earlier work of Miller and Williams (1973), Miller, Williams, and Haladyna (1978),Williams (1977), and Williams and Haladyna (1982). It is also believed that the system is workable, and that the test maker can incorporate ideas presented in this chapter into everyday test item-writing practices.

The Typology

As much as possible, the advice on item development and items used to illustrate various types of content and cognitive behaviors will include conventional multiple-choice, alternate-choice, multiple-true false and context-dependent item sets. Examples are intentionally simple and familiar as opposed to esoteric.

The purposes of the typology are: (a) to enable its users to specify learner outcomes in language representing some form of cognitive behavior, including recall, and (b) to enable its users to write higher level thinking test items. As noted earlier in this chapter, the typology is also useful for constructed-response test items.

The Content Dimension

The content of a course of study or a lesson can be listed in terms of learner outcomes (objectives), textbooks or training materials, lectures, or audio or videotaped material. From these sources, all content can be classified as representing one of four categories: (a) fact, (b) concept, (c) principle, or (d) procedure.

A *fact* is a declarative statement that is undeniably true. For example:

> The capital of Iowa is Des Moines.
> Jose Canseco hit 42 home runs in 1988.
> An adverb cannot modify a noun.
> Cold involves the absence of heat.

As presented here, facts are singular entities, usually beyond dispute, widely accepted by all.

A *concept* is a class of objects or events that share a common set of characteristics. For example, a chair has the intended function of seating a person, usually has four legs, a flat surface, and a backrest. The concept *chair* is noted by these distinguishing characteristics and others that may not be as important. A table might resemble a chair, but lacks the backrest, though teenagers may use a table as a chair. Other examples of concepts include:

> love, specific gravity, cash flow, pencil, student grades, validity
> insect, politician, swimming pool, plant, power, school, value

Concepts can be abstract (such as intelligence) or concrete (such as concrete for sidewalks), and other distinctions have been drawn among concepts (see Markle & Tiemann, 1970, for a more complete discussion).

A *principle* is a statement of relationship, usually between two or more concepts. A principle often takes the form: "If . . ., then . . ." Some examples of principles are:

> If there is inflation, then interest rate will rise.
> Overconsumption of food and drink usually results in
> weight gain.
> If you exercise a muscle, then it will grow.
> Hot air rises; cold air sinks.
> For every action, there is an equal and opposite reaction.
> If you avoid unforced errors in tennis, you will usually
> win the point.
> Excessive spending usually results in debt.

Principles come in two forms: immutable laws with no exceptions and probable events. For instance, it is immutable that hot air rises on our planet and cold air sinks. Many principles of science are laws. On the other hand, principles exist that are probable with either exact probabilities or subjective probabilities (guesses). A basketball player who is tall often gets more rebounds than a player who is short. Driving without a seat belt fastened is more likely to result in serious personal injury than driving with the seat belt fastened. With more data or a statistical model, we can estimate the probability of an event.

A *procedure* is a series of related actions with an objective or desired result. The actions may be mental or physical.

Mental Procedures.

> Solving a four-step algebra problem
> Developing a plan for a company picnic
> Writing a poem or short story
> Determining how to best shop for food each week
> Fixing your car

Physical Procedures.

> Performing surgery to repair a broken bone
> Batting in a softball game
> Preparing a pot of coffee
> Playing the piano
> Performing an experiment in science class

Whether it is a mental or physical procedure, there is a mental basis in all procedures. We can easily test for knowledge of procedures, but testing for knowledge of a procedure is never a substitute for the testing for the skill of performing that procedure. The proper way to test for the acquisition of a skill is through a performance test, usually involving direct observation.

The Cognitive Operations Dimension

In this typology, five distinct mental operations are: (a) recalling, (b) defining, (c) predicting, (d) evaluating, and (e) problem solving. Because the typology is two-dimensional, 20 different combinations exist (four content classifications by five cognitive operations). However, it is difficult to conceptualize some combinations of content and operations, as we shall see.

The next sections present items that illustrate each combination that is desirable and possible. Different formats are used as they seem appropriate. With most examples, brief discussions are offered for the item-writing strategy involved.

Recalling Behavior

Recalling refers to the simple recreation of a fact, concept, principle, or procedure. This is essentially recall of something presented in class or found in printed material. Each possible type of questioning strategies is presented as an example.

Recalling a Fact.

> Who put the "ram" in the "ramma lamma ding dong?"
> A. * Dion and the Belmonts
> B.   Danny and the Juniors
> C.   The Coasters
> D.   Lawrence Welk

Recalling a Concept.

> Which of the following defines "recalcitrant?"
> A. Lazy
> B.* Hesitant
> C. Scared
> D. Wanting to do over

With this item, we assume that the learners have already been presented with the word *hesitant* as meaning *recalcitrant*.

Recalling a Principle.

> What is the principle regarding when to use evaporative cooling systems in the Sonoran Desert?
> A.* The rate of evaporation is highest with low humidity.
> B. Water vapor conducts heat.
> C. Effectiveness of evaporative cooling is
>   governed by fan speed.

Again we assume that the correct option was presented verbatim from reading or instruction and the learner was asked to select the correct principle exactly as presented in a class or from a textbook. Option B is actually a true statement, but it is not the answer to the question.

Recalling a Procedure.

> Which procedure is recommended for correcting a patient's lop ear deformity?
> A. Abbotts's
> B.* Johnson's
> C. Olsen's
> D. Costello's

As with the other examples, four procedures are presented and the correct answer is a verbatim association.

A variation of recalling a procedure is recalling a specific step in a procedure:

> What should you generally say to an important client after being
> introduced?
> A.   Tell a joke to break the ice.
> B.   Talk about yourself, so he or she can learn a little
>   about you.
> C.* Ask the client about himself or herself.
> D.   Begin talking business because time is precious.

Generally speaking, it is immaterial whether we recall a fact, concept, principle, or procedure. Recall is the simplest of behaviors. Critics of teaching and testing are well supported by studies showing that we test recalling behavior well and consistently lack the ability to test beyond the recall level. In initial stages of learning, recalling may be a necessary step, thus, the previous examples serve to provide a complete set of examples for the typology.

Defining Behavior

Defining involves the identification of a paraphrased version of an original fact, concept, principle, or procedure as presented during instruction. In other words, defining is an attempt to measure what is sometimes called *understanding* or *comprehension*.

Defining can be shown in six distinct ways. Each will be described and illustrated with several examples of defining test items. The multiple-true-false format is an excellent way to test for defining. The alternate-choice is also an effective device for measuring defining behavior.

1.   **Given a definition, ask the test taker to identify the correct fact, concept, principle or procedure from a list of plausible facts, concepts, principles, or procedures.**

Defining a Concept.

> What is the term we us to describe the use of words to reflect
> sounds, such as BANG?
> A.   Metaphor
> B.* Onomatopoeia

Defining a Principle.

Which of the following explains the relationship between the length of the test and the degree of measurement error that exists?
A. The longer the test item, the more valid the test scores.
B.* The longer the test, the more reliable it tends to be.
C. Higher quality items tend to improve reliability.
D. A longer testing period for a predetermined number of items tends to improve reliability.

Note that though the distractors are wrong, they are also true statements. These distractors do not answer the question.

Defining a Procedure.
The following item could easily be classified as *recalling a concept* if the learner had been exposed to the exact phrasing.

What is the name of the procedure for formal hearings of an employee's complaint?
A. Concern
B. Protest
C.* Grievance
D. Strike

2. **Given a concept, principle, or procedure, ask the test taker to identify the correct definition from a list of plausible definitions.**

Defining a Concept.

Which represents a "typographical error?"
A. A misspelled word
B. Missing punctuation
C.* A typing error

Defining a Principle.

Which explains the reason for a thunderstorm in the summer?
A. Two air masses, hot and cold, collide along a weather front.
B.* During a humid day, rapid heating causes hot air to rise and the rapid cooling causes a rapid, violent rainstorm.
C. Hot, moist air is pushed into a mountain; the rising air cools and becomes a violent rainstorm.

Defining a Procedure.

In tennis, what kind of stroke causes the ball to rise and
then fall abruptly, tending to bounce very high and away
from the court?
A.   Underspin
B.* Top spin
C.   Lob
D.   Slice

---

3.   **Given several plausible examples of a concept, principle, or
     procedure, ask the test taker to choose the example that exemplified
     the concept, principle, or procedure.**

This class of methods is very effective because many examples can be
generated that are free of recall associations. With the previous two classes of
methods, the threat of measuring recall instead of defining is always present because
the examinee may have encountered the exact phrasing previously.

Defining a Concept. A multiple true-false format is very useful in this
instance.

Mark A if an example and B if not an example.
Which are examples of satellites?
1.   Earth   (A)
2.   Sun   (B)
3.   Moon   (A)
4.   Asteroid   (A)
5.   Meteor   (B)
6.   Mars   (A)
7.   Meteorites (B)
8.   A person-launched space station   (A)

Defining a Principle.

Which situation below shows gravitation relationship between
two objects?
A.* The moon causing tides on earth.
B.   Solar flares disrupting our television programs.
C.   Dropping a feather from a building.
D.   An airplane taking off.

Defining a Procedure.

A patient is taken to the emergency room after a serious
auto injury. What is the first thing you should check?
A.   The patient's medical insurance or ability to pay
B.* That the patient can breathe
C.   That the patient has suffered a serious loss of blood
D.   For indications of shock

Items like the one above are easy to write. However, the danger is that the item might represent recall instead of defining.

4.   **Given the concept, principle, or procedure, ask the test taker to identify the best example from a list of several plausible examples. This differs from the previous class of defining items in that all may be correct, but one is clearly the best.**

Defining a Concept.

Which is an example of hyperbole?
A.   It is kistimary to cuss the bride.
B.   Cruel kindness
C.* Mile high mound of popcorn

This item stem is probably the most dependable for defining a concept. The word *hyperbole* could be replaced by any other word, which completes the item stem. Then, unfamiliar examples can be generated as options. This format also can be effectively converted to multiple true-false, so that each option becomes a true-false item. This changeover will increase the number of items possible for this situation.

Defining a Principle.

Which kind of person is likely to get emphysema?
A.   Habitual drinker
B.   Chronic drug user
C.* Habitual smoker
D.   Type A personality

Emphysema is a concept. Causes involve principles. The test taker must identify a cause among plausible causes. This behavior may be recalled in some instructional circumstances; here it was intended to be defining behavior.

Defining a Procedure.

What is liposuction?
A. A technique for removing lipids.
B. A type of diet and exercise regimen for weight loss
     and toning
C.* A surgical procedure for removing body fat.
D. A commercial fitness product

5. **Given several plausible characteristics of a concept, principle, or procedure, ask the test taker to identify the correct fact, concept, principle, or procedure.**

Defining a Fact.

Which river runs from north to south and empties into
the Gulf of Mexico in the southern United States?
A. Columbia
B.* Mississippi
C. Snake
D. Potomac

To a less knowledgeable learner, this item may be defining behavior, but to someone more exposed to learning about geography, this item probably would be classified as recall.

Defining a Concept.

This animal has eight legs and an external skeleton. What is it?
A. Insect
B. Amphibian
C.* Arachnid
D. Mollusk

This animal has eight legs and an external skeleton. What
is it?
A. Ant
B. Turtle
C.* Spider
D. Scallop

The previous two items illustrate a general and a specific questioning strategy using the same stem.

Defining a Principle.

Which event below demonstrates why it tends to rain in mountainous areas?
A. Hot air mixes with cold air.
B. Rapid evaporation saturates the air.
C.* Hot moist air condenses when it rises.
D. Melting snow tends to saturate the air.

Defining a Procedure.

Which term do we use to describe the act of rapidly cooking food in a pan using cooking oil?
A. Frying
B. Par boiling
C.* Saute
D. Baking
E. Broiling

6. Given a concept, principle, or procedure, ask the test taker to identify the outstanding characteristic or distinguishing feature. The plausible list also may contain characteristics and noncharacteristics, distinguishing features or nondistinguishing features.

Defining a Concept.

Which distinguishes the albatross from most other birds?
A.* Its size
B. Its reputation in mythology
C. Its appetite
D. Its tendency to protect its young

Defining a Principle.

A piece of paper ignites in your oven. What caused this?
A.* The temperature was above 451 degrees Fahrenheit.
B. Cooking oil probably covered the paper.

Defining a Procedure.

> Which of the following is necessary in repairing a thermofropple?
> A.* A Johnson rod
> B. A c-clamp
> C. A rammadingle
> D. A luscatator

Defining behavior is a simpler form of higher level thinking. In Bloom's taxonomy, defining would probably be considered translating. As shown in this section, a variety of questioning techniques can be used to test one's ability to define a fact, concept, principle, or procedure. The items are somewhat easy to prepare, and many item stems are generic in nature. One need only identify the concept, principle, or procedure, some characteristics, and some examples and nonexamples. These are the basic materials for defining test items.

Predicting Behavior

Predicting behavior involves the identification of consequences from a given situation. Predicting behavior comes primarily from the use of a principle. It is difficult to imagine predicting behavior based on any other type of content. With principles, predictions may be absolute or probable. We are mainly interested in probable events, because they represent the uncertainty in most learning involving principles.

Item stems for predicting behavior exist in several generic forms:

> If . . . , then what happens?
> What is the consequence of . . . ?
> What would happen if . . . ?

The following examples exemplify predicting-type, multiple-choice items.

> What is the main cause of the increase in national debt from 1945 to 1985?
> A. Increases in spending in education
> B. Increases in defense spending
> C. Inflation
> D.* Efforts of the Congress to meet the nation's needs

> What would be the main consequence of long term alcoholism in a male?
> A. Diseased kidneys
> B.* Debilitated liver
> C. Heart disease
> D. Cancer

Written in a multiple true-false format:

> When an object floats in water, what is certain?
> 1. The specific gravity of the object is more than 1.00
> 2. The density of the object exceeds one gram per cubic centimeter.
> 3.* The object is lighter than water.
> 4. The pressure of water is greater than the pressure of the object.
> 5. The volume of water is greater than the volume of the object.
> 6.* The weight of water for a set volume is more than the weight of the object for the same set volume.

This is a very effective format to test the thorough understanding of a principle. In this instance, it is an absolute as opposed to probable phenomenon.

As we examine more complex behavior, the varieties of questioning strategies are fewer as are the examples. Fortunately, the use of several generic item stems provides a good basis for this kind of questioning. The next chapter provides item shells that expand this technology for systematic testing.

Evaluating Behavior

All evaluating behavior requires the test taker to choose one from among several choices based on a criterion or criteria. There are many real-life examples of evaluating behavior, for example, buying a box of cereal, choosing a new car, deciding which street to take on the way to work, deciding when to go to sleep, or deciding where to take a vacation. Evaluating behavior is also important in problem solving. Three types of evaluating behavior are presented here.

The first is merely using a predetermined criterion to make a decision. For instance, considering cost, which box of cereal among four or five should one buy? The criterion might be changed to *taste, nutrition*, or *manufacturer's reputation*.

The second is when we present a problem, we ask the test taker to choose the criterion or criteria to use in making a decision. For the same cereal buying problem, the test taker might be asked to figure out which criterion is most important to the health of the family members eating the cereal.

The third requires the test taker to both select a criterion or criteria and also make a decision. Using the cereal example again, we might ask a test taker to choose both a criterion and a cereal in the same problem. The problem with this third type is that when a student misses the item, it is difficult to tell if the difficulty is in choosing a criterion or applying the criterion toward making a decision.

Evaluating behavior is the most realistic and life-like. Many test items can be drawn from real life. The item maker can draw from personal experiences to develop evaluating items or may work within the framework of case scenarios–contrived situations that provide opportunities for demonstrating evaluating behaviors. Since recent reform initiatives call for learning to be in a meaningful context (NCTM, 1989; *What Works*, 1985), evaluating questions can be easily created.

Following are examples of evaluating behavior for each type of content and evaluating question strategy.

Evaluating Facts. How does one evaluate facts? The following example shows how this is done.

> **Which is the longest way from San Francisco to San Jose?**
> A. Via Route 101
> B. Via the Junipero Serra Freeway
> C.* Via State Route 1

Although this is a fact, students who have not encountered this fact and who are presented with a map and a legend can use evaluating to answer the test item.

Evaluating Concepts. The concept of cleaning bleached hair is tested in this item. Four products are evaluated on the basis of effectiveness, and the third option is correct.

> **Which is the most effective for cleaning bleached hair?**
> A. Benzine
> B. Conditioner
> C.* A mild shampoo
> D. Any shampoo

Evaluating Principles. Whether the principle is absolute or probable, options can be written to set up evaluation based on a principle.

> What is the most effective way to cool a home in a humid climate?
> A.   Evaporative cooler
> B.* Air conditioner
> C.   Fans
> E.   Cooling tower

Although all four answers are correct, the stem calls for an evaluation in terms of the criterion of effectiveness. The item could be modified to use the criterion of cost, which would change the answer. Or the criterion could be environmental impact, in which case air conditioner might be the worst answer among the choices.

Evaluating Procedures. Given the choice of several procedures in a situation, the test taker has to choose the best answer among the options .

> What is the most effective way to treat athlete's foot?
> A.   Let nature take its course.
> B.   Wear sandals.
> C.   Using a fungicidal foot power.
> D.* Using a fungicidal salve.

As with the previous example, the criterion of effectiveness could be replaced with other criteria, such as cost, long-term effectiveness, or complications. Another variation to increase the richness of this questioning strategy is to use other problems, for example, sunburn, insect bites, or skin rashes.

Evaluating procedures can be also treated in the format of a context-dependent item set.

The item at the top of the next page is the old-fashioned mathematics story problem, but some attempt is made through the questioning strategy to break down the problem into parts that require comparisons. Some might classify the entire item set as problem solving, recognizing that it is a multistep mental procedure that mainly involves evaluating behavior. The problem is meaningful to many consumers and reflects current emphasis in mathematics instruction (NCTM, 1989).

Evaluating behavior is somewhat easy to test with the array of techniques in this section. As with predicting and defining behavior, some generic forms of questioning exist, and these are more adequately treated in the next chapter.

Problem-Solving Behavior

This type of cognitive behavior is very complex. Several steps are involved, usually requiring combinations of recalling, summarizing, predicting, and evaluating

Molly was shopping at Superfoods and has a 50-cent double coupon for a six-pack of 12-ounce Double Bubble Cola priced at $1.49. She could also buy the same Double Bubble Cola in a 32-ounce container for $0.79. If she bought two 32-ounce containers, she could use that same coupon.

1. What is the cost of the six pack when applying the double coupon?
    A. $1.49
    B. $0.99
    C.* $0.49
    D. Cannot tell from information given

2. What is the cost of the two 32-ounce containers when applying the double coupon?
    A. * $0.58
    B. $0.79
    C. $1.58
    D. Cannot tell from information given

3. Molly decides she has to buy four six-packs for the party on Friday at her house. Which combination below is the best value (LEAST EXPENSIVE)?
    A.* Four six-packs
    B. Nine 32-ounce containers
    C. One six-pack and seven 32-ounce containers
    D. Three six-packs and two 32-ounce containers
    E. Cannot tell from information given

**Fig. 5.1. Example of an Item Set Involving
Evaluating Items**

behavior. Because there are many kinds of problem solving, this term is seldom adequately defined. Cognitive psychologists are still struggling with the defining, teaching, and measuring of problem-solving behavior (Snow, 1989; Snow & Lohman, 1989). There is little doubt that this type of behavior is important. The natural testing format for problem solving is constructed-response. It is extremely difficult to set a problem-solving experience into the confines of a multiple-choice format. One major reason is that problem solving is often a multistep experience, and the conventional multiple-choice item does not conveniently allow for a step-by-step approach.

The next example of this comes from research reported by Biggs and Collis (1982) in the framework of teaching mathematical problem solving, as Fig. 5.2 shows. The stimulus condition of a test provides a basis for a variety of questions testing higher level thinking, but the item set is particularly well suited for testing problem-solving behavior.

A final example of a mathematics task prototype is taken from Mislevy (1993b). In this example, which he adopted from the National Research Council, three performance items are given that require professional judgment from one or two trained experts. Figure 5.3 presents an adapted version. Two of the three original items are easily adapted to multiple-choice formats, thus, eliminating the judgmental scoring task. The third task requires the student to build a table based on win/loss records. The underlying cognitive behaviors are arguably the same, regardless of which format is used. Researchers are now studying similarities and differences in the cognitive processes elicited by these contrasting formats when the cognitive task appears approximately the same. Indeed Snow (1993) provided an analysis of popular arguments for and against selected- and constructed-response formats as well as develops a research agenda that is very much needed. Until this research leads to more definitive guidelines, the multiple-choice format is currently desirable from the many standpoints offered in chapter 2. Ultimately, we probably will learn that in most circumstances, it is immaterial whether the item format is selected-or constructed-response for many types of mental skills. Chapter 10 provides more discussion of this important issue. Certainly the efforts of cognitive psychologists and measurement theoreticians will likely increase the complexity and appropriateness of test formats in the measurement of these highly desired higher level thinking behaviors.

Summary

This chapter has presented some ideas for how to classify content and cognitive behaviors of various types. Although the system has been successfully used in various settings, it lacks a theoretical foundation. It merely represents descriptive ways for item writers to phrase questions that appear to measure something beyond factual recall. Use of the typology is recommended for both formal and informal testing programs, but test interpretations should not be strictly based on these classifications without validation research.

Validation research of this type has been missing from validation studies in the past, because the measurement of higher level thinking has been chronically problematic. Research validating types of higher level thinking will always be troubled by the level of experience or familiarity of test takers. It has been difficult to know when a test taker chooses or constructs a correct answer whether some form of higher level cognitive behavior was used or the test taker simply remembered something. Cognitive psychologists view this as how well-developed schemas exist when confronted with a problem. A well-developed schema may accommo-

This is a machine that changes numbers. It adds the number you put in three times and then adds 2 more. So, if you put in 4, it puts out 14.

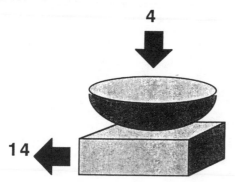

1. If 14 is put out, what number was put in?
   A. 2
   B. 3
   C.* 4
   D. Cannot say from information given.

2. If we put in a 5, what number will the machine put out?
   A. 4
   B. 14
   C.* 17
   D. Cannot say from information given.

3. If we got out a 41, what number was put in?
   A. 5
   B. 12
   C.* 13
   D. Cannot say from information given.

4. If x is the number that comes out of the machine when the number y is put in, write down the formula that will give us the value of y whatever the value of x is.
   A.* y = 3 times x plus 2
   B. x = 3 times y plus 2
   C. y = 3 plus y plus 2 times 3
   D. x = 3 plus y plus 2 times 3

Fig. 5.2. Mathematic Problem-Solving

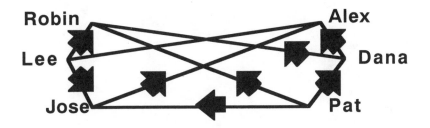

1. Who won the game between Pat and Robin?
    A.* Pat
    B.   Robin
    C.   Cannot tell from this information

2. Who is in first place?
    A.   Robin
    B.   Lee
    C.   Jose
    D.* Pat
    E.   Dana
    F.   Alex

3. Dana and Lee have not yet played each other. Who do you
    think will win?
    A.   Dana
    B.* Lee
    C.   Cannot tell without more information

4. What information is needed to answer item 3?
    A.   How Dana and Lee did against Alex
    B.* Their won-and-loss records
    C.   Who the better player is

Fig. 5.3. A mathematics task prototype.

date a very complex problem and solve it with a minimum of thought.

A recurring theme in this chapter has been that the experience of the learner has everything to do with the type of cognitive behavior being exhibited. Thus, our interpretations of test results are inherently flawed. Despite this frustrating dilemma, at best we can purposefully define various types of higher level thinking, and teach and test accordingly with the hope that the encounters are genuinely higher level and not simply recall.

6

ITEM SHELLS

Overview

Item writing is a very slow and painful process for most item writers. Experience shows that despite best intentions, even carefully written and edited items often fail to perform as intended. Methods are needed that accelerate the item-writing process and, at the same time, produce higher quality items. The item shell technique provides a means for accomplishing these two goals. A variant of the item shell, item modeling, also accomplishes these goals.

The item shell technique is primarily intended for item writers who lack formal item-writing training and experience in multiple-choice item writing. These item writers often have great difficulty in starting to write the multiple-choice item, though they had considerable knowledge, skill, and experience in the subject matter for which they were preparing items. As its name suggests, the item shell is a skeletal item. The item shell provides the syntactic structure of an item. The item writer has to supply his or her content, but the form of the item is written so it can be completed by one of the choices. This chapter presents the item shell and illustrates its use in a variety of settings.

An important variation of the item shell technique has been evolving at the National Board of Medical Examiners under the leadership of Tony LaDuca. Research on this method's effectiveness points to high speed production of high quality items (Shea, Poniatowski, Day, Langdon, LaDuca, & Norcini, 1992). Later in this chapter, a section is devoted to item modeling. The item-modeling technique has powerful implications for testing professional competence.

Origin of the Item Shell

As reported earlier in this book, attempts to make item writing a science have not yet been fruitful. An ambitious endeavor was Bormuth's algorithmic theory of item writing (Bormuth, 1970). He suggested a complex, item-writing algorithm that transformed prose into multiple-choice test items. His theory of achievement test item writing made item development more scientific and less subject to the caprice and whims of idiosyncratic item writers. The problem, however, was that the algorithm had too many steps that made its use impractical. Others have tried similar methods with similar lack of success, including facet theory and designs, item forms, amplified objectives, among others (see Roid & Haladyna, 1982).

The item shell was created out of a need for a more systematic method of multiple-choice item writing in the direction of these earlier efforts. However, the item shell also permits item writer freedom that, in turn, permits greater creativity in designing the item. The item shell is also seen as a more efficient process for writing multiple-choice items than those that presently exist. The method simplifies writing items that are in the desired direction of measuring higher levels of cognitive behavior.

Millman and Westman (1989) developed a computerized procedure called for the item shell. Their software elicits a series of inquiries and responses that produces item shells to match a particular type of cognitive behavior. The item writer can create a new item based on the shell provided by the computer.

Defining an Item Shell?

Haladyna and Shindoll (1989) defined an item shell as a "hollow" item containing a syntactic structure that is useful for writing sets of similar items. Each item shell is a generic multiple-choice test item.

A simple item shell is shown here:

> Which is an example of (any concept)?
> A. Example
> B. Plausible non example
> C. Plausible non example
> D. Plausible non example

One could take this blank item stem and substitute almost any concept or principle in any field or subject matter. Writing the stem is only one part of multiple-choice item writing, but often it is the most difficult part. Writing a correct option and several plausible distractors is also difficult, but once we write the stem, an important part of that item-writing job is done.

A limitation of the item shell technique is that you may develop an abundance of items that all have the same syntactic structure, such as shown on the previous page. Some test makers and test takers may perceive this situation negatively and want a greater variety in questioning strategies. Because appropriate sampling of content is a major concern in achievement and ability testing, the test items should representatively sample from different types of taught and learned content. Therefore, the use of a variety of item shells is recommended rather than generating hundreds of items from a single shell, which is entirely possible and even easy to do.

Another limitation of the item shell technique is that it does not apply equally well to all content. There are many instances where the learning task is specific enough so that generalization to sets of similar items is simply not possible.

As will be shown later in this chapter, the item shell can be adapted for a variety of types of content and cognitive operations, as described in chapter 5. In fact, chapters 5 and 6 are good complements for one another.

Developing Item Shells

There are generally two ways to develop item shells. The first and easiest way is to co-opt the generic shell presented in Table 6.1. These shells are nothing more than item stems taken from successfully performing items. The content expert should identify the fact, concept, principle, or procedure being tested and the type of cognitive behavior desired (that is, recalling, defining, predicting, evaluating, or problem solving).

A second way is to transform highly successful items into item shells. To do so, one should follow certain steps. Table 6.2 shows a variety of item shells for medical problem solving. To transform items into shells several conditions must be met. First an item must be identified as a successful performer. Chapter 8 discusses the criteria for item performance. Second, the type of cognitive behavior represented by the item must be identified. Third, the content that the item tests must be identified. Fourth, a series of item-writing steps might be followed. These steps are:

1. Identify the stem of a successfully performing item.

> A 6-year-old child is brought to the hospital with contusions over the abdomen and chest as a result of an automobile accident. What should be the initial treatment?

2. Underline key words or phrases representing the content of the item.

> A <u>6-year-old child</u> is brought to the hospital with <u>contusions over the abdomen and chest</u> because of an <u>automobile</u> accident. What should be the initial treatment be?

Table 6.1
Generic Item Shells
Classified by Cognitive Operation

Defining—Concepts
Which is the best definition of. . . ?
Which is the meaning of. . . ?
Which is synonymous with. . . ?
Which is the correct definition for . . . ?
Which is like. . . ?
Which is characteristic of. . . ?
Which is an example of. . . ?
Which distinguishes. . . ?

Defining—Principles
Which is the best definition of . . . ?
Which is the principle of. . . ?
Which is the reason for. . . ?
Which is the cause of. . . ?
Which is the relationship between. . . and. . . ?
Which is an example of the principle of. . . ?

Predicting—Principles
What would happen if. . . ?
If. . . , what happens?
What is the consequence of . . . ?
What is the cause of . . . ?

Evaluating—Facts and Concepts
Which is the most or least important, significant, effective. . . ?
Which is better, worse, higher, lower, farther, nearer, heavier,
     lighter, darker, lighter,. . . ?
Which is most like, least like. . . ?
What is the difference between . . . and . . . ?
What is a similarity between . . . and . . . ?

Evaluating—Principles
Which of the following principles best applies to. . . ?

Evaluating—Procedures
Which of the following procedures best applies to the problem of. . . ?

Applying—Concepts, Principles, Procedures
What is the best way to. . . ?
How should one . . . ?

Table 6.2
Examples of Item Shells
for Medical Problem Solving

Defining

What are the main symptoms of . . . ?

Comment: This item shell provides for the generation of a multitude of items dealing with the symptoms of patient illnesses.

Predicting

What is the most common (cause, or symptom) of a (patient problem)?

Comment: This very general item shell provides for a variety of combinations that mostly reflects anticipating consequences or cause-and-effect relationships arising from principles. Understanding of concepts is also important for successful performance on such items.

Evaluating

Patient illness is diagnosed. Which treatment is likely to be most effective?

Comment: This item shell provides for a variety of patient illnesses, according to some taxonomy or typology of illnesses and treatment options. Simply stated, one is the best. Another questioning strategy is to choose the reason why a particular treatment is most effective.

Applying

Information is presented about a patient problem. How should the patient be treated?

Comment: The item shell provides information about a patient disease or injury. The completed item will require the test taker to make a correct diagnosis and to identify the correct treatment protocol, based upon the information given.

Note. From "Item shells: A method for writing effective multiple-choice test items" by T. M. Haladyna & R. R. Shindoll. *Evaluation in the Health Professions, 12*, 97-104. © 1989 by Sage Publications. Adapted with permission.

3. Identify variations for each key word or phrase.

Age of person: infant, child (ages 3-14), adolescent (ages 13-18), young adult (ages 19-31), middle age (ages 32-59), elderly (ages 60 and over).

Trauma injury and complications: Cuts, contusions, fractures, internal injuries.

Type of accident: Automobile, home, industrial, recreational

4. Select an age, trauma injury or complication, and type of accident from personal experience.

5. Write the stem.

> An infant is brought to the hospital with severe abrasions following a bicycle accident involving the mother. What should initial treatment be?

6. Write the correct answer.

> A. * Conduct a visual examination.

7. Write the required number of distractors, or as many plausible distractors as you can with a limit of four, since most automated scoring permits up to five options comfortably.

> A. * Conduct a visual examination.
> B.   Treat for infection.
> C.   Administer pain killers to calm the infant.
> D.   Send for laboratory tests.
> E.   Clean the wounds with an antiseptic.

Steps 4 through 7 can be repeated for writing a set of items dealing with a physician's treatment of people coming to the emergency department of a hospital. The effectiveness of the item comes with the writing of plausible distractors. However, the phrasing of the item, with the three variations, makes it possible to generate many items covering a multitude of combinations of ages, trauma injuries and complications, and types of injuries. The item writer need not concern himself or herself with the "trappings" of the item but can, instead, concentrate on content. For instance, an experienced physician who is writing test items for a certification examination might draw heavily from clinical experience and use the item shell to generate a dozen different items representing the realistic range of problems encountered in a typical medical practice. In these instances, the testing events can be transformed into context-dependent item sets.

An item shell for eighth-grade science is developed to illustrate the process. The unit is on gases and its characteristics:

Step One: Identify the stem.

> Which is the distinguishing characteristic of hydrogen?

Step Two: Underline the key word or phrase.

> Which is the distinguishing characteristic of <u>hydrogen?</u>

Step Three: Identify variations for each key word or phrase.

> Which is the distinguishing characteristic of (gases studied
> in this unit)?

Step Four: Select an instance from the range of variations.

> Oxygen

Step Five: Write the stem.

> Which is the distinguishing characteristic of oxygen?

Step Six: Write the correct answer.

> A. It is an element in water.

Step Seven: Write the distractors.

> B. It has a lower density than hydrogen.
> C. It can be fractionally distilled.
> D. It has a lower boiling point than hydrogen.

The last word in the stem can be replaced by any of a variety of gasses, easily producing many item stems. The difficult task of choosing a right answer and several plausible distractors remains.

Although the process of developing item shells may seem laborious, as illustrated on the preceding pages, keep in mind that many of these seven steps become automatic in the development of item shell. In fact, once a good item is discovered, several steps can be performed simultaneously arriving at a new item soon after the original item is identified.

Item shells have the value of being used formally or informally, as part of a careful item development effort, or informally for classroom testing. Clearly the value of the item shell is its versatility to operate at different cognitive operations with the four types of content (facts, concepts, principles, and procedures) and in different subject matter areas.

Evaluation of Item Shells

According to Haladyna and Shindoll (1989), the item shell has several attractive features:

1.   The item shell helps inexperienced item writers phrase the item in an attractive and effective manner, because the item shell is based on a previously used, successfully performing item.
2.   Item shells can be applied to a variety of types of content (facts, concepts, principles, and procedures), types of cognitive behaviors (recalling, summarizing, predicting, evaluating, and problem solving), and various subject matters.
3.   Items shells are easily produced, and lead to the rapid development of useful items.
4.   Item shells can be used in item-writing training, as a teaching device.
5.   Item shells can be used to help item writers polish good ideas for items. Once they have ideas, they can select from generic shells, as Table 6.1 shows, or from a specially prepared set of shells, as Table 6.2 shows.
6.   Item shells complement traditional methods of item writing, so that a variety of item formats exists.
7.   Finally, item shells help crystallize our ideas about the content of a test. The item shell provides the most basic, operational definition of what really is measured. In fact, the item shell comes close to resembling instructional objectives or other types of content identifiers.

In summary, the item shell is a very useful device for writing multiple-choice items because it has an empirical basis and provides the structure for the content expert who wishes to write items. The technique is flexible enough to allow a variety of shells fitting the complex needs of most formal and informal testing programs. Millman and Westman (1989) showed that this technique can be computerized, even further streamlining the process. Thus, the future of the item shell as an item-writing aid seems bright.

Generic Item Sets

Chapter 3 presents and illustrates the context-dependent item set as a means for testing various types of higher level thinking with meaningful scenarios or vignettes. This format is becoming increasingly popular because of its versatility. Testing theorists are also developing new models for scoring item sets (Thissen, Steinberg, & Mooney, 1989). This section uses the concept of item shells in a more elaborate format, the item set. This work is derived principally from Haladyna (1991) but also has roots in the earlier theories of Guttman and Hively (discussed in Roid & Haladyna, 1982).

Item Shells for Item Sets

The production of test items that measure various types of higher level thinking are problematic, as noted in previous chapters. Item shells presented in this chapter lessen this problem. With the problem-solving type item set introduced in chapter 3, a systematic method for producing large numbers of items for item sets using shell-like structures has been developed (Haladyna, 1991). This section provides the concept and methods for developing item shells for item sets.

Generic Scenario

The generic scenario is a key element in the development of these items. A scenario (or vignette) is a short story containing relevant information to solve a problem. Sometimes the scenario can contain irrelevant information, if the intent is to have the examinee discriminate between the relevant and irrelevant information.

These scenarios can have the general form, as shown for a beginning graduate level statistics course:

> Given a situation where bivariate correlation is to be used, the student will (1) state or identify the research question/hypothesis, (2) identify the constructs (Y and X) to be measured, (3) write or identify the statistical null and alternate hypotheses, or directional, if indicated in the problem, (4) identify the criterion and predictor variables, (5) assess the power of the statistical test, (6) determine alpha, (7) draw a conclusion regarding the null/alternate hypotheses, when given results, (8) determine the degree of practical significance, (9) discuss the possibility of Type I and Type II errors in this problem, and (10) draw a conclusion regarding the research question/hypothesis.

The previous example involved one statistical test, product-moment correlation. A total of 18 common statistical tests are taught. With the use of each test, four variations exist: (a) statistically and practically significant, (b) statistically but not practically significant, (c) not statistically but potentially practically significant, and (d) neither statistically nor practically significant. Thus the achievement domain contains 72 possibilities. Once a scenario is generated, the four conditions may be created with a single scenario. For example:

> Two researchers studied 42 men and women for the relationship between amount of sleep each night and calories burned on an exercise bike. They obtained a correlation of .28, which has a two-tailed probability of .08.

This problem can be varied in terms of its sample size and its correlation to simulate the four conditions described in the previous paragraph. Thus, with the writing of a single scenario, four actual scenarios are developed.

With each scenario, a total of 10 test items is possible. With the development of this single scenario and its four variants, the item writer has created a total of 40 test items. Some item sets can be used in an instructional setting for practice, while others should appear on formative quizzes and summative tests. For formal testing programs, item sets can be generated in large quantities to satisfy needs without great expense.

Table 6.3 presents a fully developed item set. This set is unconventional, because it contains a subset of multiple true-false items. Typically not all possible items from an item set domain would be used in a test for several reasons. One, too many items are possible and it might exceed the need that is called for in the test specifications. Two, an item set is best confined to a single page or facing pages in a test booklet. Three, item sets are known to have inter-item cuing, so the use of all possible items may enhance undesirable cuing. With the scenario presented in Table 6.3, minor variations in the sample size, the correlation and its associated probability, and a directional test can essentially create a new problem.

Evaluation of Generic Item Sets

This method provides a basis for testing complex, multistep thinking that may be scenario-based. In most circumstances, such thinking would be tested using open-ended response format. In fact, the generic item set makes no assumption about the test item format. However, the generic item set technique is very well suited to simulating complex thinking with the objectively scorable multiple-choice format.

The method is rigid in the sense that it has a structure and organization. But, this is important in facilitating the development of many relevant items. On the other hand, the item writer has the freedom to write interesting scenarios and

Table 6.3
A Fully Developed Scenario-Based Problem Solving Item Set

Two researchers were studying the relationship between amount of sleep each night and calories burned on an exercise bike for 42 men and women. They were interested if people who slept more had more energy to use during their exercise session. They obtained a correlation of .28, which has a two-tailed probability of .08. Alpha was .05.

1. Which is an example of a properly written research question?
   A.* Is there a relationship between amount of sleep and energy expended?
   B. Does amount of sleep correlate with energy used?
   C. What is the cause of energy expended?
   D. What is the value of rho?

What is the correct term for the variable amount of sleep?
Mark A if correct or B if incorrect.
2. Criterion (A)
3. Independent (B)
4. Dependent (A)
5. Predictor (B)
6. y (A)
7. x (B)

8. What is the correct statistical null hypothesis?
   A. There is no correlation between sleep and energy expended.
   B.* Rho equals zero.
   C. r equals zero.
   D. Rho equals r.

9. If power is a potentially serious problem in this study, what remedies should you take?
   A.* Set alpha to .10 and do a directional test.
   B. Set alpha to .05 and do a directional test.
   C. Set alpha to .01 and do a non directional test.
   D. Set alpha to .05 and do a non directional test.

10. What conclusion should you draw regarding the null hypothesis?
    A.* Reject
    B. Accept
    C. Cannot determine without more information

11. What is the size of the effect?
    A. Zero
    B.* Small
    C. Moderate
    D. Large

12. What are the chances of making a Type I error in this problem?
    A.* .05
    B. Very small
    C. Large
    D. Cannot determine without more information

13. What are the chances of making a Type II error in this problem?
    A. Zero
    B.* Very small
    C. Large
    D. Cannot determine without more information

14. What conclusion should you draw regarding this study?
    A. The correlation was significant.
    B. The correlation was not significant.
    C.* A small relationship exists.
    D. No relationship exists.

identify factors within each scenario that may be systematically varied. The generic questions also can be a creative endeavor, but once they are developed can be used for variations of the scenario. The writing of the correct answer is somewhat straightforward, but the writing of distractors requires some inventiveness.

As noted earlier and well worth making the point again, item sets have a tendency for inter item cuing. In technical terms, this is called local dependence (Hambleton & Swaminathan, 1987), and the problem is significant for item sets (see Haladyna, 1992a; Thissen, Steinberg, & Mooney, 1989). Item writers have to be careful to minimize the tendency for examinees to benefit from other items appearing in the set. This is why it is recommended that not all possible items in the set should be used for each set at any one time.

The generic item set seems to apply well to quantitative subjects, like the statistics examples. But how well does it apply to nonquantitative content? These item sets have been successfully used in national licensing examinations in accountancy, medicine, nursing, and pharmacy, among others. Haladyna (1991) provided an example in art history. So it seems that this method can be used for other types of content.

This method derives from the earlier work with item forms by Hively and with facet theory by Guttman, whose theories are discussed by Roid and Haladyna (1982). These earlier efforts failed because the methods were too cumbersome to use and the items did not perform as desired. Nonetheless, these earlier methods provide a theoretical rationale for this method, and hopefully, for other proposals which will be discussed in chapter 10.

Item Modeling

Although item modeling has many traits in common with item shells, it is distinguished in several important ways. This section presents a case of an operational definition of professional practice, justifies the use of item modeling as a basis for the content validation of resulting test scores, and illustrates the item-modeling procedure.

Operational Definition Versus Construct Definition

As presented earlier in this book, construct validation is recommended when developing measures of a constructs (Messick, 1989). However, Cronbach (1987), among others, maintained that operational definitions are preferable over constructs because such definitions leave no doubt about what we are trying to measure. Unfortunately, we have few instances where we can operationally define constructs and thus avoid the necessity of construct validation.

In the operationist perspective, there is one and only one measure of a concept. Independent test builders working from the same understanding will build identical tests, if an operational definition is adequate. In contrast, construct validity admits that this is not possible; that we have to build alternative measures and collect evidence regarding their similarities. For example, two measures of a construct should be highly correlated, and measures of unrelated constructs should not be highly correlated. The observation of this behavior is one aspect of what is done in construct validation.

A Rationale for Item Modeling

LaDuca (in press) contended that in professional practice, we have used a behavioral-based knowledge-skills model for discrete learning of chunks of information. That is, traditional tests of ability and achievement view cognitive behavior as existing in discrete parts, and each test item systematically samples specific classes of behaviors, thus domain-referenced interpretations result that give us information about how much learning has occurred. Mislevy (1993a) refers to this mode of construct definition and the resulting tests as representing "low-to-high proficiency." Some writers maintain that this view is outmoded and inappropriate for most settings (Shepard, 1991; Snow, 1993).

This point of view is consistent with the modern reform movement in education calling for greater emphasis on higher level thinking (Nickerson, 1989). For nearly two decades, mathematics educators have promoted a greater emphasis on problem solving, in fact, arguing that problem solving is the main reason for studying mathematics (Prawat, 1993). Other subject matters are presented as fertile for problem-solving teaching and testing. In summary, the impetus of school reform coupled with advances in cognitive psychology are calling for a different view of learning and, in this setting, competence. LaDuca (in press) submitted that "competent practice resides in appropriate responses to the demands of the encounter."

LaDuca proposed that licensure tests for a profession ought to be aimed at behavior that unimpeachably relates to effective practice. The nature of each encounter presents a problem that needs an effective solution to the attending physician. Conventional task analysis and role delineation studies identify knowledge and skills that tangentially related to competence, but the linkage is not so direct. In place of this approach is problem-solving behavior that hinges on all possible realistic, professional encounters.

LaDuca's ideas apply directly to professional licensing and competency testing, but it may be adapted to other settings. For instance, item modeling might be used in consumer problems (e.g., buying a car or appliance, food shopping, painting a house or a room, remodeling a house, fixing a car, or planning landscaping for a new home).

An Example of Item Modeling

This section briefly presents the structural aspects of LaDuca's item-modeling procedures. (Readers interested in the fuller discussion should refer to LaDuca, in press; LaDuca & Downing, in press; LaDuca et al. (1986), and Shea et al. (1991).

For clinical encounters, several faceted dimensions exist for the development of the vignette (clinical encounter) driving content of the item. These facets are used by the expert physician in writing a content-appropriate test item. The existence of these facets makes item writing more systematic.

FACET ONE: SETTING

1. Unscheduled patients/clinic visits
2. Scheduled appointments
3. Hospital rounds
4. Emergency department
5. Other encounters

This first facet identifies six major settings involving patient encounters. The weighting of these settings may be done through studies of the profession or through professional judgment about the criticalness of each setting.

FACET TWO: PHYSICIAN TASKS

1. Obtaining history and performing physical examination
2. Using laboratory and diagnostic studies
3. Formulating most likely diagnosis
4. Evaluating the severity of patient's problem(s)
5. Managing the patient
6. Applying scientific concepts

This second facet provides the array of possible physician activities, in sequential order. The last activity, applying scientific concepts, is somewhat disjointed from the others, because it connects patient conditions with diagnostic data as well as disease or injury patterns and their complications. In other words, it is the complex step in treatment that the other categories do not conveniently describe.

FACET THREE: CASE CLUSTER

1a. Initial workup of new patient, new problem
1b. Initial workup of known patient, new problem
2a. Continued care of known patient, old problem
2b. Continued care of known patient, worsening old problem
3. Emergency care

This third facet provides four types of patient encounters, in three discrete categories with two variations in each of the first two categories. A sample question provides the application of these three facets:

> A 19-year-old archeology student comes to the student health service complaining of severe diarrhea, with 15 large-volume watery stools per day for 2 days. She has had no vomiting, hematochezia, chills or fever, but she is very weak and very thirsty. She is just returned form a 2-week trip to a remote Central American archeological research site. Physical examination shows a temperature 37.2 degrees Centigrade (99.0 degrees Fahrenheit), pulse 120/min, respirations 12/min and blood pressure 90/50 mm Hg. Her lips are dry and skin turgor is poor. What is the most likely cause of the diarrhea?
>
> A. Anxiety and stress from traveling
> B. Inflammatory disease of the large bowel
> C. An osmotic diarrheal process
> D.* A secretory diarrheal process
> E. Poor eating habits during her trip

This item has the following facets:

Facet One: Setting-2. Scheduled appointment
Facet Two: Physician Task-3. Formulating most likely diagnosis
Facet Three: Case Cluster-1a. Initial workup of new patient, new problem

Interestingly, the item pinpoints a central task (3) of diagnosis, but necessarily involves the successful completion of the first two tasks in the task taxonomy. The vignette could be transformed to a context-dependent item set that includes all six physician tasks. The genesis of the patient problem comes from the rich experience of the physician/expert, but systematically fits into the faceted vignette so that test specifications can be satisfied.

Evaluation of Item Modeling

This approach to automated item writing has many virtues to recommend its use. These include the following:

1.   Its foundation is in generating an operational definition. In many settings, particularly in a profession, encounters seem appropriate and realistic. The ability to define a domain consisting of all encounters is at the heart of item modeling.

2.   The method is flexible and adaptive to many settings and situations.
3.   The method has a high degree of credibility, because it rests upon the judgments of experts in a field of study or profession.
4.   The method accelerates the item-writer's ability to write test items, something that nonprofessional item writers greatly need.
5.   In its most sophisticated form, distractors are systematically created.
6.   Item specifications are created that are standardized and uniform.
7.   The method can provide a basis for instruction as well as formative testing because the item model can be used in teaching just as easily as in testing.
8.   Although not explicit, item modeling can be revised to the item set format that more closely models multistep thinking.

Its greatest difficulty appears to be that a lack of imagination would render it useless. Experts in a selected field will need to collectively use that expertise and invent vignettes that systematically define the domain of possible encounters in a field of study. For instance, in auto mechanics, it may be possible to use vignettes to define all possible electrical problems that may occur in the training and licensing of a certified automotive mechanic.

Summary

Item shells, generic item shells for item sets, and item modeling were discussed, illustrated, and evaluated. These methods have much in common. The item shell technique is merely prescriptive, and depends upon using existing items. The generic item set approaches item modeling in concept, but has a fixed questioning structure. Item modeling has a fixed structure of item stems that allows for a domain definition of encounters.

Although these are somewhat new methods, each seems to have great potential for improving both the quality and efficiency of item writing as we know it. The greatest reservation in using either method is the preparation required at the onset of item-writing training. Experts need to identify a vignette structure and systematically define the facets that are varied. Although item shells and item modeling have much in common, further developments will probably favor item modeling because of its inherent theoretical qualities that strike at the foundation of professional competence. But the greatest efficiency and hope for modeling problem solving will come from the merging of item modeling with item sets.

VALIDATING TEST ITEMS

7

REVIEWING MULTIPLE-CHOICE ITEMS

Overview

After we write the item, several reviews can be performed with the purpose of improving the item. Both research and experience have shown that many multiple-choice items are flawed in some way, so these reviews are much needed. The time invested in these reviews will reap rewards in a direct way. The more polish we apply to items, the better the items become. But, some of these activities are significantly more important than others and deserve more attention.

A Rationale for Item Review

Although the scientific basis for writing test items is emerging, the practice of item writing is not yet a highly scientific endeavor, such as the practices of analyzing and scoring test items. In a formal testing program, the reviews to be recommended are essential, whereas in informal testing programs such reviews are desirable but often impractical. Nonetheless, the improvement of any testing program hinges on the ability of test makers to design and write test items properly and also the ability to review and improve these items.

Messick (1989) made a very important point about the value of reviews. Any factor contributing to the increased or reduced difficulty of the test or lack of discrimination that is external to the test content is a form of bias. It contaminates the inferences we require from test results. Thus Messick views the various activities that comprise item review as essential. *The Standards for Educational and Psychological Testing* (APA, 1985) also supported this important practice.

Among the reviews to be recommended, the first is the review of items with respect to the item-writing rules presented in chapter 4. Next, the *editorial review* examines faults due to spelling, capitalization, punctuation, abbreviation, and grammatical errors. This review also concerns clarity of writing. The *key check* is another important review, verifying that each right answer is indeed correct. Another important review is a *content check* for each item to verify that the item represents the content intended. The review for bias takes two forms, judgmental and statistical. Both are recommended, but the latter is appropriately treated in chapter 9. The *bias review* in this chapter involves the study of test items that might favor one subgroup of test takers over another subgroup. Finally, *test taker review* is a desirable type of review where test items are administered to small groups of prospective test takers to determine the validity of using these items in the intended test. In formal testing programs, this action is highly recommended. In classroom testing programs, this kind of review should be conducted with students in class after the test is administered.

Review of Items for Item-Writing Errors

Chapter 4 presented 43 item-writing rules and examples of the use or misuse of each rule. Every test item should be subject to a review to decide if items were properly written. While the 43 rules are provided as guidelines, no one should think of these rules as rigid laws of item writing. As noted previously in this book and in other sources (e.g., Haladyna & Downing, 1989a, 1989b), the degree of consensus about many rules is questionable and the amount of empirical research supporting many rules is lacking. Violating these rules does not necessarily lead to bad items. On the other hand, following these rules probably will result in a test that not only "looks" better but more likely performs according to expectations.

Once these rules are mastered, the detection of item-writing errors is a skill that can be developed to a high degree of proficiency. Items should be revised accordingly. Table 7.1 summarizes these rules. A convenient and effective way to use Table 7.1 in reviewing items is to use each rule number as a code for items that are being reviewed. The persons performing the review can read each item and enter the code on the test booklet containing the offending item. Such information can be used by the test developers to consider redrafting the item, revising it appropriately, or retiring the item.

Editorial Review

Regardless of the type of the testing program or the resources available for the development of the test, it is desirable to have each test professionally edited. The editor is someone usually formally trained in the canons of English grammar and composition.

There are several good reasons for the editorial review. First, edited test items present the cognitive tasks in a clearer fashion than unedited test items. Not only is this an item-writing rule, it is common sense. Items should clearly and accurately present the problem and the options. Second, editorial errors tend to distract test takers. Because great concentration is needed on the test, such errors detract from the basic purpose of testing, to find the extent of knowledge of the test taker. Third, errors reflect badly on the test maker. Face validity is the tendency for a test to look like a test. If there are many editorial errors, the test takers are likely to think that

---

Table 7.1
Summary of 43 Item-Writing Rules

General Item Writing (Procedural)
1. Use either the best answer or the correct answer format.
2. Avoid complex multiple-choice (Type K) items.
3. Format the item vertically not horizontally.
4. Allow time for editing and other types of item revisions.
5. Use good grammar, punctuation, and spelling consistently.
6. Minimize examinee reading time in phrasing each item.
7. Avoid trick items, those that mislead or deceive test takers into answering incorrectly.

General Item Writing (Content Concerns)
8. Base each item on an educational or instructional objective.
9. Focus on a single problem.
10. Keep the vocabulary consistent with the examinee's level of understanding.
11. Avoid cuing one item with another; keep items independent of one another.
12. Use examples as a basis for developing your items.
13. Avoid overspecific knowledge when developing the item.
14. Avoid textbook, verbatim phrasing when developing the item.
15. Avoid items based on opinions.
16. Use multiple-choice to measure higher level thinking.
17. Test for important or significant material; avoid trivial material.

Stem Construction
18. State the stem in the question form instead of the completion form.
19. When using the completion format, do not leave a blank for completion in the beginning or middle of the stem.
20. Ensure that the directions in the stem are clear, and that wording lets the examinee know exactly what is being asked.
21. Avoid window dressing (excessive verbiage) in the stem.
22. Word the stem positively; avoid negative phrasing.
23. Include the central idea and most of the phrasing in the stem.

Table 7.1 (continued)

General Option Development
24. Use as many plausible distractors as are feasible.
25. Place options in logical or numerical order.
26. Keep options independent; options should not be overlapping.
27. Keep all options in an item homogeneous in content.
28. Keep the length of options fairly consistent.
29. Avoid, or use sparingly, the phrase "all of the above."
30. Avoid, or use sparingly, the phrase "none of the above."
31. Avoid the use of the phrase "I don't know."
32. Phrase options positively, not negatively.
33. Avoid distractors that can clue testwise examinees; for example, avoid clang associations, absurd options, formal prompts, or semantic (overly specific or overly general) clues.
34. Avoid giving clues through the use of faulty grammatical construction.
35. Avoid specific determiners, such as "never" and "always."

Correct Option Development
36. Position the correct option so that it appears about the same number of times in each possible position for a set of items.
37. Make sure there is one and only one correct option.

Distractor Development
38. Use plausible distractors; avoid illogical distractors.
39. Incorporate common errors of students in distractors.
40. Use technically phrased distractors.
41. Use familiar yet incorrect phrases as distractors.
42. Use true statements that do not correctly answer the item.
43. Avoid the use of humor when developing options.

---

the test falls short in the more important areas of content and item-writing quality. Thus, the test maker loses the respect of test takers.

Several areas of concern of the editorial review are given in Table 7.2. A valuable aid in testing programs is an editorial guide, which is normally several pages of guidelines about acceptable formats, abbreviations, style conventions, and other details of item preparation, such as type font and size, margins, etc. For informal testing, where no editorial guideline is feasible, consistency of style is also important.

There are some excellent references that should be part of the library of a test maker, whether professional or amateur. Some of these are:

Table 7.2
Objective of the Editorial Review

Areas of Concern	Aspects of the Review
1. Mechanics	Spelling, abbreviations and acronyms, punctuation, and capitalization
2. Grammar	Complete sentences, correct use of pronouns, correct form and use of verbs, and correct use of modifiers
3. Clarity	Item stem clearly presents the problem, and options provide coherent and plausible responses.
4. Style	Active voice, conciseness, positive statements of the problem in the stem, consistency

Achtert, W. S., & Gibaldi, J. (1985). *The MLA style manual.* New York: Modern Language Association of America.

American Psychological Association. (1985). *Publication manual of the American Psychological Association* (3rd ed.). Washington, DC: Author.

Strunk, W., Jr., & White, E. B. (1959). *The elements of style.* New York: MacMillan.

The Chicago manual of style (13th ed.). (1982). Chicago: University of Chicago Press.

Warriner, J. E. & Griffith, F. (1957). *English grammar and composition.* New York: Harcourt, Brace, & World.

A spelling checker on a word processing program is also very handy. *WordPerfect* or *Microsoft Word* are highly recommended. Spelling checkers have resident dictionaries for checking the correct spelling of many words. However, the best feature is the opportunity to develop an exception spelling list, where specialized and words not in the spelling checker's dictionary can be added. Of course, many of these types of words have to be first verified from another source before each word can be so added. For example if one works in medicine or in law, the spelling of various medical terms can be checked in a specialized dictionary, such as Stedman's *Medical Dictionary* or Black's *Law Dictionary*. The former has over 68,000 medical terms and the latter uses over 16,000 legal terms.

Key Check

The key check is a method for ensuring that there is one and only one correct answer. Checking the key is an important step in test development, and never should be done superficially or casually.

Why is it necessary to check the key? Because several possibilities exist after the test is given and the items are statistically analyzed:

1. There may be no right answers.
2. There may be a right answer, but it is not the one that is keyed.
3. There may be two or more right answers.

What should be done if any of these three circumstances exist after the test is given?

In the unlikely event of the first situation, all examinees should be given credit for the item. The principle at stake is that no test taker should be penalized for the test maker's error. Another possibility is to omit that item from the test and rescale the test—the practice of rescaling means that the shorter test will constitute the "valid" version.

If the second or third conditions exist, right answers should be rekeyed and the test results should be rescored to correct any errors created by the problems. The alternate action is to remove the item, as suggested in the previous paragraph.

These kinds of drastic actions can be avoided through a thorough, conscientious key check.

Performing the Key Check

The key check should always be done by a content expert or a panel of content experts. After the test is given, methods discussed in the next chapter are useful in revealing potential key errors. However these methods are of a different nature than this key check.

The original item writer will often key the item. The expert reviewers or panel should self-administer the item and then decide if their response matches the key. If it fails to match the key, then the item should be reviewed, and through consensus judgment, the key should be determined. If a lack of consensus exists, then the item is inherently ambiguous or otherwise faulty.

Another way to validate a key is to provide a reference to the right answer from an authoritative source, such as a textbook or a journal. This is a common practice in medical certification testing and other professional licensing tests. The practice of providing references for test items also ensures a faithfulness to content that may be part of the test specifications.

In any testing program where important decisions are made based on test scores, the failure to deal with key errors is unfair to test takers.

Content Review

The central issue in content review is relevance. Messick (1989) stated:

> Judgments of the relevance of test items or tasks to the intended score interpretation should take into account all aspects of the testing procedure that significantly affect test performance. These include, as we have seen, specification of the construct domain of reference in terms of topical content, typical behaviors, and underlying processes. Also needed are test specifications regarding stimulus formats and response alternatives, administration conditions (such as examinee instructions or time limits), and criteria for item scoring. (p. 276)

As Popham (1993) pointed out, the expert judgment regarding test items has dominated validity studies. Most classroom testing and formal testing programs seek a type of test score interpretation relating to some well defined content (Fitzpatrick, 1981; Kane, 1982; Messick, 1989). Under these conditions, content is believed to be definable in terms of a domain of knowledge (for instance, a set of facts, concepts, principles, and procedures). Under these circumstances, each test is believed to be a representative sample of the total domain of knowledge. As Messick noted, the chief concerns are (a) clear construct definition, (b) test specifications that call for the sample of content and behaviors desired, and (c) attention to the test item formats and response conditions desired. He further adds administration and scoring conditions to this area of concern.

The technology, as noted by Popham previously, is use of content experts, persons intimate with the content who are willing to review items to ensure that each item represents the content and level of cognitive behavior desired. The expert or panel of experts should ensure that each item is (a) relevant to the domain of content being tested and (b) properly identified in terms of this content. For example, if auto mechanics' knowledge of brakes is being tested, then each item should be analyzed to figure out if it belongs to the domain of knowledge for which the test is designed and if it is correctly identified.

Although this step may seem very mundane, it is sometimes surprising to see items misclassified by content. With classroom tests designed to measure student achievement, students can easily identify items that are instructionally irrelevant. In formal testing programs, there are an ever growing number of detection techniques that inform users about items that may be out of place. This chapter discusses judgmental review, whereas chapters 8 and 9 discuss statistical methods.

Methods for performing the content review are suggested by Rovinelli and Hambleton (1977). In selecting content reviewers, these authors make excellent points:

1. Can the reviewers make valid judgments regarding the content of items?

2. Is there agreement among reviewers?
3. What information is sought in the content review?
4. What factors affect the accuracy of content judgments of the reviewers?
5. What techniques can be used to collect and analyze judgments?

Regarding the last point, the authors strongly recommend using the simplest method available.

Toward that end, the review of test items can be done in formal testing programs by asking each content specialist to classify the item according to an item classification guide. Rovinelli and Hambleton (1977) recommended a simple three-point rating scale:

1. Item is correctly classified.
2. Uncertain
3. Item is incorrectly classified.

These authors also provide an index of congruence between the original classification and the content specialists classification. The index can be used to identify those items having content classification problems. If the cognitive level of each item is of concern, the same kind of rating can be used.

Figure 7.1 provides a simplified example of ratings from content experts using the mythical Azalea Growers' Certification Test. As shown at the top of the figure, the test specifications provide the proportions of items required in the test, whereas the bottom provides the actual ratings of content. In most testing programs, the four topics shown would be further subdivided into subtopics in outline fashion, and content experts would be asked to provide a more exacting type of review than simply to identify the main topic.

The science of content review has been raised beyond merely expert judgment and simple descriptive indicators of content agreement. Crocker, Llabre, and Miller (1988) proposed a more sophisticated system of study of content ratings involving generalizability theory. They described how the theory can be used to generate a variety of study designs that not only provide indices of content rater consistency but also identify sources of inconsistency. They reminded us that the study of test items is growing more sophisticated, necessitated by the "high stakes" nature of many testing programs, and the importance of ensuring that the content of tests is as "advertised."

Content review has been a rather mundane aspect of test design. As Messick (1989) noted, although capable test development includes these important steps, we do not have much systematic information in the literature that informs us about what to use and how to use it. Hambleton (1984) provided the most current and comprehensive summary of methods for validating test items.

	Watering	Fertilizer	Light	Soil
Recalling	4%	6%	4%	6%
Defining	2%	4%	8%	6%
Predicting	10%	2%	2%	6%
Evaluating	8%	4%	4%	4%
Problem solving	12%	8%	0%	0%

Item Number	Original Class.	Reviewers #1	#2	#3
82	Watering	3	3	3
83	Fertilizer	1	1	1
84	Soil	1	2	1
85	Soil	2	3	2
86	Light	1	1	1

Fig. 7.1. Excerpt of reviews from three content reviewers against original classification for the Azalea Growers Certification Test

Judgmental Item Bias Review

Bias is a complex concept relating to unfairness of both test score interpretations and uses. Bias can be observed at the test score and item response levels. Evidence of bias comes in either judgmental or empirical forms, and the argument for bias optimally would include both forms (Cole & Moss, 1989; Messick, 1989). This section will deal with judgmental item bias, which is any aspect of the test item that treats a subgroup of test takers stereotypically or otherwise pejoratively. Chapter 9 treats the empirical form of evidence of item bias. For instance, the most common forms of judgmental item bias involved negative or stereotypical references to gender, ethnic groups, or racial minorities.

The concept of judgmental item bias has received very little scholarly attention. Few primary references in the field of educational measurement provide more than a paragraph to a page of general discussion. *The Standards for Educational and Psychological Testing* (American Psychological Association, 1985) provided in standard 3.10 a single paragraph of commentary that explains the nature of item bias and the responsibility of test makers: "When previous research indicates the need for studies of item or test performance differences for a particular kind of test for members of age, ethnic, cultural, and gender groups in the population of test takers, such studies should be conducted as soon as is feasible. Such research should be designed to detect and eliminate aspects of test design, content, or format that might bias test scores for a particular groups" (p. 27).

This standard emphasizes empirical forms of item bias at the expense of judgmental forms. A stronger standard, a more prudent policy, might include judgmental item bias review as a standard practice for standardized testing programs, particularly those with "high stakes" interpretations and uses. Classroom testing should routinely be monitored for insensitive references as mentioned in this standard.

Current textbooks on educational measurement give very little attention to this topic. However, there are several good reasons for more concern. First and foremost, Zoref and Williams (1980) noted a high incidence of gender and ethnic stereotyping in several prominent intelligence tests. They cited several studies done in the 1970s where similar findings existed for achievement tests. To what extent this kind of bias exists in other standardized tests currently can only be speculation, but any incidence of this stereotyping is to be avoided in the future. Second, for humanistic concerns, all test makers should ensure that items do not stereotype diverse elements of our society. Third, such stereotyping is inaccurate, due to overgeneralization. Fourth, stereotyping may cause reactions during the test taking process.

Table 7.3 provides some criteria for judging item bias, adapted from Zoref and Williams (1980). Despite the attempt in that table to categorize forms of item bias, this area is in much need of more systematic and extensive study than it has received in the past. We lack both a complete rationale and a technology for performing judgmental item bias reviews.

Test-Taker Review

A good source of information about the quality of a test item is the test taker. In fact, one of several good sources of evidence in construct validation is the collection of qualitative data regarding test item performance. If the setting for testing is instructional, this is strongly recommended, because each student's analysis of wrong answers can actually aid in the learning process. If the setting for testing is a formal testing program, this type of inquiry is more problematic and logistically difficult. Nonetheless, several compelling reasons exist to recommend this practice.

Classroom Testing

The next class period following a classroom test should be spent discussing test results. The primary purpose is to help students learn from their errors. If learning is a continuous process, a posttest analysis can be very helpful in subsequent learning efforts. A second purpose, however, is to detect items that fail to perform as intended. The expert judgment of classroom learners can be marshalled for the purpose of exposing ambiguous or misleading items.

After a classroom test is administered and scored, it is recommended that students have an opportunity to discuss each item and provide alternative reasoning for their wrong answers. Sometimes, they may demonstrate the inherent weakness in the item and the correct rationale for their answer. In these circumstances, they

Table 7.3
A Typology for Judgmental Item Bias Review

Gender	Race/Ethnic
Representation: Items should be balanced with respect to gender representations. Factors to consider include clothes, length of hair, facial qualities, and make-up. Nouns and pronouns should be considered (he/she, woman/man).	Representation: Simply stated, if the racial or ethnic identity of characters in test items is present, it should resemble the demographics of the testing taking population.
Characterization: Two aspects of this are role stereotyping (RS) and apparel stereotyping (AS). RS would include any verbal or pictorial referring to qualities such as intelligence, strength, vigor, ruggedness, historical contributions, mechanical aptitude, professionalism, and/or fame being assigned to males exclusively. Female examples of RS include depicting women in domestic situations, passiveness, weakness, general activity, excessive interest in clothes or cosmetics, and the like. AS is viewed as the lesser of the two aspects of characterization. AS refers to clothing and other accoutrements that are associated with men and women, for example, neckties, cosmetics. This latter category is used to support the more important designation of the former category in identifying gender bias in an item.	Characterization: White characters in test items may be stereotypically be presented in leadership roles, wealthy, professional, technical, intelligent, academic, and the like. Minority characters are depicted as unskilled, subservient, under-educated, poor, or in professional sports.

Note. From "A look at content bias in IQ tests" by L. Zoref & P. Williams. *Journal of Educational Measurement, 17*, 313-322. © 1980 by the National Council on Measurement in Education. Adapted by permission of the publisher.

deserve credit for their responses. Such informal polling also may determine that certain items are deficient because the highest scoring students are chronically missing the item or the lowest scoring students are chronically getting an item right. Standard item analysis also will reveal this, but the informal polling method is practical and feasible. In fact it can be done immediately after the test is given, if time permits, or at the next class meeting. Further there is instructional value to the activity, because students have the opportunity to learn what they did not learn before being tested. An electronic version of this polling method is reported by Sato (1980), but such a technique would be difficult to carry out in most instructional settings because of cost. On the other hand, the informal polling method can provide appeals for the correct scoring of the test and also provide some diagnostic teaching and remedial learning.

An analysis for any single student can reveal the nature of the problem. Sometimes, a student may realize that overconfidence, test anxiety, lack of study or preparation, or other factors legitimately affected performance, or it may reveal that the items were at fault. In some circumstances, a student can offer a correct line of reasoning that justifies an answer that no one else in the class or the teacher thought was right. In these rarer circumstances, credit could be given. This action rightfully accepts the premise that item writing is seldom a perfect process and that such corrective actions are sometimes justified.

Another device for obtaining answer justification is the use of a form where the student writes out a criticism of the item or the reasoning used to select his or her response. The instruction might read:

> Present any arguments favoring the answer you chose on the test.

Such written commentary often reveals the thought processes of students in arriving at a wrong answer. If the process was valid, perhaps the item was flawed and prevented the student from choosing the desired answer. It is surprising how flaws are discovered by the test taker even after the items passed through all other reviews.

Formal Testing

In formal testing programs, the *think-aloud* procedure has been used to study the thought processes of students during a test. The *developmental field test* is also designed to accomplish a similar end, to analyze student behavior during a test to determine if an item is working as intended. The procedures for the think-aloud and the developmental field test are essentially the same. Students are grouped at a table and asked to answer a set of questions. During the time allotted, the administrator sits at the table and talks to the students, probing to find out what prompted certain answers. The setting is friendly and collegial, and each student is urged to talk about the test.

The basis for the think-aloud procedure comes from studies of cognitive behavior. Norris (1990) provides an excellent review of the both the history and the rationale for verbal reports of test-taking behavior. However, seeing the link to construct validity, test specialists have recommended this practice. Indeed, test taker reports of student perceived thought processes involved in answer selection or answer creation can be very revealing about the actual thought processes involved. Some impetus for this kind of test score validation comes from cognitive psychology, where information processing theory can be studied au naturel. Norris provides a useful taxonomy of elicitation levels, shown in Table 7.4.

One conclusion that Norris drew from his experimental study of college students is that the use of the six levels of elicitation of verbal reports had no effect on cognitive test behavior. Some benefits of this kind of probing, he claimed, include detecting misleading expressions, implicit clues, unfamiliar vocabulary, and alternative justifiable answers.

Another recent study by Farr, Pritchard, and Smitten (1990) shed more light on verbal reports of test takers. Their study involved reading comprehension of passages, involving the context-dependent item set for measuring comprehension, as discussed in chapter 3. Their interest was to find out if the multiple-choice format controls the kind of cognitive behavior desired. Various critics of using multiple-choice to measure reading comprehension claim that this format encourages test takers to perform surface reading as opposed to the more desired indepth reading. They experimented with 26 college students using a standardized reading comprehension test and planned probes to obtain verbal reports of their thinking processes. Four distinctly different strategies were identified for answering these context-dependent passages. The most popular of these strategies was to read the passage, then read each question, then search for the answer in the passage. Without any doubt, all test takers manifested question-answering behavior. In other words, they were focused on answering questions, as opposed to reading the passage for surface or deep meaning. Although these researchers concluded that the multiple-choice reading comprehension test is a special type of reading comprehension task, it seems to have general value to the act of reading comprehension. These researchers concluded that this study answers critics who contend that surface thinking only occurs in this kind of test. Further, they say that the development of items (tasks) actually determines the types of cognitive behaviors being elicited. Their sample includes highly able adult readers who used effective reading skills in locating the correct answers. Descriptive studies like this one are rare but they help us understand better the underlying cognitive processes actually used to answer questions.

As Norris (1990) summarized verbal reports of test taking: "Verbal reports of thinking would be useful in the validation of multiple-choice critical thinking tests, if they could provide evidence to judge whether good thinking was associated with choosing keyed answers and poor thinking was associated with unkeyed answers" (p. 55).

Table 7.4
Descriptions of Elicitation Levels

Elicitation Level	Description
Think Aloud	Subjects were instructed to report all they were thinking as they worked through the items and to mark their answers on a standardized answer
Immediate Recall	Subjects were instructed to mark their answers to each item on a standardized answer sheet and to tell immediately after choosing each answer why they chose it.
Criteria Probe	Subjects were instructed to mark their answers to each item on a standardized answer sheet, and were asked immediately after marking each answer whether a piece of information pointed out in the item had made any difference to their choice.
Principle Probe	Subjects were treated as in the criterion problem group with an additional question asking whether their answer choice was based upon particular general principles.
No Elicitation	Subjects were not interviewed, but were instructed to work alone and to mark their answers on a standardized sheet.

Note.   From "Effects of eliciting verbal reports of thinking on critical thinking test performance." by S. P. Norris. *Journal of Educational Measurement, 27*, 41-58. © 1990 by the National Council on Measurement in Education. Adapted by permission of the publisher.

Although this method is time consuming and logistically difficult, it seems well worth the effort if one is serious about validating test results.

Summary

This chapter has sought to inform readers about the benefits of reviewing new test items. These reviews are complementary. The *item-writing rule review* is desirable because it allows reviewers the chance to look for obvious item-writing violations that may lead to faulty performance. The *editorial review* is essential to preserving the "looks" of the test, as well as the clarity of presentation of test items. The *key check* is essential to ensure that the keyed options are correct. If experts can not agree on the correct answer to the test item, then the item probably should not be used. The *content classification review* is also essential in preserving the fidelity between the choice of items for a test and the test specifications. A *judgmental item bias review* is essential for high-stakes testing programs and desirable for all other testing programs, including informal testing. But the judgmental item bias review is only part of a total study of bias, because statistical methods for detecting bias also may be used and are described and reviewed in chapter 9. The *test-taker review* is very desirable in all types of testing programs and testing situations and has many good qualities. Answer justification is useful in a classroom setting where teacher-made tests may be evaluated by the consumer, the student. Think-aloud procedures can be used to validate test items in formal testing programs.

8

ANALYZING ITEM RESPONSES

Overview

This chapter presents methods for improving test items through the analysis of item responses. The nature of this analysis includes the tabulation of item responses, graphical methods, and statistical analysis. Some theories, research, and technologies are very new and not yet ready for implementation in testing, but they provide a basis for future theory building, research, and new technologies. Among the methods studied, some are recommended for use, whereas others are not.

The Nature of Item Responses

In chapter 1, the nature of a test item and examinees' responses to test items is discussed. Some of these topics are presented again in this chapter but are treated more comprehensively.

Responses to test items tend to develop patterns. Items with desirable response patterns contribute to developing an effective test, whereas items with undesirable item response patterns weaken test score validity. Thus, the primary objective in this chapter is to learn how to analyze item responses. Once analyzed, items can be discarded, retained for future use, or improved. The attainment of this primary objective is complicated by the particular test theory we use. The problem of analyzing item response patterns will be addressed using classical test theory, but then later in this chapter we will shift to item response theory. Some methods do not reside within either theory but are useful in better understanding the dynamics of item performance.

Another complication we face is the choice of the scoring method. For nearly a century, test analysts have treated distractors and items equally. That is, all right answers score one point each and all wrong answers score no points. This is sometimes called *zero-one* or *binary* scoring. With coming of item response theory, the weighting of right answers is realized with the two- and three-parameter models. Both in a classical and item response theory frameworks, theoreticians have developed polytomous scoring models that consider the differential information offered in distractors (Haladyna & Sympson, 1988). Haladyna and Crehan (1993) have showed that the evaluation of test items and options differs between dichotomous and polytomous scoring methods. This chapter describes and illustrates both orientations. Methods of polytomous scoring allow us to probe more deeply into the item response patterns and reveal the intrinsic worth of each distractor in meaningful ways.

Instruction/Training/Human Development Context

To understand how to use item response patterns to evaluate items, we must place the item in a context, the test itself and what it is supposed to measure. One significant context is when a test is intended to measure the degree of accomplishment of learners who are being instructed or trained. Instruction/training assumes that a certain domain of achievement is being learned, and the test, as a sample of this achievement domain, helps us estimate the extent of each student's knowledge and the group's status in this domain. If the test measures status in a domain for certifying competence in a profession, licensing a professional, certifying completion of a course of study, or the like, we are again interested in accomplishment relevant to a domain. An added responsibility is to decide if the test score truly falls above or below the passing score. This matter pertains to test score reliability, or more specifically, the precision of test scores. Item quality is a major factor in determining the precision of test scores.

Item Performance Patterns

There are several ways to study performance patterns and draw inferences about the effectiveness of each item. Each will be presented and discussed. These methods are usually complementary, but some interesting and important distinctions exist among these methods that may lead to different results. Some of these variations deal with the test theory used, whereas other variations deal with whether results are dichotomously or polytomously scored. Readers who are conversant with traditional and item response theory item analysis will find this section to be a review of familiar concepts and procedures. However, some additional and innovative procedures are introduced and illustrated. This section has two parts. The first examines characteristics of test items, and the second examines distractor characteristics.

Item Difficulty

The natural metric for item difficulty is percentage correct for the group answering the item. The ceiling of any multiple-choice item is 100% and the floor is determined by the probability of a correct response when all examinees are guessing. With a four-option item, the floor is 25%. The nomenclature for item difficulty is *p-value*, which stands for the proportion or percentage of examinees correctly answering the item.

In classical test theory, every item has a natural difficulty; one that is based on all persons for whom the test is intended. This p-value is very difficult to estimate accurately unless you are testing a very representative group of test takers. This is one reason why classical theory is criticized, because the estimation of the p-value is potentially biased by the sample upon which the estimate is based. If the sample contains well instructed, highly trained, or well developed persons, the tests and its items appear very easy, usually above .90. If the sample contains uninstructed, untrained, or undeveloped persons, the test and the items appear very hard, usually below .40.

Item response theory allows for the estimating of item difficulty without consideration for exactly who is being tested. With classical test theory as just noted, the performance level of the sample strongly influences the estimation of difficulty. With item response theory, the composition of the sample is generally immaterial to parameter estimation, and item difficulty can be estimated without bias. There are many item response theory models. Most of these models are applicable to large testing programs, involving 500 or more test takers. If a testing program is that large and the content domain is somewhat unidimensional, item response theory can be very effective for constructing tests that are adaptable for many purposes and types of examinees. The one-, two-, and three-parameter binary-scoring models will typically lead to similar estimates of difficulty, and these estimates will be highly correlated to classical estimates of difficulty. Because difficulty is under or overestimated with classical test theory, the ability to accurately estimate parameters, like difficulty, provide a clear advantage for item response theory.

Controlling Item Difficulty. What causes an item to be difficult or easy? Studies about factors that control item difficulty are scarce. One possible cause of a p-value is the extent to which instruction, training, or development has occurred with those being tested. Consider an item with a p-value of .66. Was it the composition of the group being tested, the effectiveness of instruction or training, or the extent of development that caused this p-value? One clue is to examine test performance of instructed and uninstructed, trained or untrained, developed or undeveloped individuals and groups. This concept is instructional sensitivity, and it is more fully discussed in a subsequent section of this chapter. Another possible cause of a p-value is that the item is really not relevant to the content domain being tested. In this circumstance, we would not expect the item performance pattern to be unintelligible because the item has really nothing to do with the instruction, training, or development.

Green and Smith (1987), Smith (1986), and Smith and Kramer (1990) conducted some interesting experiments on controlling item difficulty. This aspect of item design is a promising research topic. The production of items at a known level of difficulty provides an advantage over the current hit or miss methods we typically use. If tasks could be graded a priori to item development, we would have more intelligent control of item difficulty and, perhaps, item quality as well.

Item Discrimination

Item discrimination is a characteristic of an item that addresses the ability of an item to measure sensitively individual differences. If test takers are known to differ in their performances, then each test item should mirror the tendency for test takers to vary. Thus, with a discriminating item, those choosing the correct answer must necessarily differ in total score from those choosing any wrong answer. This is not a characteristic of putative *norm-referenced tests*, but a characteristic of any measuring instrument where repeated trials (items) are used.

Item discrimination can be estimated in several ways, and pitfalls exist in its measurement. Some major differences exist depending upon which statistical theory of test scores is used.

In classical theory, item discrimination is simply the product-moment (point-biserial) relationship between item and test performance. Some theorists believe that the biserial correlation (a sister to the point-biserial) is more appropriate. For instance, a highly discriminating item is one where the average performance level of those test takers answering correctly is very high, for example about 90%, and the average performance level of those answering incorrectly is very low, for example about 50%. The size of the discrimination index is informative about the relation of the item to the total domain of knowledge, as represented by the total test score. It can be shown statistically and empirically that test score reliability depends upon item discrimination. The weakness of using classical item discrimination in instructional testing is that if the range of scores is restricted, when instruction is effective and student effort is high, the discrimination index is greatly underestimated. In fact, if all performers answer correctly, the discrimination index will be zero. But this is misleading. If the sample included nonlearners, we would find out more about the ability of the item to discriminate. One can obtain an unbiased estimate of discrimination in the same way as one can obtain an unbiased estimate of difficulty—by obtaining a representative sample that includes the full range of behavior for the trait being measured. Restriction in the range of this behavior is likely to affect the estimation of discrimination.

In item response theory, we have a variety of traditional, dichotomous scoring models as well as newer polytomous scoring models from which to choose. The one-parameter item response model (referred to as the *Rasch model*) is not concerned with discrimination, as all items are assumed to be equally discriminating. The Rasch model has one parameter—difficulty. The model is popular because it is simple to apply, and it provides satisfactory results despite this implausible assumption about discrimination. Critics of this model will appropriately point out that the model is too simplistic and ignores the fact that items do vary with respect to discrimination. With the two-parameter and three-parameter models, item discrimination is proportional to the slope of the option characteristic curve at the point of inflexion (Lord, 1980). This shows that an item is most discriminating in a particular range of scores. One item may discriminate very well for high-scoring test takers, whereas another item may discriminate best for low-scoring test takers. Figure 8.1 illustrates an option characteristic curve for the correct choice. A test consisting of items with the same discrimination would provide the most precise estimates of test scores at that point. In Fig. 8.1, this steep slope is the middle of the test score scale. In designing tests guided by item response theory, discrimination pays handsome dividends. Interested readers should consult one of the excellent books on this topic that provide more complete discussions (e.g., Hambleton & Swaminathan, 1987; Hulin, Drasgow, & Parsons, 1983; Lord, 1980).

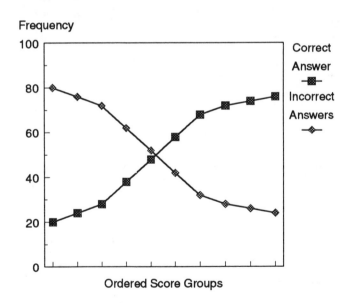

**Fig. 8.1. Trace lines for
correct and incorrect answers for an item.**

Several excellent computer programs are available for a variety of computer environments that provide estimates of parameters. These include *Rascal* (Assessment Systems Corporation, 1992), *Ascal* (Assessment Systems Corporation, 1989), *Bigsteps*, (Wright & Linacre, 1992), *Bilog* (Mislevy & Bock, 1990), and *Bimain* (Muraki, Mislevy, & Bock, 1992), to name a few that are easily obtainable and easy to use. *Parscale* (Muraki & Bock, 1993) provided for equating when multiple-choice and performance tests are used.

A third method to estimate item discrimination is the *eta coefficient*. This statistic can be derived from the one-way analysis of variance, where the dependent variable is choice mean (the average score of persons selecting that option), and the independent variable is the option choice. In analysis of variance, three estimates of variance are obtained: sums of square between, sums of squares within, and sums of squares total. The ratio of the sums of squares between and the sums of squares total is the squared eta coefficient. In some statistical treatments, this ratio is also the squared correlation between two variables (R^2). The eta coefficient is similar to the traditional product-moment discrimination index. In practice, the eta coefficient differs from the product-moment correlation coefficient in that the eta considers the differential nature of distractors, whereas the product-moment makes no distinction among item responses to distractors.

Haladyna and Crehan (1993) provided an example of two items that have approximately the same product-moment discrimination index but different eta coefficients, as Table 8.1 shows.

The first item has a high discrimination index but a low eta coefficient. Notice that the average scores of those choosing each option (*choice means*) are relatively closely bunched. The second item also has a high discrimination index but also a high eta coefficient, owing to the fact that the choice means of the distractors are more separated. In dichotomous scoring, point-biserial may be appropriate, and the discrimination parameter in the two- and three-parameter models may be appropriate with dichotomous scoring. However, with polytomous scoring, the eta coeffi-

Table 8.1
Point-biserial and Eta Coefficients for Two Items

	Item 1	Item2
Point-biserial	.512	.552
Eta Coefficient	.189	.326
Choice Means		
Option A	33.9%	33.4%
Option B	23.5%	24.8%
Option C	27.0%	29.6%
Option D	26.4%	30.7%

cient provides different information that is appropriate for studying item performance relative to polytomous scoring.

What we can learn from this section is that with dichotomous scoring, one can obtain approximately the same information from using the classical discrimination index (the product-moment correlation between item and test performance) or the discrimination parameter from the two- or three-parameter item response models. But with polytomous scoring these methods are inappropriate, and the eta coefficient gives us unique and more appropriate information.

Dimensionality and Discrimination. One vexing problem that exists with the estimation of discrimination is the dimensionality of the test. Generally, tests ought to be as unidimensional as possible with the present day theories and methods we use. For instance, with item response theory, unidimensionality is a prerequisite of the item response data. Hattie (1985) provided an excellent review of this issue. When using the two- or three-parameter logistic response model, the computer program will fail to converge if multidimensionality exists. With the use of classical theory, discrimination indexes, obtained from product-moment correlations or biserial correlations, will be lower than expected and unstable from sample to sample. Thus, one has to be cautious that the underlying test data is unidimensional when estimating discrimination. A quick-and-dirty method is to estimate KR-20 internal consistency reliability. If lower than expected for the number of items in the test, then this is a clue that the data may be multidimensional. A more dependable method is to conduct a factor analysis, but this has some difficulties as well (Gorsuch, 1983; Hambleton & Swaminathan, 1987; Hattie, 1985). Chapter 9 provides more discussion of this problem.

Instructional Sensitivity

If instruction/training has been successful, persons instructed or trained, should perform at the upper end of the test score scale, whereas those not instructed or trained or those not having developed the necessary knowledge will perform at the lower end of the scale, as illustrated in Fig. 8.2. This is not true in instances where bias exists, or the test taker is performing erratically, or the test is in some way inappropriate, say too hard to too easy or the test simply does not represent that domain.

In Fig. 8.2, the uninstructed group displays low performance on a test and its items, and the instructed group displays high performance on a test and its items. This idealized performance pattern shows effective instruction, good student effort, and a test that is *sensitive to this instruction*. Other terms used to describe this phenomenon are *instructional sensitivity* or *opportunity to learn* (Haladyna & Roid, 1981). Instructional sensitivity can be estimated using classical or item response theory. The concept of instructional sensitivity incorporates the concepts of item

xx   xx
xxx   xxx
xxxxxx   xxxxxx
xxxxxxxxxx   xxxxxxxxxx
— —
Low performance   High performance
Before instruction   After instruction

**Fig. 8.2. Idealized performance of
instructed and uninstructed students.**

difficulty and item discrimination (Haladyna, 1974; Haladyna & Roid, 1981; Herbig, 1976).

Item difficulty varies because of the group of students tested has received differential instruction. Advanced students perform well on an item, whereas less advanced students do not perform very well. Therefore, it is possible to observe several conditions involving item difficulty that help us find which items are working as predicted and which items have performance problems that require closer analysis.

First, the simplest of the instructional sensitivity indexes will be used to illustrate several possible conditions. Then instructional sensitivity and how it can be measured several ways and estimated without complete information will be shown.

Instructional sensitivity is a helpful concept in analyzing several important instructional conditions. These conditions include (a) effective instruction, (b) ineffective instruction or lack of instruction, (c) unneeded instruction, or (d) item is too easy. With each condition, several plausible, alternate hypotheses exist. The index must be used with someone who is intimate with the instructional setting.

Pre-to-Post Difference Index (PPDI). This index, first introduced by Cox and Vargas (1966), provides the simple difference in item difficulty based two samples of test takers known to differ with respect to instruction. For instance, the first group can be typical students who have not yet received instruction, while the second group can be typical students who have received instruction.

Pre-Instruction	Post-Instruction	PPDI
40%	80%	40

This simple illustration suggests that the item is moderately difficult (60%) for a typical four-option multiple-choice item, when the sample has an equal number of instructed and uninstructed students. The change in difficulty for the two conditions represents the amount of learning gained from instruction, as reflected by a single item.

Because a single item is a somewhat undependable measure, and because it is somewhat biased by its intrinsic difficulty, it is far better to aggregate several items across the test to make an inference about instructional effectiveness or growth.

Other conditions exist for this index that provides useful descriptive information about item performance:

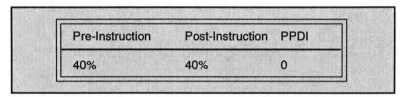

Pre-Instruction	Post-Instruction	PPDI
40%	40%	0

This kind of performance might suggest ineffective instruction or lack of treatment of the content on which the item was based. A second, plausible and rivaling hypothesis is that the item is so difficult that few can answer it correctly, despite the effectiveness of instruction. A third plausible hypothesis is that the item is unrelated to the purposes of the test, therefore no amount of instruction is relevant to performance on the item. The instructional designer and test designer must be careful to consider other, more plausible, hypotheses and reach a correct conclusion. Often this conclusion is augmented by studying the performance patterns of clusters of items. Having a single item perform like above is a different matter, but having all items perform as above is entirely another matter. A single item may be unnecessarily difficult, but if all items perform similarly, then the problem may lie with instruction, or the entire test may be content invalid for this purpose.

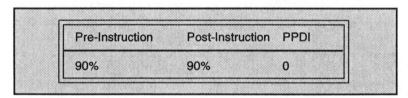

Pre-Instruction	Post-Instruction	PPDI
90%	90%	0

Like the previous example, the PPDI is zero, but unlike the previous example, the performance of both samples is high. Several rivaling hypotheses explain this performance. First, the material may have already been learned, and both uninstructed and instructed groups perform well on the item. Second, the item may have a fault that is cuing the correct answer; therefore, most astute students are picking the right answer despite whether they have learned the content represented by the item. Third, the item is inherently easy for everyone. The item fails to reflect the influence of instruction, because the item fails to discriminate what content is to be measured due to the inherent easiness of the item.

Other Indexes. Obtaining a sample of test behavior from a preinstructed or uninstructed group is often impractical. Haladyna and Roid (1981) examined a set of other instructional sensitivity indexes, including one derived from the Rasch model and a Bayesian index. They found a high degree of relation among these indexes. They also found that the postinstruction difficulty is a very dependable predictor of PPDI, but the use of this index will be incorrect in the condition reported above where pre- and postinstruction performance of test takers is uniformly high. Thus, this short-cut method for estimating PPDI is useful but one should always consider this inherent weakness in analyzing the instructional sensitivity of items by using post-instruction difficulty alone.

In this setting, the validity of these conclusions is not easy to prove based on statistical results alone. Analysis of performance patterns requires close observation of the instructional circumstances and the judicious use of item and test scores to draw valid conclusions. Instructional sensitivity is a useful combination of information about item difficulty and discrimination that contributes to the study and improvement of items designed to test the effects of teaching or training.

Guessing

All multiple-choice test items contain an element of guessing. Any test taker when encountering the item either knows the right answer, has partial knowledge that allows for the elimination of implausible distractors and a guess among the remaining choices, or simply a guess in the absence of any knowledge.

In classical test theory, one can ignore the influence of guessing completely, if that guessing is balanced by the laws of probability that will take control if the test is long enough. The probability of getting a higher-than-deserved score by guessing is very small as the test gets longer. Some test developers have used correction-for-guessing formulas.

Statistical indicators exist for studying the extent and influence of guessing with each item. Specifically, in the three-parameter item response model, the third parameter is guessing. Hambleton and Swaminathan (1987) discussed the guessing parameter, identifying it as a pseudo-chance level for the item. This parameter is not intended to model the psychological process of guessing but merely to establish that a reasonable floor exists for the difficulty parameter. This guessing parameter is used along with item difficulty and discrimination to compute a test taker's score. The influence of the guessing parameter is small in relation to the influence of the discrimination parameter. Several polytomous scoring models that also use correct and incorrect responses incorporate information about guessing into scoring procedures (Sympson, 1983, 1986; Thissen & Steinberg, 1984).

Distractor Evaluation

Previous sections dealt with characteristics of test items that depend upon the correct answer, without regard for distractors. This section pertains to the evaluation of distractors. Since we know that distractors are functionally related to the trace line for the correct response, the development of good distractors will help the item perform as intended.

Traditional treatments of distractor evaluation in the authoritative *Educational Measurement* are brief (Wesman, 1971; Millman & Greene, 1989). Textbooks seldom give an in depth treatment of this subject, probably because not much is known about how to evaluate distractors.

Thissen, Steinberg, and Fitzpatrick (1989) stated that test users and analysts should consider that the distractor is an important part of the item. Indeed, nearly 50 years of continuous research has revealed a relationship between distractor choice and total test score (Haladyna & Sympson, 1988; Levine & Drasgow, 1983; Nishisato, 1980). In fact, there is a compelling rationale and more recent evidence to suggest that the study of distractors is necessary for sound item and test development.

Performance on the test item is governed by many factors, one being the quality of distractors. Although it may be obvious that the correct answer must be correct, the distractors must be incorrect. Experience has shown that we may accidentally have more than one correct answer for a test item, and that item response patterns for distractors seldom reflect what we expect (Haladyna & Downing, in press). Distractors will occasionally resemble correct answers or more often will exhibit no interpretable pattern. Expert, consensus judgment is critical in determining the rightness and wrongness of options. But this is not enough. Option analysis provides insights into potential errors of judgment and also inadequate performances of distractors. As with test items in their entirety, distractors that fail to perform should either be revised, replaced, or removed. Thus, our objective is to detect poorly performing distractors and then take remedial action.

Three different yet complementary ways to study responses to distractors exist. First, we have the frequency table (Levine & Drasgow, 1983; Wainer, 1989) that provides a tabulation of option choices as a function of ordinal score groups. Second, a graphical procedure, trace lines, has been proposed (Thissen, Steinberg, & Fitzpatrick, 1989). Third, a family of statistical indexes can be used to determine which distractors are working and which are not working.

To summarize, the conceptual rationale underpinning the creation of a distractor is that it should appeal to low scorers, those who have not mastered the domain of knowledge, whereas high scorers, who have shown a high degree of mastery of the domain of knowledge should avoid distractors. Distractors that are seldom chosen by any test taker should be removed or replaced. These kinds of distractors are likely to be so implausible to all test takers that hardly anyone would choose one of these. Distractors essentially unrelated to test performance should be replaced, because

Table 8.2
Frequency Tables for Two Four-Option Multiple-Choice Items

		Options		
Score Group[1]	A*	B	C	D
80-99	17%	1%	0%	2%
60-79	14%	2%	0%	4%
40-59	10%	5%	2%	3%
20-39	8%	9%	1%	2%
1-19	6%	10%	1%	3%
Total	55%	27%	4%	14%

		Options		
Score Group[1]	A*	B	C	D
80-99	19%	1%	0%	0%
60-79	14%	3%	1%	2%
40-59	8%	4%	2%	6%
20-39	8%	9%	1%	2%
1-19	6%	12%	1%	1%
Total	55%	29%	5%	11%

*Correct Answer
[1]In percentile ranks

they fail to contribute to the functioning of the item as illustrated in Fig. 8.1. As we study the three approaches to studying distractor performance, the main idea is that distractors should appeal to low scoring test takers and not appeal to high scoring test takers. Any contradiction to this state of affairs signals an ineffective distractor.

Frequency Table. The frequency table is a distribution of responses for each option according to score groups. Each score group represents an ordered fractional part of the test score distribution. Table 8.2 shows the frequency tables for the two items. In this table, there are five score groups, representing five distinct ordered achievement levels. For small samples of test takers, five score groups can be used, whereas with larger samples, 10 to 20 score groups might prove useful. The sum of frequencies (in percent) for each score group is the fractional equivalent of the number of test takers in that score group to the total sample. Because we have five score groups, each row equals about 20%, one-fifth of the total sample. (Sometimes, because more than one person received the same score, it is not possible to have exactly 20% in each score group.) The column totals represent the frequency of response to each option.

For the first item, the correct answer, option A, was chosen 55% of the time,

19% by the highest score group, 14% by the next highest score group, and 6% by the lowest score group. This is a typical and desirable pattern of response for a correct answer.

Option B, a distractor, has a low response rate for the higher groups and a higher response rate for the lower groups. This is a desirable pattern for a good performing distractor. As described earlier, all distractors should have a pattern like this.

Option C displays a low response rate across all five score groups. Such distractors are useless, probably due to extreme implausibility. Such distractors should be removed from the test item or be replaced.

·Option D displays a rather unchanging performance across all score groups. No orderly relationship exists between this distractor and total test performance. Such distractors should be removed or replaced from the test item because it is not working as intended.

The second item exhibits a distractor pattern that presents problems of interpretation and evaluation. Option D is more often chosen by the middle group and least often chosen by the higher and lower groups. This pattern is nonmonotonic in the sense that it increases as a function of total test score and then decreases. Is this pattern a statistical accident or does the distractor attract middle achievers and not attract high and low achievers? Distractors are not designed to produce such a pattern, because the general intent of a distractor is to appeal to persons who lack knowledge. The nonmonotonic pattern shown in option D implies that the information represented by option D is more attractive to middle performers and less attractive to high and low performers. The nonmonotonic pattern appears to disrupt the orderly relation between right and wrong answers illustrated in options A and B. For this reason, nonmonotonic trace lines should be viewed as undesirable.

Trace Lines. The *trace line* is a depiction of item performance as a function of total performance (Nunnally, 1967). Data from Table 8.2 were used to construct trace lines in Fig. 8.3, although trace lines can be estimated using polytomous item response theory (Thissen, 1993). A four-option item can have up to five trace lines representing various aspects of performance of the item. One trace line exists for each option, and one for nonrespondents. Because nonresponse is seldom a problem in modern tests, this trace line may be unnecessary. Where correction-for-guessing is employed, nonresponse is significant and a trace line for nonresponse is necessary because test takers are encouraged not to guess.

An effectively performing item contains a trace line that is monotonically increasing, as illustrated in Fig. 8.1. This figure shows that the probability or tendency to choose the right answer increases with the person's status in the ability/ achievement being measured by the test. The collective performance of distractors must monotonically decrease in opposite corresponding fashion, as illustrated in Fig. 8.1. The figure shows that any examinee's tendency to choose any wrong answer decreases with the person's ability/achievement.

The correct answer option A for the first item in Table 8.2 has a trace line that is monotonically increasing. This trace line is lower with low achieving test takers and increases as total test scores increase. This is a desirable pattern for a correct answer. Correspondingly, a distractor should have a monotonically decreasing trace line, as option B illustrates. Lower scoring test takers tend to choose this option, while moderate and higher scores tend to avoid it. Option C shows a low response trace line, and option D shows a somewhat flat performance across score groups.

Trace lines can be constructed by using a standard computer graphics program, such as *Harvard Graphics*, *Excel*, or *Freelance*. Some of these computer programs have the option of taking the data from the frequency tables and providing smoothed

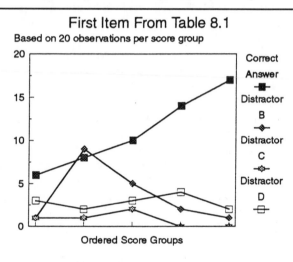

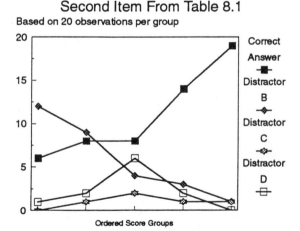

Fig. 8.3. Trace lines for items shown in Table 8.1.

curves for easier interpretation of the trace lines. One of these computer programs on a personal computer using a laser printer produced Figs. 8.1, 8.2, and 8.3.

Item analysts like Wainer (1989) and Thissen, Steinberg, and Fitzpatrick (1989) favored using trace lines. They argued that trace lines make item analysis more meaningful and interpretable. Statistical approaches can be daunting to many practitioners, and trace lines offer a valid method for studying distractor performance.

Statistical Methods. Several statistical methods can be used to study distractor performance. These methods do not necessarily measure the same characteristic (Haladyna & Crehan, 1993). Among these methods, two have serious shortcomings and probably should not be used, whereas the last, based on the trace line, is probably the best.

The first is the *product-moment correlation* between distractor performance and total test score. This is the point-biserial discrimination index that is found in most item analysis computer programs. This index considers the average performance of those selecting the distractor versus the average of those not selecting the distractor. A statistically significant positive correlation would be expected for a correct choice, whereas a statistically significant negative correlation would be expected for a distractor. Low response distractors would be eliminated from this analysis; the low response would suggest that such distractors are so implausible that only a few random guessers would select this option. Nonmonotonic distractors would produce negative correlations, but would be subject to the test for statistical significance. This correlation would more likely not be statistically significant, because the non-monotonic trace line mimics the trace line of a correct answer in part. Also, because the number of test takers choosing distractors is likely to be

Table 8.3
Choice Means for Two Items from a Test

	Item #32 Choice Mean	Item #45 Choice Mean
Option A*	66%	88%
Option B	54%	86%
Option C	43%	84%
Option D	62%	85%
F-ratio	22.44	1.04
probability	.000. . .	.62
R-squared	.12	.02

*Correct choice

Table 8.4
Contingency Table for Chi-Squared Test for an Option

	First Score Group	Second Score Group	Third Score Group	Fourth Score Group	Fifth Score Group
Expected	20%	20%	20%	20%	20%
Observed	6%	14%	20%	26%	34%

small, the statistical tests lack the power to reject the null hypothesis that the population correlation is zero. To increase the power, a directional test should be used and alpha should be set at .10. A bootstrap method is suggested for overcoming any bias introduced by the nature of the sample (de Gruijter, 1988), but this kind of extreme measure points out an inherent flaw in the use of this index. It should be noted that the discrimination index is not robust. If item difficulty is high or low, the index is attenuated. It maximizes when difficulty is moderate. The sample composition has much to do with the estimate of discrimination. Distractors tend to be infrequently chosen, particularly when item difficulty exceeds .85. Thus, the point-biserial correlation is often based on only a few observations, which is a serious limitation. Henrysson (1971) provided additional insights into the inadequacy of this index for the study of distractor performance. Because of these many limitations, this index probably should not be used.

Another related method is the *choice mean* for each distractor. As noted earlier in this chapter, the choice mean of distractors should be lower than the choice mean of the correct answer. The *eta coefficient* informs us about the degree of discriminability among distractors, but it does not provide a clear answer to the question of how well each distractor works. Referring to Table 8.3, however, we can note that the choice mean for each distractor differs from the choice mean of the correct answer. The difference in these choice means can serve as a measure of distractor effectiveness; the lower the choice mean, the better the distractor. This difference can be standardized by using the standard deviation of test scores, if a standardized *effect-size* measure is desired. The choice mean seems useful to study distractors, because the lower the choice mean, the more effective the distractor. Yet, it should be noted that a bias exists in this procedure, because when the right answer is chosen by most high-scoring test takers, the low-scoring test takers divide their choices among the three distractors plus the correct answer. So, distractors will always have lower choice means, and statistical tests will always reveal this condition. Any exception would signal a distractor that is probably a correct answer.

As indicated earlier, the trace line has many attractive characteristics in the evaluation of item performance. These characteristics apply equally to distractor analysis. Haladyna and Crehan (1993) also showed that trace lines reveal more about an option performance than a choice mean. Whereas choice means reveal the average performance of all examinees choosing any option, the trace line accurately characterizes the functional relationship between item and total test performance as is inferred by the concept of item discrimination. For example, a distractor may have a low choice mean but a flat trace line, showing that it fails to discriminate among the score groups. So the trace line is superior to the choice mean for evaluating a distractor.

Up to this point, the trace line has not been evaluated statistically. Haladyna and Downing (in press) showed that the trace line can be subjected to statistical criteria using a chi-square test of independence. Table 8.4 illustrates a contingency table for option performance. Applying a chi-square test to these categorical frequencies, a statistically significant result would signal a trace line that is not flat. In the above case, it is monotonically increasing, which is characteristic of a correct answer.

Thus, with the notion of option discrimination for the right choice, we expect monotonically increasing trace lines, positive point-biserial discrimination indexes, positive discrimination parameters with the two- and three-parameter models, and choice means that exceed the choice means for distractors. For the wrong choice, we expect monotonically decreasing trace lines, negative discrimination, negative discrimination parameters for the two- and three-parameter models (which are very unconventional to compute), and choice means that are lower than the choice mean for the correct option.

The trace line appears to offer the best, most sensitive, and revealing look at option performance, because it graphically illustrates patterns that can be easily understood, as well as providing statistical evidence. The other statistical methods all have limitations that suggest that they should not be used.

Summary

This chapter has focused on the task of examining item response patterns to evaluate item performance and, if necessary, improve item performance. A variety of perspectives and methods have been described and illustrated. Tabular methods provide clear summaries of response patterns, but graphical methods are easier to understand and interpret. Statistical methods are necessary to distinguish between real trends and random variation. Binary scoring suggests one set of procedures, polychotomous scoring another.

9

USING ITEM RESPONSE PATTERNS TO STUDY SPECIFIC PROBLEMS IN TESTING

Overview

Chapter 8 provided basic information about analyzing item response patterns, which included traditional and new methods. An objective in this chapter is to review the extensive and growing literature on item bias (equity) and differential item functioning (DIF). The existence of DIF detracts from the validity of test score interpretations and uses. Therefore, in construct validation, the study of DIF can be viewed as essential not simply desirable. Another objective is the study and detection of patterns that inform us about the validity of a test score or a group of test scores. Specifically, we may want to know if a pattern of item responses may suggest (a) cheating, (b) test anxiety, (c) inattention, (d) non response, (e) idiosyncratic marking, (f) plodding, (g) language or reading difficulties, or (h) marking errors. Finally, item response patterns may be used to study the relationships among important aspects of the instructional program, namely curriculum, instruction, and achievement tests. In this setting, the focus is on the relationships between curriculum and instruction with item responses instead of total test scores.

Item Bias (Differential Item Functioning)

Strictly speaking when two groups perform differently on a test and no differences are believed to exist between two groups, bias is producing these differences. Various specialists in this field have described bias in different ways. For example, Messick (1989) described bias as "construct irrelevant variance" (p. 34). Bias contaminates test score interpretations and uses. It is unwanted or unneeded. It obscures what we are trying to measure. Cole and Moss (1989) described bias as "differential validity of a given interpretation of a test score for any definable relevant subgroup of test takers" (p. 205). With the Cole and Moss definition, group identity is a critical factor in detecting bias. Cole and Moss additionally observed that bias is a more encompassing concept that includes construct definition, the creations of tests, and construct validation. The very essence of validity, test score interpretations and use, are intertwined with bias. The essential question is: Is any interpretation less valid for any group, for example, an ethnic group or persons from a certain region of the nation.

Chapter 7 discusses *item bias review* as a logical/judgmental process for accumulating evidence of item bias. This chapter considers the statistical process for studying item bias. These two alternate forms of analysis, although often providing unique views of item bias, should both be considered important, complementary sources of evidence in construct validation.

Regarding terminology, the term *bias* has meant systematic under or overestimation of a parameter to statisticians, but it means something very different and undesirable to the public (Dorans & Potenza, 1993). Thus the term *differential item functioning (DIF)* will be used consistently in this section instead of item bias.

As described so far, DIF is a property of the interpretation of test scores. Consistent with the approach adopted in chapter 1, the item is the sub-unit of the test, and the same standards and procedures applied to test scores also apply to item responses. Therefore, the study of DIF is critical to the study of test score bias.

A barbering examination in Oregon in the late 1800s is one of the earliest examples of testing for a profession. Since then, test programs for certification, license, or credential have proliferated (Shapiro, Stutsky, & Watt, 1989). Well-documented racial differences in test scores led to widespread discontent, culminating in the Golden Rule Insurance Company versus Mathias case in the Illinois Appellate Court in 1980. Federal legislation led to policies that promoted greater monitoring of black-white racial differences in test item difficulties. The reasoning was that if a black-white difference in item difficulty was greater than the observed test score difference, this was taken as evidence of DIF. Over a decade later, we have witnessed an explosion in the quantity and variety of methods for studying DIF.

Several statistical methods exist, some having more success than others, some having been studied more than others, and some having greater simplicity than others. For example, one can study correlations among items for differing subgroups. Such studies can be improved through confirmatory factor analysis, to determine if a factor structure is resilient to different subgroups of examinees. A logical extension of this is to use causal modeling to determine if a causal network can be sustained from one subgroup to another (e.g., men to women for analogical reasoning). Failure here would signal that the test differentially measures what it purports to measure.

The most direct and simplest method is the comparison of item difficulties. One seeks item-by-group interactions as evidence of DIF. However, Cole and Moss

(1989) among others were very critical of this procedure, pointing out that the method fails to incorporate the role of discrimination, can miss real item bias, as well as identify items mistakenly as biased.

With the coming of item response theory and heightened interest in DIF, the option characteristic curve became a basis for studying DIF. But these methods are impractical, because large sample sizes are needed and the procedures are cumbersome.

Another approach involves subgroup analysis of the types used in Table 8.1 and Fig. 8.2 in chapter 8. Score groups are defined for each group being compared and then the pattern of choices is compared. This method necessarily involves fit statistics, the most promising, widely studied, and accepted is the *Mantel-Haenszel statistic* (Mantel & Haenszel, 1959). This statistic considers the odds of two different groups correctly answering an item when ability of the groups is already statistically controlled. Specific details on its calculation and uses can be found in Holland and Thayer (1988). The use of logistic regression is another natural application for DIF studies (Swaminathan & Rogers, 1990), but its limitation is its complexity.

Only recently have theorists extended the study of DIF to rating scales, thus including performance tests (Dorans & Potenza, 1993; Miller & Spray, 1993). This decade researchers will very likely develop and refine both theory and statistical methods for DIF with polytomously scored items involving both multiple-choice and rating scale items.

DIF is a healthy and actively growing field of study. The emerging technology provides test users with important and necessary tools to improve test items and hence improve the validity of test score interpretations and uses. Readers desiring more information about DIF are referred to the most current and comprehensive summary to date in Holland and Wainer's *Differential Item Functioning* (1993).

Using Item Response Patterns to Study Specific Problems in Testing

A general term used to describe this class of activities is *appropriateness measurement*. The objective of appropriateness measurement is the statistical detection of invalid test scores. Such invalid test scores can arise in many ways, and there are many detection methods. First, types of test performance problems that might be encountered will be identified, then theories and methods will be identified and reviewed. A prefatory evaluation of this field is that it is somewhat immature, and not much theoretical development and empirical research has yet been done. On the other hand, its potential to uncover invalid test scores is considerable.

Cheating

Cheating is undesirable because the test scores arising from cheating are inflated (biased). Thus, the interpretations and uses of test scores arising from cheating are invalid. In many circumstances, the use of test scores inflated by cheating may have harmful effects on the public, such as a passing score obtained by an incompetent physician, pharmacist, nurse, architect, or automotive mechanic. The problem of cheating is significant, and statistical detection a worthy objective.

According to Frary (1993), methods to combat cheating in high stakes testing programs involve scrambling of test items from form to form, multiple test forms each consisting of different sets of items, or careful monitoring of test takers during test administration. Given that these methods fail to prevent cheating, test administrators need to identify potential instances of cheating and obtain evidence in support of an accusation. The statistical methods enabled through appropriateness measurement are one form of evidence.

There is an extensive literature relating to the detection of patterns of answer copying by test takers. For example, Bellezza and Bellezza (1989) reported in their review of this problem, that about 75% of undergraduate college students resort to some form of cheating. They suggested an error-similarity pattern analysis based on binomial probabilities. Bellezza and Bellezza's index resembles earlier indexes suggested by Angoff (1974) and Cody (1985). They offer a FORTRAN computer program that can be used with a personal computer. Such a program could be written for a mainframe computer to deal with larger testing programs. The method identifies outliers, performances so similar with respect to wrong answers, that it may have occurred through copying. It is important to understand that the study of patterns of right answers may be misleading, because it is possible for two persons studying together to have similar patterns of right answers, but it is unlikely that wrong answer patterns will be similar because distractors have differential attractiveness and most tests have three or four distractors per item.

Test Anxiety

A prevailing problem in any standardized and classroom testing setting is anxiety that results from the pressure of testing. Hill and Wigfield (1984) estimated that about 25% of the population has some form of debilitating test anxiety. The depressed performance of test takers has harmful effects. Detection of this depressed performance by pattern analysis cannot only correct an invalid test scores but identify persons in need of treatment. Test anxiety can be clinically treated.

Inattention

Test takers who are not well motivated or easily distracted may choose multiple-choice answer carelessly. Wright (1977) referred to such test takers as "sleepers." Such people are likely to obtain lower scores by failing to answer correctly test items that they might ordinarily correctly answer. Such patterns can be identified, and scores treated accordingly, such as removing offenders from the sample of test scores, or otherwise invalidating these results, keeping in mind that such scores often influence results of research, evaluation, or policy studies.

Nonresponse

Under conditions of guessing when the correct answer cannot be identified, testwise examinees usually mark all answers available on a test, so that nonresponse is not a problem. In some testing situations, test takers are encouraged to omit an answer instead of guessing. Depending upon the testing condition, test takers may inadvertently not respond due to timidity or other personality factors, and the identification of test takers may remove this source of test score bias.

Idiosyncratic Answering

Under conditions where the test does not have important consequences to the test taker, some test takers may mark in peculiar patterns, to give the appearance that they are seriously taking the test. Such behavior introduces a negative bias in the testing process, affecting both individual and group performances. Some examples could be pattern marking, for example, ABCDABCDABCD..., or BBBCCCBBBCCC... The identification and removal of offending scores helps improve the accuracy of group results. Also pattern marking like this might lead to undesirable individual score interpretation and use. The detection of individual idiosyncratic behavior may be a deterrent to a future of such behavior, for instance, in public schools where standardized achievement tests are often the target of such behavior. An issue here is the seriousness of such tests. Tests without serious consequences with older children will be more subject to idiosyncratic pattern marking. A common motivation among school age children to mark idiosyncratically has been documented in several studies (e.g., Paris, Lawton, Turner, & Roth, 1991). Thus, the problem is more significant in situations where the test takers have little or no reason to do well.

Plodding

Under conditions of a timed test, some test takers may not have enough time to answer all items. These persons are very careful and meticulous in approaching each item and also may lack test-taking skills that encourage time management strategies. Thus, they do not to answer items at the end of the test. The result is a lower score than deserved, assuming speed is not the primary trait being measured. It is not possible to extend the time limit for most standardized tests; therefore, the prevention of the problem lies in better test-taking training. The detection of these persons can be done by methods discussed in the next section.

Some reasons for plodding may be (a) lack of motivation, (b) personal style, (c) lack of testwiseness, or (d) lack of proficiency in the English language. Any of these conditions might cause a test taker not to finish, and the resulting score is not an accurate measure of knowledge due to this inhibitory condition. Plodders should be detected. Their problems should be treated, and their scores could be invalidated.

Coaching

In testing situations where the outcomes are especially important, such as licensing examinations, there are many test coaching services that provide specific content instruction that may be articulated with a portion of the test. Another context for coaching is with college admissions testing. Reviews of the extant research on admissions testing coaching by Becker (1990) and Linn (1990) provided evidence that most coaching gains are of a small nature, usually less than one fifth of a standard deviation. Linn makes the important point that the crucial consideration is not how much scores have changed, but how much the underlying trait that the test purportedly measures has changed. If coaching involves item-specific strategies, then interpretation of any gain should be that test behavior does not generalize to the larger domain that the test score represents. If coached test takers are compared to non coached test takers, the subsequent interpretations might be flawed. Haladyna, Nolen, and Haas (1991) called this practice a source of *test score pollution*, arguing that such coaching may boost test performance without substantially affecting the domain that a test score represents.

The detection of coaching can be done through any techniques identified and discussed in the section on differential item functioning in this chapter. The necessary precondition to using these techniques is to identify two groups, one coached and one uncoached. Items displaying differential item functioning provide evidence of the types of items, content, and cognitive demand that affect test scores. But research of this type about coaching effects has not yet been reported. In fact, Becker (1990) provided indications that the quality of most research on coaching is inadequate.

Another important issue about coaching is what action to take with test takers who have received specific coaching. Because such scores may be argued to be invalid in some circumstances, should sponsoring organizations invalidate scores of persons who have been coached for a test, or should interpretations of coached results be tempered.

Language Deficiency

Test takers may have a high degree of knowledge about a domain but fail to show this knowledge because the test taker's primary language is not English. In these instances, any interpretation or use of a test score should be declared invalid. Standard 6.10 in the *Standards for Educational and Psychological Testing* (American Psychological Association, 1985) urged caution in test score interpretation and use when the language of test exceeds the linguistic abilities of test takers.

Marking Errors

Test responses are often made on optically scannable answer sheets. Sometimes, in the midst of this anxiety-provoking testing situation, test takers may mark in the wrong places on the answer sheet. Marking across instead of down, or down instead of across, or skipping one place and marking in all other places, so that all answers are off by one position. Although such carelessness is often inexcusable, the detection problem is possible. The policy to deal with the problem is again another issue. Mismarked answer sheets produce invalid test scores. Therefore, it seems reasonable that these mismarked sheets must be detected and removed from the scoring and reporting process, or the test taker should be given an opportunity to correct the error.

Using Item Response Patterns to
Study Specific Problems in Testing

In this section four types of methods for detecting unusual item response patterns are presented. This field is somewhat new. In most instances, computer software for the study of these unusual response patterns is not yet available. Thus a ready-made technology does not exist for studying the kinds of problems discussed in the previous section. However, the value of this section is to give readers an insight into logic of the study of response patterns with an eye toward the eventual implementation of computer software programs to perform this work. Certainly research is needed in this field. Meanwhile, informal, nonstatistical methods are also possible that provide a reasonable substitute for the more sophisticated, computer-based methods of the future.

Appropriateness Measurement

This first approach is powerful enough to detect a variety of test performance problems, but it is limited by the need for large samples of test behavior. The chief characteristic of these methods is the use of an explicit statistical model, usually an item response model. The objectives of appropriateness measurement include the estimation of ability/achievement, cultural differences, instructional effects, and causes of low scores. In many high-stakes testing situations, it is important to allow for challenges made to a test result by test takers. Appropriateness measurement should offer evidence that a test score may be invalid. This array of uses shows the extensiveness of appropriateness measurement to greater problems than are the object of this section.

The context or purpose for the index is important. Drasgow and Guertler (1987) stated that several subjective judgments are necessary. For instance, if one is using a test to make a pass/fail certification decision, the location of a "dubious" score relative to the passing score and the relative risk one is willing to take have much to do with these decisions. Other factors to consider in using these indexes are (a) the cost of retesting, (b) the risk of misclassification, (c) the cost of misclassification, and (d) the confidence or research evidence supporting the use of the procedure.

According to Drasgow, Levine, and Williams (1985), aberrant response patterns are identified by first applying a model to a set of normal responses and then using a measure of goodness of fit, an appropriateness index, to find out the degree to which anyone deviates from normal response patterns. In an early study, Levine and Rubin (1979) showed that such detection was achievable, and since then there has been a steady progression of studies involving several theoretical models (Drasgow, 1982; Levine & Drasgow, 1982, 1983). These studies were initially done using the three-parameter item response model, but later studies involved polytomous item response models (Drasgow, et al., 1985). Levine and Drasgow (1988) provided a good summary of this work and further distinguished between these two approaches.

In summary, about one decade's worth of study has been conducted on appropriateness measurement; consequently it is not yet ready for widespread implementation. Not only must software be developed that is user-friendly, but policies must be created for use in professions and education to frame the defensible uses of appropriateness measurement in a proper context. With the advent of such computer software, more extensive research could be conducted affecting these emerging testing policies and procedures.

Instructional Pattern Analysis

The second approach to be discussed in this section involves indexes expressly designed to reveal unusual item response patterns in an instructional setting. In this category are found the once popular Sato caution index (Sato, 1975, 1980) and several other indexes. This group of methods may not be sensitive to all problems presented in the previous section, but these methods make these problems simpler to understand and solve. For instance, the Sato approach is applicable to classroom tests consisting of several items (problems) and students, usually 10–20 items and 15 students. The intent is to examine a matrix of students' right and wrong responses for determining or diagnosing learning difficulties. The concept exhibited in the S–P chart is that high-scoring students should not miss easy items and low-scoring students should not correctly answer hard items. The systematic study of the S–P matrix of responses reveals both instructional and item difficulties. The term *pattern analysis* will be used to refer to this line of research and development.

As mentioned previously, Sato (1975) introduced a simple pattern analysis for a classroom based on the idea that some scores deserve a cautious interpretation. Like appropriateness measurement, the caution index and its derivatives have a broad array of applications, but this section will be limited to only those problems discussed earlier.

   The Student-Problems (S-P) Chart. The focus of pattern analysis is the S–P chart that is a visual display of right and wrong answers for a class. Table 9.1 is adapted from Tatsuoka and Linn (1983) contains the right and wrong responses to 10 items for 15 students. Not only does the S–P chart identify aberrant student scores, but it also identifies items with aberrant item response patterns.

   The S–P chart is based on two boundaries, the S–curve and the P–curve, and a student/item matrix of item responses. Students are ordered by scores, and items are placed from easy on the left side of the chart to hard on the right.

   The S–curve is constructed by counting the number-correct for any student and constructing the boundary line to the right of the item response for that student. For the 15 students, there are 15 boundary lines that are connected to form the S–curve. If a student answers items correctly outside of the S–curve (to the right of the S–curve), this improbable result implies that the score should be considered cautiously. Similarly, if a student misses an item inside of the S–curve, to the left of the S–curve, this improbable result implies that the student failed items that a student of this achievement level would ordinarily answer correctly. In the first instance, the student passed items that would normally be failed. Referring to Table 9.1, student 9 answered items 6, 8, and 9 correctly, which normally would be missed by students at this level of achievement. Student 9 also missed three easy items. A total of six improbable responses for student 9 points to a potential problem of interpretation of this student score of 5 of 10 (50%).

   The P–curve is constructed by counting the number right in the class for each item and drawing a boundary line below that item response in the matrix. For example, the first item was correctly answered by 13 of 15 students so the P–curve boundary line is drawn below the item response for the 13th student. Analogous to the S–curve, it is improbable to miss an item above the P–curve and answer an item below the P–curve correctly. Item 6 shows that two high scoring students (3 and 6) missed this item while four low scoring students answered it correctly. Item 6 has an aberrant response pattern that causes us to look at it more closely.

   A variety of indexes is available that provides numerical values for each student and item (see Tatsuoka & Linn, 1983). However, a simple count, such as used above provides an effective means for identifying persons and items with unusual response patterns.

Item Response Theory

Item analysis has been extended to include the study of item response patterns to detect many test taker patterns that may invalidate test scores (Wright & Masters, 1982; Wright & Stone, 1979). The development of new computer software *Iparm* by Richard Smith (1993) provides item analysts with a new tool to study person-item response patterns. Smith, Kramer, and Kubiak (1990) reported that about 25% of the response patterns in a graduate admissions test had at least one of these recognizable performance pattern problems. Smith provided the most extensive

Table 9.1
Students/Problems (SP) Chart for a Class of 15 Students on a Ten-Item Test

student	1	2	3	4	5	6	7	8	9	10	Tot.
1	1	1	1	1	1	1	1	1	1	1	10
2	1	1	1	1	1	1	1	1	1	0	9
3	1	1	1	1	1	0	1	1	0	1	8
4	1	0	1	1	1	1	0	1	0	0	6
5	1	1	1	1	0	1	0	0	1	0	6
6	1	1	1	0	1	0	1	0	1	0	6
7	1	1	1	1	0	0	1	0	0	0	5
8	1	1	1	0	1	1	0	0	0	0	5
9	1	0	0	1	0	1	0	1	1	0	5
10	1	1	0	1	0	0	1	0	0	1	5
11	0	1	1	1	1	0	0	0	0	0	4
12	1	0	0	0	1	1	0	0	0	0	3
13	1	1	0	0	0	1	0	0	0	0	3
14	1	0	1	0	0	0	0	0	0	0	2
15	0	1	0	0	0	0	0	0	0	0	1
Item Diff.	13	11	10	9	8	8	6	5	5	4	
p-value	87	73	67	60	53	53	40	33	23	27	

Note. Adapted from "Indices for detecting unusual patterns: Links between two general approaches and potential applications." by K.K. Tatsuoka and R. L. Linn, 1983, *Applied Psychological Measurement*, 7, 81-96. © 1983 by Applied Psychological Measurement. Adapted with permission.

writing to date on this interesting and promising use of item response theory.

With item response theory, a person's achievement estimate is governed by the results of encounters with items. Items that are too hard are often missed and items that are too easy are often answered correctly. It is the frequency of exceptions to this rule that creates conditions for *person fit statistics*. When a high-achieving test taker misses too many easy items or a low-achieving test taker gets too many hard items right, these patterns can be detected.

Smith (1993) stated that for every item/person interaction, the difference between expected and actual item responses can be residualized and transformed into a variable by dividing by its standard deviation. The result is a person/item fit statistic. Another way of saying this is that a person's achievement status should be invariant across sets of items. No matter how we group these items, subscores should be nearly perfectly correlated in a unidimensional test, and these subscores should be at approximately the same magnitude.

The example provides an illustration of person/item interactions on a 100-item test. Student 1 has a normal pattern. The four percentage point fluctuation is equivalent to one raw score point. Student 2 did poorly in the fourth quarter of the test. *Iparm* can be used to scale these results and determine if this aberration is statistically notable, which it is in the second instance. Diagnostically, such a result could be due to an overly strict time limit, fatigue, or another relevant factor. *Iparm* will compute scores that both include and eliminate the aberrant section. Thus student two could have a score based on the agreeable first three quarters of the test or a score based on the full 100-item test. With mitigating circumstances, *Iparm* can be used to identify and correct invalid scores.

	Items 1-25	Items 26-50	Items 51-75	Items 76-100
Student 1	80%	84%	80%	84%
Student 2	84%	80%	84%	50%

Smith provided an excellent array of examples of different person fit problems. These problems were described in seminal discussions by Wright (1977) and Wright and Stone (1979), but are now part of the arsenal of techniques that are ready to use due to the emergence of *Iparm*.

Item person maps contain a personal account of each test taker's performance relative to expectations. Fit statistics (infit and outfit) are used to identify aberrant response patterns. Generally the normal range of these statistics varies from .6 to 1.5. When infit and outfit statistics fall outside this range, a specific response pattern has been detected, and each pattern provides a basis for speculating about the causes. Further investigation is then warranted. Linacre and Wright (1993) provided a diagnostic chart for misfit that includes dichotomously scored test items, rating scale items, person patterns, and judging patterns. This chart provides a basis for expanding our technology for studying item response pattern problems, as well as relativity of items to person response pattern problems.

One very attractive feature of *Iparm* is the ability to identify the categorical variable that may introduce bias, for example, male-female differences or item format effects. Some brief examples from Smith's discussion will illustrate how useful *Iparm* and person fit analysis can be. Smith describes one test taker who misses several items at the beginning of a test, which is characteristic of test anxiety. Two scores, one based on earlier items and one based on later items, offers a stark contrast in performance. Which score is correct? Or should total score be used? Traditional thinking would favor a total score, but person fit reveals that total score may be biased due to some external factor such as text anxiety.

Another example is a person who did not finish the test (a plodder). The test score estimated with omits as wrong answers was considerably lower than the score based on items tried. If speededness is a factor in the test, then the scoring policy is clear, use the total score. However, speededness is usually undesirable and a plodder is penalized by the severe time limit. The plodder's score is biased under this condition. *Iparm* estimates both scores, and test users can invalidate the original score and accept the score based on fewer items.

Conclusions

By using influences that systematically inflate or deflate test scores, we can make an interpretation or use of these scores less valid. The use of methods for detecting unusual response patterns is becoming increasingly important. As tests continue to be used to make important decisions regarding employment, selection to a program or school, certification, or the ability to practice in a profession, the use of methods to detect aberrant responses should increase. Unfortunately, the theories and technologies for many of these methods are somewhat new and untested. Software for the study of patterns is very limited. Nonetheless, construct validation and the *Standards for Educational and Psychological Testing* make clear the need for such studies and corrective actions to reduce the threat of test score bias.

The Study of Curricular and Instructional Emphases

With the evaluation of any instructional program, one is always concerned with the linkage between curriculum and instruction, and the extent to which the tests are integrated with instruction (Nitko, 1989). These linkages are critical to the use of achievement measures as one measure of instructional program effectiveness. Once we have established these linkages, item response patterns can be used to study the emphasis that curriculum receives in instruction and the extent that the instructional program has succeeded.

Harnisch (1983) provided excellent insights into the questions that item response patterns will answer. When test results are reported within any unit of analysis, for example, a state, school district, or class, we really do not know what extent students have mastered the knowledge and skills represented by each test item. Further, the study of item response patterns, when tied to content, can help identify the effects of certain instructional strategies on acquisition, retention, and transfer of learning. Patterns of errors can be used to decide which, if any, instructional strategies worked, and what kind of remedial instruction is needed.

It is important to note that the literature does not address the effectiveness of these methods, nor does a well developed technology for pattern analysis exist that can detect curricular emphasis and instructional effectiveness. This is an emerging science.

Ideally, content needs to be defined in such ways that one can study the interrelationships among units of content, instruction bearing on these units of content, and the test items representing each unit. One commonly used unit is the instructional objective. In an instructional context, it is important to determine exactly what content represents the "instructional intent," and the outcome of instruction. The summative achievement test must represent this instructional intent. Linn and Harnisch (1981) referred to the lack of correspondence as "instructional bias." So the task is to determine if such bias exists that would invalidate a specific test use, for example, to evaluate the effects of curriculum or instruction. Or we might decide to salvage nonbiased items from such a test.

Once decided that objectives, instruction, and test items can be linked through content expert judgments, as described in chapter 7, it is then important to study patterns of response to items. Linn and Harnisch (1981) described various ways to compare performances. One compares trace lines, another compares item difficulty in different contexts, and still another compares test scores over the same content from different contexts.

Issues for Study

The context for any study of item patterns is the instructional program and the purposes for testing. If we are evaluating a program, ideally we want a perfect correspondence between the curriculum/content and the test. Since many published tests lack this match, the best we can hope for is to identify those items representing objectives that are part of the curriculum, and then use item pattern analysis to determine the success of the instructional program. Three kinds of analyses are suggested:

1. Match between content and test.
2. Match between instruction and test or opportunity to learn.

3.   Instructional sensitivity.

Match Between Content and Test. Normally we would identify a panel of teachers and curriculum specialists to make judgments about the match between each objective of the curriculum and the test items. All items are classified as (a) matched, (b) uncertain, or (c) unmatched. Only matched items are considered in evaluation. Chapter 7 discusses this activity.

Match Between Instruction and Test. Instructional emphasis is virtually impossible to document in the classroom (Linn, 1983). Nonetheless, some have attempted to do this. One method is to use teacher judgments. For example, Leinhardt and Seewald (1980) suggested that teachers be asked to estimate the percentage of students in a class who were taught enough to answer a specific item correctly. But this method produced ambiguous results. Another approach determines what topics were covered in the class by interviewing teachers. Leinhardt and Seewald found that both curriculum and instructional match methods predicted achievement equally well. A series of studies in the late 1980s by Mehrens and Phillips (1986; 1987) and Phillips and Mehrens (1987) established that methods of tagging items by instructional emphasis did not provide strong evidence of differential effectiveness. Although their results may be taken as negative regarding the practice of subsetting items by instructional emphasis, the real problem may exist with the type of test used—a standardized instrument. With tests expressly designed for a specific curriculum, the methods and results of their studies might have proven more conclusive. Yoon, Burstein, Gold, Chen, and Kim (1990) reported an exploratory study of the validity of teachers' judgments of instructional emphasis on tests designed for instruction at the secondary level. They found support for a six level rating system (newly taught, extended, reviewed, assumed, taught later, and not in curriculum). This kind of survey not only informs teachers about what they should be covering in these classes, but more closely links instruction to the testing process. Because the essence of criterion-referenced testing movement is this integration of teaching and testing, this method promises to provide a strong inference system to instructional testing and the evaluation of instruction.

Statistical Methods of Study

Expert Judges Content Analysis. Popham (1993) observed that expert judges are typically needed to "validate" items because we lack criterion variables. Thus, we are compelled to rely on human judgment. This kind of judgment also provides a type of face validity in test development. Some content experts have approved the items and that the items do measure what they should measure. The criterion-referenced movement of the 1970s generated a high level of activity in the construction of achievement tests linked to objectives and content domains. At one time, expert judges' content analysis was a mainstay, and a technology evolved with statistical indexes that are easily understood and used effectively (see Rovinelli & Hambleton, 1977). Popham lamented in his review and appraisal, which was limited to teaching licensing tests, that we know very little about conducting these reviews, constituting high degrees of agreement, and analyzing data from these reviews. Quite naturally, considerable variety exists among proposed methods, and the evolution of a refined science of content analysis has not yet materialized. This may be due, in part, to the chronic problem of definition of achievement that has troubled us for decades. Despite the immaturity of this field, a strong commitment to continuing content reviews exists.

Factor Analysis. Human judgment may be useful for many reasons discussed in the previous chapter for the confirmation of item content and cognitive behavior, but statistical methods exist that provide a sound basis for helping test developers improve their tests and thus helping improve their interpretations and uses of test data. Confirmatory item factor analysis is a basis for grouping items into content categories. Such methods also can verify the reasoning that goes into test specifications, ensuring that an empirical evidence exists for the content categories of a test. Another important consideration here is that factor analysis can help in the study of the dimensionality of test scores. Because classical and item response models currently used require unidimensional test data, factor analysis becomes an important tool.

However, the analysis of item response using factor analysis is not without difficulty. Lord (1980) discussed some of these problems. His advice was to use tetrachoric correlations and hope that a dominant factor appears. Hambleton and Swaminathan (1987) reviewed some history of item factor analysis and reaffirmed the problems encountered. One of these is factor analysis will likely produce difficulty factors that must be considered as nuisance findings. Gorsuch (1983) recommended item groups of like items to form miniscales, which results in a more satisfactory factor resolution, since item responses tend to be so undependable.

Testfact, computer software developed by Wilson, Wood, and Gibbons (1992), performs item analysis and test scoring. More importantly, *Testfact* includes Minres principal factor analysis of tetrachoric correlations and optional full information item factor analysis. This program represents an important breakthrough in the study of dimensionality since standard computer packages for statistical analysis are generally unfriendly to binary-scored test data. This program has great versatility and capacity for handling the largest tests and examinee sizes. The study of dimensionality via factor analysis is strongly recommended for item analysts. The validation of item responses can be greatly affected by assuming that a test is unidimensional when it is not.

Item Response Theory. As just described, most IRT models in use require one dimensional data. Failure to use such data will result in convergence problems with the two- and three-parameter models, which is very frustrating in item analysis. On the other hand, when data is multidimensional, one is then compelled to analyze each dimension independent of the others, thus making the use of IRT much more complex than usually anticipated. The existence of differential instructional sensitivity, or, more specifically, the opportunity to learn, may invalidate the use of IRT. For example, if one is testing geometry in a junior high school setting in a school district, the teaching of some concepts and procedures may destroy the unidimensionality of the geometry subtest, making IRT analysis problematic. Smith (1993) described a method using person/item fit methods for detecting content disturbances on tests, which might be related to this issue of instructional sensitivity/opportunity to learn. This may be a fruitful method in the future for the study of curriculum/instruction/testing interactions.

Instructional Sensitivity. Earlier in this chapter this topic was introduced as a method for studying and evaluating items in an instructional setting. This characteristic can be directly applied to the study of instructional patterns with the item serving as the unit of analysis. By grouping or clustering items according to content and collecting item difficulties one can ascertain the effectiveness of instruction at any level. Haladyna (1982) provided some examples drawn from criterion-referenced and item response theory applications that show data displays. In Table 9.2, we see instances of item clusters where students were (a) introduced, (b) developed, or (c) reinforced. Item data should reflect what we believe is happening instructionally. The examples in Table 9.2 use item response theory, and the scale was created to range between 150 and 450 for the elementary grades curriculum. The instructional emphasis (introduced, developed, and reinforced) creates levels of expectations about performance that the fall and spring testing

---

Table 9.2
Example of Instructional Sensitivity Indexes for Content

Topic	Introduced Grade Four		Developed Grade Five		Reinforced Grade Six	
	Fall	Spring	Fall	Spring	Fall	Spring
Objective 23	170	178	174	208	210	224
Objective 24	200	212	210	231	232	238
Objective 25	185	199	202	222	216	244

The achievement scale derives from the use of item response theory and ranges between 150 and 450 for elementary school levels.

---

should reflect. When results are contrary to our beliefs about what should be happening we can examine the curriculum for appropriateness of what was taught or sequencing problems, instruction for deficiencies, or the items for invalidity.

Summary

This chapter complements the previous chapter. This chapter reviewed the field of item bias, described the logic and methods for detecting suspicious test scores, based on aberrant item and person response patterns, and reported on patterns of item responses or clusters of item responses toward the end of studying curriculum-instruction articulation or evaluating instructional program effectiveness.

Item bias has been a topic of great interest currently, and the science of studying item bias has become increasingly more complex. The term *differential item functioning* is now commonly used to describe this science. These methods should become routine features of item analysis in the future, because they identify important kinds of flaws in test items.

Pattern analysis involves the study of item response patterns for the purpose of determining if a test score truly represents ability or achievement or if some intervening factor has caused the score to be higher or lower than it should be. Many types of conditions have been identified, but statistical tools for determining if these patterns exist are just being developed. One such tool, *Iparm*, provides some useful methods for studying these patterns.

Finally, the last part of this chapter was devoted to the role of item response in studying curricular emphasis, instructional effectiveness, and instructional sensitivity. This application of item responses in these ways is also quite young and immature, but also very promising.

Most of the theory and methods for studying item response patterns to solve specific problems are somewhat new. Considerably more research and development is needed. In particular, computer software is needed to more widely use these methods and explore their potential for uncovering response patterns that will help improve teaching.

THE FUTURE OF ITEM WRITING
AND ITEM RESPONSE VALIDATION

10

NEW DIRECTIONS IN ITEM WRITING AND
ITEM RESPONSE VALIDATION

Overview

This final chapter assesses the futures of item development and item response validation, but first a context is described that affects these futures. This context includes (a) the role of policy at national, state, and local levels, politics, and educational reform, (b) the emergence of cognitive psychology and the retrenchment of behaviorism, (c) changes in conception of ability and achievement, and (d) emergence of statistical test score theories that are more in step with recent cognitive psychology approaches to developing ability and achievement.

Factors Affecting the Future of
Item Writing and Item Response Validation

Policy, Politics, and School Reform

Education consists of various communities, the combination of which provides educational opportunities to millions of people in a variety of ways, including infant learning and preschool classes, elementary and secondary education, undergraduate education, graduate programs, professional training, military training, business training, professional development, and adult continuing education reflecting recreational, personal or human development.

One of these communities within education is a group of policy makers including elected and appointed federal and state officials and school board members. Their responsibility is to make policy and allocate resources.

Though many of these policy makers are not well informed about schools, schooling, theories, research on schooling, cognitive psychology, or statistical test score theories, they have considerable influence on educational practices. With respect to policy, policy makers will control the direction of changes in testing in the nation, in states, and in school districts.

House (1991) characterized educational policy as heavily influenced by economic and social conditions and political philosophies. He traced recent history regarding the status of schools relative to our economic and social conditions in two rivaling political positions—liberal and conservative. In the liberal view, increases in spending on education will lead to better trained people who will be producers as opposed to consumers of our resources. In the conservative view, the failure of education to deal with the poor has resulted in undisciplined masses who have contributed heavily to economic and social woes. With respect to changes in testing in the nation, states, and local school districts, the education platforms of political parties have a major influence on the testing policies and practices in each jurisdiction.

School reform appears to have received its impetus from the report *A Nation At Risk* (National Commission for Educational Excellence, 1983). Another significant movement is restructuring of schools, which is more systemic and involves decentralized control of schools involving mainly parents, teachers, and students. One of many forces behind the reform movement has been the misuse of standardized test scores. In recent years, test scores have been used in ways unimagined by the original developers and publishers of these tests (Mehrens & Kaminski, 1989; Nolen, Haladyna, & Haas, 1992). Haladyna, Nolen, and Haas (1991) estimated that over 29 different uses of test scores currently exist, and most are not construct validated. The need for accountability has created a ruthless *test score improvement* practice where vendors and educators routinely raise test scores in high stakes cognitive tests (Cannell, 1989; Nolen, Haladyna, & Haas, 1992; Mehrens & Kaminski, 1989). With respect to school reform, traditional ideas and practices must be reexamined and reevaluated. This reform movement will lead to new testing paradigms where some of these traditional ideas and practices will survive, but others will not. Indeed, this is already underway. The authentic assessment movement has had a profound effect on both educational testing in the nation, in states, and in classrooms, and also on teaching.

Central to the intent of this book, the multiple-choice format is again under attack. Critics believe that this format limits test takers to low level mental activity that is undesirable (Frederiksen, 1984; Snow, 1993). Shepard (1993) seriously charged that multiple-choice testing has created harmful multiple-choice teaching. Strong statements like these characterize the zeal for performance testing as the only authentic assessment. Snow (1993) provided a more balanced view of this issue about item formats and proposed a research agenda that thoughtfully examines the rationale for item formats. One thing is clear from these discussions: We must learn quite a bit more about the effects of item format on cognitive learning before we can make confident statements about the effectiveness of any format. Research is needed that shows the optimal formats for measuring newly defined abilities and various forms of higher level achievement.

The multiple-choice item will survive these attacks because it has many good qualities, as noted in chapter 2. But the reform movement has dictated a more balanced position regarding what is taught and what is measured. Thus, the overreliance on multiple-choice formats to measure school ability and achievement has ended, and practitioners are more aware of misuses of test results.

Cognitive Psychology

Behaviorism is well established in teaching and testing. Most varieties of systematic instruction have behaviorist origins and characteristics. These include, for example, objective-based learning, outcome-based learning, mastery learning, the personalized system of instruction, competency-based instruction, and the Carroll model for school learning. These teaching technologies have the common elements of unit mastery, well defined learning outcomes, and criterion-referenced tests closely linked to learner outcomes.

Criterion-referenced testing became prominent in the 1970s and 1980s. This testing approach is behavioral in origin. Such tests are designed from behavioral (instructional) objectives, and, in effect, provide an operational definition of desired student learning, where teaching to the test in a precise way is a paramount concern (Cohen, 1987). Criterion-referenced testing may be a casualty of the school reform movement that features authentic assessment instead. In fact, attention to this topic at annual meetings of the American Educational Research Association and the National Council on Measurement in Education and in journals has declined substantially in this decade. Instead essays and research on performance testing and authentic assessment populate these meetings and journals. Despite the increasing popularity of authentic assessment, fueled by advances in cognitive psychology, the residue of behaviorism in the schools will probably last a long time, but clearly educational behaviorism is in decline.

Cognitive psychology cannot yet be characterized as a unified science of cognitive behavior. Snow and Lohman (1989) described this field as a loose confederation of scientists studying various aspects of cognitive behavior. Terminology varies considerably. For instance, knowledge structures are variously referred to as *mental models, frames,* or *schemas* (Mislevy, 1993a). Despite this heterogeneity in the theoretical bases for research, most cognitive psychologists appear to be working on the same problems in much the same way with a common theoretical orientation, namely that (a) learners develop their working internal models to solve problems, (b) these models develop from personal experience, and (c) these models are used to solve other similar situations encountered in life. The most intelligent behavior consists of a variety of working models (schemas, the building blocks of cognition) that have greater generality. The issue of learning task generality to other problems encountered is critical to learning theory and testing.

Snow and Lohman (1989), among others, called for a unification of cognitive and test theories to better address teaching and learning. The main goal of this unification seems to be a deeper understanding and the ability to develop complex learning. Dibello, Roussos, and Stout (1993) proposed such a unified theory drawing heavily from earlier work by Tatsuoka (1985) and her colleagues. An emergent unified theory of school learning hopes to explain how students acquire, organize, and use knowledge. The emerging theory will:

1. likely derive from current and past information processing theories.

2. incorporate concepts of declarative, procedural, and strategic knowledge, as opposed to more traditional dichotomy of knowledge and skills. Dibello et al. (1993) also proposed schematic and algorithmic knowledge.

3. provide a basis for organizing both declarative and procedural knowledge using schemata, and a more complete understanding of how these will lead to more effective teaching methods.

4. place emphasis on problem solving and other types of higher level thinking. Problem solving will be more complex than we realize. In fact, there is evidence to suggest that a variety of problem solving methods are content bound (see Snow & Lohman, 1989).

5. be confirmed or disconfirmed by both qualitative and quantitative inquiry.

6. focus on practical applications of principles and procedures to classroom instruction. In this context, the instructional program becomes the focus; its constituent parts are curriculum, instruction, and integrated testing.

7. include a way to diagnose learning difficulties using student incorrect responses.

8. incorporate a componential conceptualization of abilities into the curriculum. Abilities will be developed over longer periods of time (Gardner & Hatch, 1989; Sternberg, 1985). Test scores reflecting these abilities will not be dramatic in terms of showing growth, because such growth is irregular and slow.

9. involve the idiosyncratic nature of each school learner, a condition that has direct implications for individualized instruction and individual education plans.

10. recognize the context of exogenous factors. The personal/social context of each learner has a strong influence on the quality and quantity of learning. Such factors as test anxiety, economic status, parental support for schooling, nutrition, personal or social adjustment, physical health, and the like become critical aspects of both theory and technology of school learning.

11. Have a component consisting of a statistical theory of option response patterns that will be more compatible with complex, multi-step thinking.

Although we are far from realizing such a learning theory, the groundwork is being laid for this transition from a behavioral orientation to a cognitive approach that emphasizes more complex forms of thinking. Leading theorists and educational reformers consistently increase the intensity of their efforts toward this reformation, and the results are already manifest in the authentic assessment movement.

Given these 11 qualities of this emerging unified theory of school learning, present day teaching and testing practices seem almost obsolete. The futures of item development and item response validation should be quite different from current practices.

Redefining of Ability and Achievement

Two barriers exist that affect the future of item development and item response validation. The two are related, but are different problems.

Cognitive psychologists and others have used a plethora of terms representing higher level thinking, including metacognition, problem solving, analysis, evaluation, comprehension, conceptual learning, critical thinking, reasoning, strategic knowledge, schematic knowledge, and algorithmic knowledge, to name a few. The first stage in construct validity is definition. These terms are seldom adequately defined so that we can identify or construct items that measure these traits. Thus, the most basic step in construct validity, construct definition, continues to inhibit both the development of many higher level thinking behaviors and their measurement.

A second barrier is the absence of a validated taxonomy of complex cognitive behavior. Studies of teachers' success with using higher level thinking questions leads to inconclusive findings due to a variety of factors, including methodological problems (Winne, 1979). Many other studies and reports attest to the current difficulty of successfully measuring higher level thinking with the kind of scientific rigor required in construct validation. Recently, Royer, Cisero, and Carlo (1993) presented a taxonomy of higher level behavior and reviewed research on its validity. This impressive work is based on a cognitive learning theory proposed by J. R. Anderson (1990). Although the taxonomy is far from being at the implementation stage, it provides a reasonable structure that invites further study and validation.

Item writing in the current environment cannot thrive due to the existence of these two barriers. Advances in theory should lead to better construct definitions and organization of types of higher level thinking that will sustain more productive item development leading to higher quality teacher-produced and standardized tests of higher level thinking.

Statistical Theories of Test Scores

Any theory ultimately must stand empirical tests. Once constructs are defined and variables are constructed, testing provides one basis for the empirical validation of test score construct interpretations and uses. In this context, a statistical theory of test scores is used.

Classical test theory has its roots settled in the early part of this century and has grown substantially. It is still widely accepted and used in testing programs despite the rapid and understandable emergence of item response theories. For many reasons enumerated in chapter 8 and in other sources (e.g., Hambleton & Jones, 1993; Hambleton & Swaminathan, 1987), classical theory has enough deficiencies to limit its future use. Nonetheless, its use is encouraged by its familiarity to the mainstream of test users.

Generalizability theory is a neoclassical theory that allows users the ability to study sources of error in cognitive measurement (see Brennan, 1982). Brennan (1993) showed how generalizability theory can be used to study the influences of context in test development. Although generalizability theory is somewhat new, it seems to have a dimmer future than traditional item response theory, because of the same problems we face with classical theory.

Dichotomous (binary) item response theories have developed rapidly in recent years, largely due to the efforts of theorists like Rasch, Birnbaum, Lord, Bock, and Wright, to name a few. These theories are increasingly applied in large scale testing programs. Linn (1990) observed that probably item response theories do not produce more valid test score interpretations and use. However, they have changed the way we think about test design and validation.

Although dichotomous item response theory receive a high degree of support among theoreticians and some practitioners, its complexity and dependence upon unidimensional test data and large samples limit its applications. The applicability of item response theory to classroom instruction is problematic, for several reasons. First, because item response theory requires large samples, it seldom is useful at the classroom level, unless, tests are designed for many classrooms. Second, the construct represented by a test must be unidimensional if item response theory is used. Instruction increasingly involves integrating subjects and multidimensionality. Third, item parameter estimates may fluctuate because of differential instruction, where some concepts, principles, and procedures are taught while other content is not taught. Disturbances in parameter estimates have been linked to class and school effects (Hess, 1994). If a test contains taught and untaught material, unidimensionality fails, and estimates of item parameters in the two- and three-parameter model will fail to converge. Thus, analysis of achievement tests closely linked to ongoing instruction is likely to lead to unstable item parameter estimates.

Linear polytomous scoring (option weighting) procedures have been supported by over 50 years of intermittent research that consistently shows slightly higher reliability when compared to dichotomous scoring (Haladyna & Sympson, 1988). Theoretically, the method of reciprocal averages, introduced by Guttman (1941) for a multiple-choice format, actually maximizes coefficient alpha (Lord, 1958). This research finding is remarkable when one considers that the development of effective distractors plagues item writing. In a recent study Haladyna and Downing (in press) evaluated distractors in four standardized tests. They found that most items have only one or two working distractors. Thus, conventional option weighting would not seem very effective with these tests, yet the research continues to show that linear polytomous scoring produces more reliable scores when compared to binary scoring.

More recently, polytomous item response theories have been developed by Bock (1972), Samejima (1979), Sympson (1983, 1986), and Thissen and Steinberg (1986). This theoretical work has led to the development of computer software that initiates studies bearing on the comparative effectiveness of these proposed models (Linacre & Wright, 1993; Muraki & Bock, 1993; Sympson, 1990; Thissen, 1991). Given that future item development methods produce better distractors, polytomous scoring's future is brighter than doubters like Wang and Stanley (1970) earlier believed.

In *Test Theory for a New Generation of Tests*, Frederiksen, Mislevy, and Bejar (1993) assembled an impressive and comprehensive treatment of ongoing theoretical work, representing a new wave of statistical test theory. This collection of papers seems aimed at realizing the goal of unifying cognitive and measurement perspectives with emphasis on complex learning. Mislevy (1993a) distinguished much of this recent work as departing from low-to-high proficiency testing where a total score has meaning to pattern scoring where wrong answers have diagnostic value. In this setting, the total score does not inform us about *how* a learner reached the final answer to a complex set of activities. An appropriate analysis of patterns of responses may inform us about the effectiveness of a process used to solve a problem. In other words, patterns of responses, such as derived from the context-dependent item set, may lead to inferences about optimal and suboptimal learning. Theoretical developments by Bejar (1993), Embretsen (1985), Fisher (1983), Haertel & Wiley (1993), Jannarone (1988), Tatsuoka (1990), and Wilson (1989) captured the rich array of promising new choices. Many of these theorists agree that traditional classical test theory and even present-day item response theories may quickly become *passe*, because they are inadequate for handling complex cognitive behavior. As with any new theory, extensive research leading to technologies will take considerable time and resources. Thus, it will be a while before these theories are fruitfully applied.

These statistical theories have significant implications for item response validation. Traditional item analysis was concerned with estimating item difficulty and discrimination. Newer theories will lead to option response theories where right and wrong answers provide useful information, and patterns of responses also provide information on the success of learners on complex tasks.

The Future of Item Development

The previous section was devoted to describing trends and other factors that will affect the future of item development and item response validation. In this section, item writing's past is reviewed and its future discussed in this context of influences. In construct validity, an explicit relationship exists between item writing and test building, between test scores and item responses. Figure 10.1 shows the relationship between tests and items for the three steps in construct validation. Given this joint dependence between item and test and between formulation and explication, item writing must be considered as an integral aspect of construct validation.

In this section, two topics will be addressed. First, the state-of-the-art of item writing is described as a starting point. Then the characteristics of future item development will be identified and described. As new theories of item writing emerge, they should possess certain qualities that will make item writing a science rather than nontheoretical prescriptive technology that it is today.

The Item-Writing Legacy

Critics noted that item writing is not a scholarly area (e.g., Cronbach, 1970; Nitko, 1985). Item writing seems characterized by the collective wisdom and experience of measurement experts who often convey this knowledge in textbooks. Another problem is that item writing has not been an integral part of test development or validation. Previous discussions of item development in *Educational Measurement* (Lindquist, 1951; Linn, 1989; Thorndike, 1970) have treated item writing in isolation of other topics, such as validity, reliability, item analysis, among other topics. Cronbach (1971) in his classic chapter on validation provided scant attention

Formulation	Explication	Construct Validation
The process of defining a construct, its uses or interpretations, and the social consequences of these uses or interpretations	The process of creating measures of the construct	The collecting of evidence to support test score interpretations and uses in a particular context
Test specifications from domain definition	Test development	Test score validation
Item specifications from domain definition	Item development	Item response validation

Fig. 10.1.   Relationship between items and tests in construct validation.

to the role of items and item responses in test validation. Messick (1989), on the other hand, made very specific reference to the importance of various aspects of item development and item response validation on construct validity. The current unified view of validity explicitly unites many aspects of item development and item response validation with other critical aspects of construct validation. But this is only a recent development.

The criterion-referenced testing movement brought sweeping reform to test constructors at all levels by focusing attention on instructional objectives. Each item needed to be linked to an instructional objective, and the integration of teaching and testing produced predictable results, high degrees of learning, if student time for learning was flexible to fit slow learners. The dilemma was how specific to make the objective. Too specific limited the degree to which we could generalize; too vague produced too much inconsistency in item development that resulted in disagreement among context experts about the classifications of these items. The widespread use of instructional objectives in education and training is remarkable.

The current reform movement and the shift to performance testing has caused a reconsideration of the usefulness of the instructional objective. Even instructional systems have shifted away from using the term *instructional objective* to the term *learner outcome*. Because criterion-referenced testing is objective-driven, it may be replaced by a more current concept, *authentic assessment*, because of the latter's close relationship to cognitive psychology.

Haladyna and Downing (1989a) assessed the collective knowledge about item writing by examining 45 leading textbooks and other references. A taxonomy of 43 item-writing rules was created. For some rules, a lack of consensus existed among the 45 sources, illustrating what critics have said, that item writing is hardly a science. Haladyna and Downing (1989b) also reviewed over 90 studies bearing on these item-writing rules. They found an uneven distribution in the number of studies that were done to the number of rules that exist. Nearly half the rules had received no study at all. These studies and others subsequently published contributed to the conclusion that item writing continues to lack a scientific foundation.

Theories of item writing provide a more systematic basis for generating items that map content domains of ability and achievement. For this main reason, item-writing theories are desirable. Roid and Haladyna (1982) examined and evaluated several item writing theories. Bormuth proposed an item-writing theory based upon algorithms that transformed prose passages into multiple-choice items. Guttman proposed a facet theory that automated item writing by using mapping sentences containing facets that were systematically varied. Hively's item forms provided a similar approach. Although these theories are no longer studied or were inadequately tested, they provide a basis for thinking about future item-writing theories.

A series of integrative reviews by Albanese (1992), Downing (1992), Frisbie (1992), and Haladyna (1992a) provided guidance about the variety of multiple-choice formats available for item writing. This work provided an important basis for the use of some formats and the discontinuation of other formats, such as the complex multiple-choice and true-false.

This legacy of item writing is characterized by a checkered past, consisting of many thoughtful essays and chapters in textbooks about how to write items. While most of this advice is good, it fails to qualify as a science. Attempts at theory building have been ambitious but have failed due to neglect and other factors. However, these failures provide a basis for planning new theories. The next section describes desirable aspects of new theories.

Characteristics of New Approaches to Item Writing

New theories of item writing should be integrated within this emerging unified theory of learning. This section addresses some characteristics that the new generation of item-writing theories must possess to meet the challenge of measuring complex behavior. These characteristics draw heavily from current thinking in cognitive psychology but also rely on this legacy of item writing.

Inference Networks

Traditional item writing focuses on a single behavior. The stem communicates a single task; the options provide the correct and several plausible choices. Some theorists (Royer et al., 1993) portrayed this type of testing as representing micro skills, simple cognitive behaviors that, while often important, are not as important as macro skills. The latter represents the various types of higher level thinking.

Although the instructional objective was the basis for writing the item in the teaching technology in the 1970s and 1980s, defining and measuring macro skills using the objective is quite difficult, perhaps contributing to this extensive failure by practitioners to write this type of test items.

Cognitive psychology seems to be working toward an opposite end. Constructs are more complicated, reflecting how we learn instead of what we learn. Instead of aggregating knowledge, like filling a storeroom, learning is viewed as more patchwork. The schema is the mental structure for organizing this knowledge. Mislevy (1993b) provided examples of inference networks, which are graphical representations that reflect the cluster and connectedness of micro tasks that comprise a complex cognitive behavior. These networks have a statistical basis, reflecting the reasoning about the causality of factors that we can observe. The inference network may contain both multiple-choice and constructed-response elements, each providing for a certain kind of inference. Mislevy described both a causal model of reasoning about observations and an appropriate statistical theory that can be used to model student behavior during learning. Thus, the unification of cognitive learning theory and statistical test score theory takes place. Such inference networks can illustrate the pattern of behavior in a complex process or simply proficiency—the outcome of the process.

Inference networks provide a new way to view content and cognitive behavior in a complex type of learning. The inference network can be expanded to include the instructional strategy needed for each micro skill and the formative and summative aspects of learning. Item writing becomes an interesting challenge, because items must model the range of behaviors that distinguish students with respect to the trait being learned and measured. Mislevy provided several examples from different fields, illustrating that inference networks will help develop effective measures of complex behavior in a variety of settings.

In summary, the instructional objective and related criterion-referenced test, as products of behaviorism, seem doomed to extinction. Inference networks and complex, multi-step thinking will lead item writing into a new era. When new item-writing theories use inference networks and abandon the objective, the problem of writing items to measure types of higher level thinking will be alleviated.

Item-Generating Ability

Present-day item writing is a slow process, and item writers can expect that roughly 40% of their items will fail to perform as intended. This characterizes even further how item writing needs to improve. Ideally any new item-writing theory should lead to the easy generation of many content-relevant items. A simple example can show how item generating schemes can benefit item writing. In dental education, an early skill is learning to identify tooth names and numbers using the Universal Coding System. Two objectives can be used to quickly generate 104 test items:

> Given a letter code, identify the tooth name.
> Given the tooth name, identify the letter code.

Because we have 32 teeth in the adult dentition, a total of 64 items defines the domain. The primary dentition has 20 teeth, so 40 more items are possible. Each item can be multiple-choice, or we can authentically assess a dental student's actual performance using a patient. Also, a plaster or plastic model of the adult or child dentition can be used. If domain specifications were this simple in all educational settings, the problems of construct definition and item writing would be trivial. Unfortunately, we have not cleverly devised enough useful tasks like this to use such algorithms.

Historically, Bormuth's algorithmic procedures for prose passage, Hively's item forms, and Guttman's facet theory are all excellent examples of highly productive item-generating procedures (Roid & Haladyna, 1982). Each of these theories provided a basis for generating great numbers of items. Additionally, these procedures limited the creative expression of item writers by reducing what Bormuth (1970) felt was undesirable subjectivity. Indeed, an experimental study by Roid and Haladyna (1978) showed when freedom in item writing exists, bias does creep in that affects item characteristics.

Chapter 6 discusses three distinctly different approaches to item-generating procedures. The item shell provides a syntax for item writers based on successfully performing items. The algorithmic context-dependent item set attempts to measure higher level thinking through realistic encounters, portrayed in scenarios (vignettes) with key facets to vary that systematically change each scenario. Item modeling is a more systematic process that resembles Guttman's facet theory but appears more workable. Reports of its productivity are impressive. None of these methods are particularly based on an item-writing theory, but item modeling comes closest. Subsequent work on it may distinguish it as a highly useful item writing theory for tapping clinical problem solving in the professions.

With respect to new item-writing theories, Bejar (1993) proposed a response generative model (RGM) as a form of item writing that is superior to these earlier theories because it has a basis in cognitive theory, while these earlier generative theories have behavioristic origins. The RGM proposes to generate items with a predictable set of parameters, from which clear interpretations are possible. Bejar presented some research evidence from a variety of researchers, including research in areas such as spatial ability, reasoning, and verbal ability. The underlying rationale of the RGM is that item writing and item response is linked predictably. Every time an item is written, responses to that item can confirm the theory. Failure to confirm would destroy the theory's credibility. Bejar maintained that this approach is not so much an item writing method, a content specification scheme, or a cognitive theory, but a philosophy of test construction and response modeling that is integrative.

The RGM has tremendous appeal to prove or disprove itself as it is used. It has the attractive qualities of earlier generative item-writing theories, namely (a) the ability to operationalize a domain definition, (b) the ability to generate objectively sufficient numbers of items, and (c) the ease with which relevant tests are created with predictable characteristics. Additionally RGM provides a basis for validating item responses and test scores at the time of administration. What is not provided in Bejar's theory thus far are the detailed specifications of the use of the theory and the much needed research to transform theory into technology. Like earlier theories, significant research will be needed to realize the attractive claims for this model.

Misconception Strategies

A third characteristic of new item-writing theories will be the diagnostic value of wrong choices. Current item-writing wisdom suggested that distractors should be based on common errors of students (Haladyna & Downing, 1989a). Although this method of creating distractors may seem simplistic, one has only to administer items in an open-ended format to appropriately instructed students to develop credible distractors. This process applies to open-ended performance testing. The scoring rubric for open-ended tests would derive from an analysis of student errors, thus making the process very much like the design of a multiple-choice item.

Tatsuoka (1985) and her colleagues proposed a model for diagnosing cognitive errors in problem solving. This impressive research uses her rule space model based on task analyses of mathematics skills.   Mathematics seems the most readily adaptable to these theoretical developments.   We lack applications to more challenging subject matters, for example, biology, philosophy, history, women's studies, political science, speech, reading, literature studies, psychology, and art appreciation.   Because a desirable feature of achievement tests is diagnostic information leading to reteaching, these misconception methods are highly desirable.

Lohman and Ippel (1993) provided a comprehensive discussion of a general cognitive theory that examines processes that uncover misconceptions in student learning. The nature of complex learning compels cognitive psychologists to reject traditional test models that focus on the meaning of total test scores.   These researchers go further to assert that even measures of components of process that are often quantitative may be inappropriate, because step-by-step observations do not capture the essence of what makes individuals different in the performance of a complex task. Lohman and Ippel looked to understandings based on developmental psychology. Instead of using quantitative indicators in a problem-solving process, they looked for qualitative evidence.   Although this work is very preliminary, it shows that cognitive psychologists are sensitive to uncovering the precise steps in correct and incorrect problem solving. This work directly affects item writing in the future. And conventional item writing does not contribute to modeling complex behavior as it emerges in these cognitive theories.

An urgent need exists to make erroneous response part of the scoring system in testing, and, at the same time, provide information to teachers and learners about the remedial efforts needed to successfully complete complex tasks. Future item-writing theories will need this component if we are to solve the mystery of writing items for higher level thinking.

This section has treated the future for item writing. Item writing lacks the rich theoretical tradition that we observe with statistical theories of test scores. The undervaluing of item writing has resulted in a prescriptive technology instead of workable item-writing theories. The item-writing theory of the future will feature a workable method for specifying content.   Perhaps the inference networks suggested by Mislevy (1993b) or the diagnostic error classification systems developed by Tatsuoka and her colleagues for over a decade will serve this purpose. Future item-writing theory will permit the ability to rapidly generate items that completely map ability or achievement domains. Finally, any emergent theory must provide a basis for creating distractors that reveal misconceptions in learning so that diagnosis and remediation can occur.

The Future for Item-Response Validation

Item analysis has been a somewhat stagnant field in the past, limited to the estimation of item difficulty and discrimination using classical or item response theory, and the counting of responses to each distractor. Successive editions of *Educational Measurement* (Lindquist, 1951; Linn, 1989; Thorndike, 1970) documented this unremarkable state of affairs. The many influences described in this chapter, coupled with growth in cognitive and item response theories, has provided an opportunity to unify item writing and item response validation in a larger context of construct validity. The tools and understanding that are developing for more effective treatment of item responses has been characterized in this book as *item response validation*. The future of item response validation will never be realized without significant progress in developing a workable theory of item writing.

Chapter 8 discusses the topic of item response validation, and chapter 9 presents methods to study various testing problems. An important linkage was made between item response validation and construct validation. Three important aspects of item response validation that should receive more attention in the future are (a) distractor evaluation, (b) a reconceptualization of item discrimination, and (c) pattern analysis. Because these concepts were more comprehensively addressed in chapter 8, the discussion will center on the relative importance of each in the future.

Distractor Evaluation

The topic of distractor evaluation has been given little attention in the past. Even the most current edition of *Educational Measurement* provides a scant three paragraphs on this topic (Millman & Greene, 1989). However, Thissen, Steinberg, and Fitzpatrick (1989) supported the studying of distractors. They believe that any item analysis should consider the distractor as an important part of the item. Wainer (1989) provided additional support, claiming that the graphical quality of the trace line for each option makes the evaluation of an item more complex but also more complete. Because trace lines are graphical, they are less daunting to item writers who may lack the statistical background needed to deal with item discrimination indexes.

The item discrimination index provides a useful and convenient numerical summary of item discrimination, but it tends to overlook the relative contributions of each distractor. Because each distractor contains a plausible incorrect answer, item analysts are not afforded enough guidance about which distractors might be revised or retired to improve the item performance. Changes in distractors should lead to improvements in item performance, which, in turn, should lead to improved test scores.

There are at least three good reasons for evaluating distractors. First, the distractor is part of the test item and should be useful. If it is not useful, it should be removed. Useless distractors have an untoward effect on item discrimination. Second, with polytomous scoring, useful distractors contribute to more effective scoring, which has been proven to positively affect test score reliability. Third, as cognitive psychologists lead efforts to develop distractors that pinpoint misconceptions, distractor evaluation techniques will permit the empirical validation of distractor responses and by that improve our ability to provide misconception information to instructors and students.

Item Discrimination

The concept of item discrimination has evolved over most of the century. An earlier discrimination index consisted of noting the difference between mean item performance of a high-scoring group and the mean item performance of a low-scoring group. Such high-group/low-group comparisons were mathematically and calculationally simple. Statistical indexes like the biserial and point-biserial were theoretically more satisfactory, and routinely produced with the coming of the computer. However, these traditional item discrimination indexes have many deficiencies to recommend against their use (Henrysson, 1971). Two- and three-parameter binary-scoring item response theories provide discrimination that is highly related to traditional discrimination. Like traditional discrimination, the differential discriminating abilities of distractors is immaterial.

In polytomous scoring, discrimination has a different conceptualization. As discussed in chapter 8, polytomous scoring views the differential information contained in distractors more sensitively than with binary scoring. Because discriminating distractors are infrequent, according to studies like Haladyna and Downing (in press), multiple-choice items in the future may be necessarily leaner, containing only two or three distractors.

This reconceptualization of item discrimination compels item analysts to evaluate distractors, as well as consider the response pattern of each distractor relative to one another. Items that have distractors that have similar response patterns, unless reflecting uniquely different misconceptions, may not be very useful in item design.

Response Pattern Analysis

Complex behavior requires many mental steps. New theories have begun to model such behavior with new statistical theories that examine patterns of responses among items as opposed to traditional item analysis that merely examines the pattern of item response to total test score (Frederiksen, Mislevy, & Bejar, 1993; Mislevy, 1993b).

Some significant current work is being done with context-dependent item sets. Wainer and Kiely (1987) conceptualized item sets as testlets. Responses to testlets involve the chaining of response, and specific patterns have more value than others. While this pattern analysis does not fulfil the promise of cognitive psychologists regarding misconception analysis, testlet scoring takes a major first step into the field of item analysis for multi-step thinking and the relative importance of each subtask in a testlet. Chapters 8 and 9 discuss item response models and computer software that exist for studying various scoring methods. As cognitive psychologists develop constructs to the point that item writing can produce items reflecting multi-step thinking, response pattern analysis will become more statistically sophisticated and useful.

Summary and Conclusion

In this chapter, we have noted several prominent influences that will likely affect how we test ability and achievement. Clearly, a unification among the diverse and too often independent fields of cognitive learning theory and statistical test score theory is imminent. As Snow and Lohman (1989) observed, representatives from both sides have much to learn, both from each other and from partnerships. Item writing will cease to be prescriptive, such as the taxonomy proposed by Haladyna and Downing (1989a), and it will begin to be part of this unified theory that involves construct definition, test development, and construct validation both at the item and test score units of analysis. Toward that end, the creative act of item writing probably will be replaced with more algorithmic methods to control item writing biases, and creativity will take place at an earlier stage with some content specification procedures, like inference networks, that will almost automate the item writing process. How automated item writing will become remains to be seen.

With item response validation, polytomous scoring will open more opportunities to write more effective distractors and use these distractors in scoring test results. Consequently, more attention will be given to distractor response patterns that diagnose wrong thinking in a complex behavior, and the trace line will be a useful and friendly device to understand the role that each distractor plays in building a coherent item.

Both item writing and item response validation are important steps in test development and validation. As cognitive psychologists better define constructs and identify the constituent steps in complex thinking, item writing and item response validation will evolve to meet the challenge. Both item writing and item response validation will continue to play an important role in test development, but each must receive more scholarly attention than they have received in the past. Both will require significant study in the context of this emerging unified theory involving both ability and achievement.

REFERENCES

Ackerman, T. A., & Smith, P. L. (1988). A comparison of the information provided by essay, multiple-choice, and free-response writing tests. *Applied Psychological Measurement, 12,* 117-128.

Albanese, M. A. (1992). Type K items. *Educational Measurement: Issues and Practices, 12,* 28-33.

Albanese, M. A., Kent, T. A., & Whitney, D. R. (1977). A comparison of the difficulty, reliability, and validity of complex multiple-choice, multiple response, and multiple true-false items. *Annual Conference on Research in Medical Education, 16,* 105-110.

Albanese, M. A., & Sabers, D. L. (1988). Multiple true-false items: A study of interitem correlations, scoring alternatives, and reliability estimation. *Journal of Educational Measurement, 25,* 111-124.

American Psychological Association, American Educational Research Association, National Council on Measurement in Education. (1985). *Standards for Educational and Psychological Testing.* Washington, DC: American Psychological Association.

Anderson, J. R. (1990). *The adaptive character of thought.* Hillsdale, NJ: Lawrence Erlbaum Associates.

Anderson, J. R., & Bower, G. H. (1972). Recognition and retrieval process in free recall. *Psychological Review, 79,* 97-132.

Anderson, R. (1972). How to construct achievement tests to assess comprehension. *Review of Educational Research, 42,* 145-170.

Angoff, W. H. (1974). The development of statistical indices for detecting cheaters. *Journal of the American Statistical Association, 69,* 44-49.

Ansley, T. N., Spratt, K. F., & Forsyth, R. A. (1988, April). *An investigation of the effects of using calculators to reduce the computational burden on a standardized test of mathematics problem solving.* Paper presented at the annual meeting of the American Educational Research Association, New Orleans.

Assessment Systems Corporation. (1992). *RASCAL (Rasch Analysis Program).* St. Paul, MN: Author.

Assessment Systems Corporation. (1989). *ASCAL (2- and 3-parameter) IRT Calibration Program*. (Computer Software). St. Paul, MN: Author.

Badger, E. (1990, April). *Using different spectacles to look at student achievement: Implications for theory and practice*. Paper presented at the annual meeting of the American Educational Research Association, Boston.

Becker, B. J. (1990). Coaching for Scholastic Aptitude Test: Further synthesis and appraisal. *Review of Educational Research, 60*, 373-418.

Bejar, I. (1993). A generative approach to psychological and educational measurement. In N. Frederiksen, R. J. Mislevy, & I. Bejar (Eds.), *Test theory for a new generation of tests* (pp. 297-323). Hillsdale, NJ: Lawrence Erlbaum Associates.

Bellezza, F. S., & Bellezza, S. F. (1989). Detection of cheating on multiple-choice tests by using error-similarity analysis. *Teaching of Psychology, 16*, 151-155.

Bennett, R. E. (1993). On the meaning of constructed response. In R. E. Bennett & W. C. Ward (Eds.), *Construction versus choice in cognitive measurement: Issues in constructed response, performance testing, and portfolio assessment* (pp. 1-27). Hillsdale, NJ: Lawrence Erlbaum Associates.

Bennett, R. E., & Ward, W. C. (Eds.), (1993). *Construction versus choice in cognitive measurement: Issues in constructed-response, performance testing, and portfolio assessment*. Hillsdale, NJ: Lawrence Erlbaum Associates.

Bennett, R. E., Rock, D. A., & Wang, M. (1990). Equivalence of free-response and multiple-choice items. *Journal of Educational Measurement, 28*, 77-92.

Bennett, R. E., Sebrechts, M. M., & Rock, D. A. (1991). *The convergent validity of expert system scores for complex constructed-response quantitative items*. (GRE Research Report No. 88-07bP. ETS Research Report 91-12). Princeton, NJ: Educational Testing Service.

Ben-Shakhara, G., & Sinai, Y. (1991). Gender differences in multiple-choice tests: The role of differential guessing tendencies. *Journal of Educational Measurement, 28*, 23-25.

Benton, S. L., & Kiewra, K. A. (1986). Measuring the organizational aspects of writing ability. *Journal of Educational Measurement, 23*, 377-386.

Biggs, J. B., & Collis, K. F. (1982). *Evaluating the quality of learning: The SOLO taxonomy (structure of observed learning outcomes)*. New York: Academic Press.

Birenbaum, M., & Tatsuoka, K. K. (1987). Open-ended versus multiple-choice response formats-it does make a difference for diagnostic purposes. *Applied Psychological Measurement, 11*, 385-395.

Birnbaum, A. (1968). Some latent trait models and their use in inferring an examinee's ability. In F. M. Lord & M. R Novick, *Statistical theories of mental test scores*. Reading, MA: Addison-Wesley.

Bloom, B. S. (1968). Learning for mastery. *Evaluation Comment, 1*, 1-12.

Bloom, B. S., Engelhart, M. D., Furst, E. J., Hill, W. H., & Kratwohl, D. R. (1956). *Taxonomy of educational objectives*. New York: Longmans Green.

Bock, R. D. (1972). Estimating item parameters and latent ability when responses are scored in two or more nominal categories. *Psychometrika, 37*, 29-51.

Bormuth, J. R. (1970). *On a theory of achievement test items.* Chicago: University of Chicago Press.

Bracht, G. H., & Hopkins, K. D. (1970). The communality of essay and objective tests of academic achievement. *Educational and Psychological Measurement, 30,* 359-364.

Braun, H. I. (1988). Understanding score reliability: Experience calibrating essay readers. *Journal of Educational Statistics, 13,* 1-18.

Brennan, R. L. (1982). *Elements of generalizability theory.* Iowa City, Iowa: American College Testing Program.

Brennan, R. L. (1993, April). *The context of context effects.* Paper presented at the annual meeting of the American Educational Research Association, Atlanta.

Bridgman, B. (1990, April). *Essay and multiple-choice tests as predictors of college freshman GPA.* Paper presented at the annual meeting of the American Educational Research Association, Boston.

Bridgeman, B., & Lewis, C. (1991, April). *Predictive validity of advanced placement essay and multiple-choice examinations.* Paper presented at the annual meeting of the National Council on Measurement in Education, Chicago.

Bridgeman, B., & Rock, D. A. (1993). Relationship among multiple-choice and open-ended analytical questions. *Journal of Educational Measurement, 30,* 313-329.

Brown, J. (1966). *Objective tests: Their construction and analysis: A practical handbook for teachers.* London: Longmans.

Burkam, A., & Burkam, D. (1993, April). *The interaction of test item format and gender with mathematics achievement.* Paper presented at the annual meeting of the American Educational Research Association, Atlanta.

Burmester, M. A., & Olson, L. A. (1966). Comparison of item statistics for items in a multiple-choice and alternate-response form. *Science Education, 50,* 467-470.

Cannell, J. J. (1989). *How public educators cheat on standardized achievement tests.* Albuquerque, NM: Friends for Education.

Case, S. M., & Downing, S. M. (1989). *Performance of various multiple-choice item types on medical specialty examinations: Types A, B, C, K, and X.* Philadelphia: National Board of Medical Examiners.

Changas, P., & Samejima, F. (1984, April). *Efficient use of distractors in ability estimation with the multiple-choice test item.* Paper presented at the annual meeting of the American Educational Research Association, New Orleans.

Chase, C. I. (1979). The impact of achievement expectations and handwriting quality on scoring essay tests. *Journal of Educational Measurement, 16,* 39-42.

Chase, C. I. (1986). Essay test scoring: Interaction of relevant variables. *Journal of Educational Measurement, 23,* 33-42.

Cizek, G. J. (1991, April). *The effect of altering the position of options in a multiple-choice examination.* Paper presented at the annual meeting of the National Council on Measurement in Education, Chicago.

Clavner, J. (1985). Essay tests. *Innovation Abstracts.* Austin, TX: National Institute for Staff and Organizational Development, University of Texas.

Cody, R. P. (1985). Statistical analysis of examinations to detect cheating. *Journal of Medical Education, 60*, 136-137.

Coffman, W. E. (1971). Essay examinations. In R. L. Thorndike (Ed.), *Educational Measurement* (2nd ed., pp. 271-302). Washington, DC: American Council on Education.

Cohen, A. S., & Kim S. (1992). Detecting calculator effects on item performance. *Applied Measurement in Education, 5*, 303-320.

Cohen, S. A. (1987). Instructional alignment: Searching for the magic bullet. *Educational Researcher, 16*, 16-20.

Cole, N. S. (1990). Conceptions of educational achievement. *Educational Researcher, 19*, 2-7.

Cole, N. S., & Moss, P. A. (1989). Bias in test use. In R. L. Linn (Ed.), *Educational Measurement* (3rd ed., pp. 201-220). New York: American Council on Education and Macmillan.

Cox, R. C., & Vargas, J. (1966). A comparison of item selection techniques for norm-referenced and criterion-referenced tests. Pittsburgh: University of Pittsburgh Learning Research and Development Center.

Crocker, L., Llabre, M., & Miller, M. D. (1988). The generalizability of content validity ratings. *Journal of Educational Measurement, 25*, 287-299.

Cronbach, L. J. (1970). {Review of *On the theory of achievement test items*}. *Psychometrika, 35*, 509-511.

Cronbach, L. J. (1971). Test validation. In R. L. Thorndike (Ed.), *Educational Measurement* (2nd ed., pp. 443-507). Washington, DC: American Council on Education.

Cronbach, L. J. (1987). Five perspectives of the validity argument. In H. Wainer & H. I. Braun (Eds.), *Test validity*. Hillsdale, NJ: Lawrence Erlbaum Associates.

Crooks, T. J. (1988). The impact of classroom evaluation practices on students. *Review of Educational Research, 58*, 438-481.

Dawson-Saunders, B., Nungester, R. J., & Downing, S. M. (1989). *A comparison of single best answer multiple-choice items (A-type) and complex multiple-choice (K-type)*. Philadelphia: National Board of Medical Examiners.

Dawson-Saunders, B., Reshetar, R., Shea, J. A., Fierman, C. D., Kangilaski, R., & Poniatowski, P. A. (1992, April). *Alterations to item text and effects on item difficulty and discrimination*. Paper presented at the annual meeting of the National Council on Measurement in Education, San Francisco.

Dawson-Saunders, B., Reshetar, R., Shea, J. A., Fierman, C. D., Kangilaski, & R., & Poniatowski, P. A. (1993, April). *Changes in difficulty and discrimination related to altering item text*. Paper presented at the annual meeting of the National Council on Measurement in Education, Atlanta.

de Gruijter, D. N. M. (1988). Evaluating an item and option statistic using the bootstrap method. *Tijdschrift voor Onderwijsresearch, 13*, 345-352.

Dibello, L. V., Roussos, L. A., & Stout, W. F. (1993, April). *Unified cognitive/psychometric diagnosis foundations and application*. Paper presented at the annual meeting of the American Educational Research Association, Atlanta.

Dorans, J. J., & Potenza, M. T. (1993, April). *Issues in equity assessment for complex response stimuli.* Paper presented at the annual meeting of the National Council on Measurement in Education, Atlanta.

Downing, S. M. (1992). True-false and alternate-choice item formats: A review of research. *Educational Measurement: Issues and Practices, 11,* 27-30.

Drasgow, F. (1982). Choice of test model for appropriateness measurement. *Applied Psychological Measurement, 6,* 297-308.

Drasgow, F., & Guertler, E. (1987). A decision-theoretic approach to the use of appropriateness measurement for detecting invalid test and scale scores. *Journal of Applied Psychology, 72,* 10-18.

Drasgow, F., Levine, M. V., & Williams, E. A. (1985). Appropriateness measurement with polychotomous item response models and standardized indices. *British Journal of Educational Psychology, 38,* 67-86.

Ebel, R. L. (1951). Writing the test item. In E. F. Lindquist (Ed.), *Educational Measurement* (1st ed., pp. 185-249). Washington, DC: American Council on Education.

Ebel, R. L. (1970). The case for true-false test items. *School Review, 78,* 373-389

Ebel, R. L. (1978). The ineffectiveness of multiple true-false items. *Educational and Psychological Measurement, 38,* 37-44.

Ebel, R. L. (1981, April). *Some advantages of alternate-choice test items.* Paper presented at the annual meeting of the National Council on Measurement in Education, Los Angeles.

Ebel, R. L. (1982). Proposed solutions to two problems of test construction. *Journal of Educational Measurement, 19,* 267-278.

Ebel, R. L., & Frisbie, D. A. (1991). *Essential of educational measurement* (5th ed.). Englewood Cliffs, NJ: Prentice-Hall.

Ebel, R. L., & Williams, B. J. (1957). The effect of varying the number of alternatives per item on multiple-choice vocabulary test items. *The Fourteenth Yearbook.* Washington, DC: National Council on Measurement in Education.

Embretsen, S. (1985). Multicomponent latent trait models for test design. In S. E. Embretsen (Ed.), *Test design: Developments in psychology and psychometrics* (pp. 195-218). Orlando, FL: Academic Press.

FairTest Examiner. (1987). *1,* 1-16.

FairTest Examiner. (1988). *2,* 1-16.

Farr, R., Pritchard, R., & Smitten, B. (1990). A description of what happens when an examinee takes a multiple-choice reading comprehension test. *Journal of Educational Measurement, 27,* 209-226.

Fischer, G. H. (1983). Logistic latent trait models with linear constraints. *Psychometrika, 48,* 3-26.

Fiske, E. B. (1990, January 31). But is the child learning? Schools trying new tests. *The New York Times,* pp. 1, B6.

Fitzpatrick, A. R. (1981). The meaning of content validity. *Applied Psychological Measurement, 7,* 3-13.

Frary, R. B. (1993). Statistical detection of multiple-choice test answer copying: Review and commentary. *Applied Measurement in Education, 6*, 153-165.

Frederiksen, N. (1984). The real test bias. Influences of testing on teaching and learning. *American Psychologist, 39*, 193-202.

Frederiksen, N., Mislevy, R. J., & Bejar, I. (Eds.). (1993). *Test theory for a new generation of tests*. Hillsdale, NJ: Lawrence Erlbaum Associates.

Frisbie, D. A. (1973). Multiple-choice versus true false: A comparison of reliabilities and concurrent validities. *Journal of Educational Measurement, 10*, 297-304.

Frisbie, D. A. (1981). The relative difficulty ratio- A test and item index. *Educational and Psychological Measurement, 41*, 333-339.

Frisbie, D. A. (1992). The status of multiple true-false testing. *Educational Measurement: Issues and Practices, 5*, 21-26.

Frisbie, D. A., & Becker, D. F. (1991). An analysis of textbook advice about true-false tests. *Applied Measurement in Education, 4*, 67-83.

Frisbie, D. A., & Druva, C. A. (1986). Estimating the reliability of multiple-choice true-false tests. *Journal of Educational Measurement, 23*, 99-106.

Frisbie, D. A., Miranda, D. U., & Baker, K. K. (1993). An evaluation of elementary textbook tests as classroom assessment tools. *Applied Measurement in Education, 6*, 21-36.

Frisbie, D. A., & Sweeney, D. C. (1982). The relative merits of multiple true-false achievement tests. *Journal of Educational Measurement, 19*, 29-35.

Gagne, R. M. (1968). Learning hierarchies. *Educational Psychologist, 6*, 1-9.

Gardner, H. (1985). *Frames of mind: The theory of multiple intelligences*. New York: Basic Books.

Gardner, H. (1986). *The mind's new science: A history of the cognitive revolution*. New York: Basic Books.

Gardner, H., & Hatch, T. (1989). Multiple intelligences go to school. *Educational Researcher, 18*, 4-10.

Gay, L. (1980). The comparative effects of multiple-choice versus open-ended on retention. *Journal of Educational Measurement, 17*, 45-50.

Glaser, R. (1993, April). *Criterion-referenced tests: Origins and unfinished business*. In *Criterion-referenced measurement: A 30-year retrospective*. Symposium conducted at the annual meeting of the American Educational Research Association, Atlanta.

Gorsuch, R. L. (1983). *Factor analysis* (2nd ed.). Hillsdale, NJ: Lawrence Erlbaum Associates.

Green, K. E., & Smith, R. M. (1987). A comparison of two methods of decomposing item difficulties. *Journal of Educational Statistics, 12*, 369-381.

Green, S. B., Halpin, G., & Halpin, G. W. (1990, April). *The emphasis on rote memory items on classroom tests: Why are teachers so interested in hearing their own lectures*. Paper presented at the annual meeting of the National Council on Measurement in Education, Boston.

Greeno, J. G. (1980). Some examples of cognitive task analysis with instructional implications. In R. E. Snow, P-A. Federico, & W. E. Montague (Eds.), *Aptitude, learning, and instruction: Vol. 2. Cognitive process analyses of learning and problem solving.* Hillsdale, NJ: Lawrence Erlbaum Associates.

Grosse, M., & Wright, B. D. (1985). Validity and reliability of true-false tests. *Educational and Psychological Measurement, 45*, 1-13.

Guilford, J. P. (1967). *The nature of human intelligence.* New York: McGraw-Hill.

Guttman, L. (1941). The quantification of a class of attributes: A theory and method of scale construction. In P. Horst (Ed.), *Prediction of personal adjustment* (pp. 321-345). (Social Science Research Bulletin 48).

Haertel, E. (1986). The valid use of student performance measures for teacher evaluation. *Educational Evaluation and Policy Analysis, 8*, 45-60.

Haertel, E. H., & Wiley, D. E. (1993). Representations of ability structures: Implications for testing. In N. Frederiksen, R. J. Mislevy, & I. Bejar (Eds.), *Test theory for a new generation of tests* (pp. 359-384). Hillsdale, NJ: Lawrence Erlbaum Associates.

Haladyna, T.M. (1974). Effects of different samples on item and test characteristics of criterion-referenced tests. *Journal of Educational Measurement, 11*, 93-100.

Haladyna, T. M. (1982). Two approaches to criterion-referenced program assessment. *Educational Technology, 23*, 467-470.

Haladyna, T. M. (1991). Generic questioning strategies for linking teaching and testing. *Educational Technology: Research and Development, 39*, 73-81.

Haladyna, T. M. (1992a). Context dependent item sets. *Educational Measurement: Issues and Practices, 11*, 21-25.

Haladyna, T. M. (1992b). The effectiveness of several multiple-choice formats. *Applied Measurement in Education, 5*, 73-88.

Haladyna, T. M., & Crehan, K. D. (1993, April). *Validating item responses.* Paper presented at the annual meeting of the American Educational Research Association, Atlanta.

Haladyna, T. M., & Downing, S. M. (1989a). A taxonomy of multiple-choice item-writing rules. *Applied Measurement in Education, 1*, 37-50.

Haladyna, T. M., & Downing, S. M. (1989b). The validity of a taxonomy of multiple-choice item-writing rules. *Applied Measurement in Education, 1*, 51-78.

Haladyna, T. M., & Downing, S. M. (in press). How many options is enough for a multiple-choice test item. *Educational & Psychological Measurement.*

Haladyna, T. M., Nolen, S. B., & Haas, N. S. (1991). Raising standardized achievement test scores and the origins of test score pollution. *Educational Researcher, 20*, 2-7.

Haladyna, T.M., & Roid, G.H. (1981). The role of instructional sensitivity in the empirical review of criterion-referenced test items. *Journal of Educational Measurement, 18*, 39-53.

Haladyna, T. M., & Shindoll, R. R. (1989). Item shells: A method for writing effective multiple-choice test items. *Evaluation and the Health Professions, 12*, 97-104.

Haladyna, T. M., & Sympson, J. B. (1988, April). Empirically based polychotomous scoring of multiple-choice test items: A review. In *New Development in Polychotomous Scoring*. Symposium conducted at the annual meeting of the American Educational Research Association, New Orleans.

Hambleton, R. K. (1984). Validating the test scores. In R. A. Berk (Ed.), *A guide to criterion-referenced test construction* (pp. 199-230). Baltimore: Johns Hopkins University Press.

Hambleton, R. K., & Jones, R. W. (1993). Comparison of classical test theory and item response theory and their applications to test development. *Educational Measurement: Issues and Practices, 12*, 38-46.

Hambleton, R. K., & Swaminathan, H. (1987). *Item response theory: Principles and applications*. Boston: Kluwer-Nijhoff Publishing.

Hancock, G. R. (1992, April). *Impact of item complexity on the comparability of multiple-choice and constructed-response test formats*. Paper presented at the annual meeting of the American Educational Research Association, San Francisco.

Hancock, G. R., Thiede, K. W., & Sax, G. (1992, April). *Reliability of comparably written two-option multiple-choice and true-false test items*. Paper presented at the annual meeting of the National Council on Measurement in Education, Chicago.

Harnisch, D. L. (1983). Item response patterns: Applications for educational practice. *Journal of Educational Measurement, 20*, 191-206.

Harnisch, D. L., & Linn, R. L. (1981). Analysis of item response patterns: Questionable test data and dissimilar curriculum practices. *Journal of Educational Measurement, 18*, 133-146.

Hattie, J. A. (1985). Methodological review: Assessing unidimensionality of tests and items. *Applied Psychological Measurement, 9*, 139-164.

Heim, A. W., & Watts, K. P. (1967). An experiment on multiple-choice versus open-ended answering in a vocabulary test. *British Journal of Educational Psychology, 37*, 339-346.

Henrysson, S. (1971). Analyzing the test item. In R. L. Thorndike (Ed.) *Educational Measurement* (2nd ed., pp. 130-159) Washington, DC: American Council on Education.

Herbig, M. (1976). Item analysis by use in pre-test and post-test: A comparison of different coefficients. *PLET, 13*, 49-54.

Hess, R. (1994, April). *Using the Rasch model to calibrate a district-wide, curriculum-based mathematics assessment*. Paper presented at the annual meeting of the American Educational Research Association, New Orleans.

Hill, G. C., & Woods, G. T. (1974). Multiple true-false questions. *Education in Chemistry, 11*, 86-87.

Hill, K., & Wigfield, A. (1984). Test anxiety: A major educational problem and what can be done about it. *The Elementary School Journal, 85*, 105-126.

Hoffman, B. (1964). *Tyranny of testing*. New York: Collier.

Hogan, T. P., & Mishler, C. (1980). Relationship between essay tests and objective tests of language skills for elementary school students. *Journal of Educational Measurement, 17,* 219-228.

Holland, P. W., & Thayer, D. T. (1988). Differential item performance and the Mantel-Haenzel procedure. In H. Wainer & H. Braun (Eds.), *Test validity* (pp. 129-145). Hillsdale, NJ: Lawrence Erlbaum Associates.

Holland, P. W., & Wainer, H. (Eds.). (1993). *Differential item functioning.* Hillsdale, NJ: Lawrence Erlbaum Associates.

House, E. R. (1991). Big policy, little policy. *Educational Researcher, 20,* 21-26.

Hsu, L. M. (1980). Dependence of the relative difficulty of true-false and grouped true-false tests on the ability levels of examinees. *Educational and Psychological Measurement, 40,* 891-894.

Hughes, D. C., Keeling, B., & Tuck, B. F. (1983). Effects of achievement expectations and handwriting quality on scoring essays. *Journal of Educational Measurement, 20,* 65-70.

Hubbard, J. P. (1978). *Measuring medical education: The tests and the experience of the National Board of Medical Examiners* (2nd ed.). Philadelphia: Lea & Febiger.

Hulin, C. L., Drasgow, F., and Parsons, C. K. (1983). *Item response theory: Application to psychological measurement.* Homewood, IL: Dow Jones-Irwin.

Jacobs, P. I., & Vandeventer, M. (1970). Information in wrong responses. *Psychological Reports, 26,* 311-315.

Jannarone, R. J. (1988). Conjunctive measurement theory: Cognitive research prospects. *Center for Machine Intelligence* (USCMI Report No. 88-12). Columbia, SC: University of South Carolina.

Jensen, A. R. (1980). *Bias in mental testing.* New York: Free Press.

Joorabchi, B., & Chawhan, A. R. (1975). Multiple-choice questions- the debate goes on. *British Journal of Medical Education, 9,* 275-280.

Kane, M. T. (1982). The validity of licensure examinations. *American Psychologist, 7,* 911-918.

Keller, F. S. (1968). Goodbye teacher . . . *Journal of Applied Behavior Analysis, 1,* 79-89.

Kintsch, W. (1970). Models for free recall and recognition. In D. A. Norman (Ed.), *Models of human memory* (pp. 313-373). New York: Academic Press.

LaDuca, A. (in press). Validation of a professional licensure examinations: Professions theory, test design, and construct validity. *Evaluation in the Health Professions.*

LaDuca, A., & Downing, S. M. (in press). Test development: Systematic item writing and test construction. In J. C. Impara & J. C. Fortune (Eds.), *Licensure examinations.* Lincoln, NE: Buros Institute of Mental Measurements.

LaDuca, A., Staples, W. I., Templeton, B., & Holzman, G. B. (1986). Item modelling procedure for constructing content-equivalent multiple-choice questions. *Medical Education, 20,* 53-56.

Leinhardt, G., & Seewald, A. M. (1980, April). *Overlap: What's tested, what's taught?* Paper presented at the annual meeting of the American Educational Research Association, Boston.

Levine H. G., & McGuire, C. H. (1971). *Journal of Medical Education, 46,* 78-85.

Levine, H. G., McGuire, C. H., & Natress, L. W., Jr. (1970). The validity of multiple-choice achievement tests as measures of competence in medicine. *American Educational Research Journal, 7*, 69-82.

Levine, M. V., & Drasgow, F. (1982). Appropriateness measurement: Review, critique, and validating studies. *British Journal of Educational Psychology, 35*, 42-56.

Levine, M. V., & Drasgow, F. (1983). The relation between incorrect option choice and estimated ability. *Educational and Psychological Measurement, 43*, 675-685.

Levine, M. V., & Drasgow, F. (1988). Optimal appropriateness measurement. *Psychometrika, 53*, 161-176.

Lewis, J. C., & Hoover, H. D. (1981, April). *The effect of pupil performance from using hand-held calculators during standardized mathematics achievement tests.* Paper presented at the annual meeting of the National Council on Measurement in Education, Los Angeles.

Linacre, J. M., & Wright, B. D. (1993). *FACETS: Computer program for many-faceted Rasch measurement.* {Computer Software}. Chicago: MESA Press.

Lindquist, E. F. (Ed.) (1951). *Educational Measurement* (1st ed.). Washington, DC: American Council on Education.

Linn, R. L. (1983). Curricular validity: Convincing the court that it was taught without precluding the possibility of measuring it. In G. F. Madaus (Ed.), *The court, validity, and minimum competency testing* (pp. 115-132). Boston: Kluwer-Nijhoff.

Linn, R. L. (Ed.). (1989). *Educational measurement* (3rd ed.). New York: American Council on Education and Macmillan.

Linn, R. L. (1990a). Admission testing: Recommended uses, validity, differential predicting, and coaching. *Applied Measurement in Education, 3*, 297-318,

Linn, R. L. (1990b). Has item response theory increased the validity of achievement test scores? *Applied Measurement in Education, 3*, 143-166.

Linn, R. L., & Harnisch, D. L. (1981). Interactions between item content and group membership on achievement test items. *Journal of Educational Measurement, 18*, 109-118.

Lohman, D. F., & Ippel, M. J. (1993). Cognitive diagnosis: From statistically based assessment toward theory-based assessment. In N. Frederiksen, R. J. Mislevy, & I. Bejar (Eds.), *Test theory for a new generation of tests* (pp. 41-71). Hillsdale, NJ: Lawrence Erlbaum Associates.

Lord, F. M. (1958). Some relations between Guttman's principal components of scale analysis and other psychometric theory. *Psychometrika, 23*, 291-296.

Lord, F. M. (1980). *Applications of item response theory to practical testing problems.* Hillsdale, NJ: Lawrence Erlbaum Associates.

Lord, F. M. (1977). Optimal number of choices per item-A comparison of four approaches. *Journal of Educational Measurement, 14*, 33-38.

Loyd, B. H. (1991). Mathematics test performance: The effects of item type and calculator use. *Applied Measurement in Education, 4*, 11-22.

Lukhele, R., Thissen, D., & Wainer, H. (1992, April). *On the relative value of multiple-choice, constructed-response, and examinee-selected items on two achievement tests.* Paper presented at the annual meeting of the American Educational Research Association, San Francisco.

MacIntosh, H. G., & Morrison, R. B. (1969). *Objective testing.* London: University of London Press.

Maihoff, N. A., & Mehrens, W. A. (1985, April). *A comparison of alternate-choice and true-false item forms used in classroom examinations.* Paper presented at the annual meeting of the National Council on Measurement in Education, Chicago.

Maihoff, N. A., & Phillips, E. R. (1988, April). *A comparison of multiple-choice and alternate-choice item forms on classroom tests.* Paper presented at the annual meeting of the National Council on Measurement in Education, San Francisco.

Mantel, N., & Haenszel, W. (1959). Statistical aspects of the analysis of data from retrospective studies of disease. *Journal of the National Cancer Institute, 22,* 719-748.

Markle, S. M., & Tiemann, P. W. (1970). *Really understanding concepts.* Champaign, IL: Stipes.

Marshall, S. R. (1990, April). *What students learn (and remember) from word problem instruction.* In *Penetrating to the Mathematical Structure of Word Problems.* Symposium conducted at the annual meeting of the American Educational Research Association, Boston.

Martinez, M. E. (1990). A comparison of multiple-choice and constructed figural response items. *Journal of Educational Measurement, 28,* 131-145.

Martinez, M. E. (1993). Cognitive processing requirements of constructed figural response and multiple-choice items in architecture assessment. *Applied Measurement in Education, 6.* 167-180.

Masters, G. N. (1982). A Rasch model for partial credit scoring. *Psychometrika, 47,* 149-174.

McGill-Franzen, A., & Allington, R. L. (1993). Flunk'em or get them classified—The contamination of primary grade accountability data. *Educational Researcher, 22,* 19-22.

Mehrens, W. A., & Kaminski, J. (1989). Methods for improving a standardized test scores: Fruitful, fruitless, or fraudulent? *Educational Measurement: Issues and Practices, 8,* 14-22.

Mehrens, W. A., & Phillips, S. E. (1986). Detecting impacts of curricular differences in achievement test data. *Journal of Educational Measurement, 23,* 185-196.

Mehrens, W. A., & Phillips, S. E. (1987). Sensitivity of item difficulties to curricular validity. *Journal of Educational Measurement, 24,* 357-370.

Merrill, M. D., Reigeluth, C. M., & Faust, G. W. (1979). The instructional quality profile: A curriculum evaluation and design tool. In H. F. O'Neill, Jr. (Ed.), *Procedures for instructional systems development.* New York: Academic Press.

Messick, S. (1975). The standard problem: Meaning and values in measurement and evaluation. *American Psychologist, 30,* 955-966.

Messick, S. (1984). The psychology of educational measurement. *Journal of Educational Measurement, 21*, 215-237.

Messick, S. (1989). Validity. In R. L. Linn (Ed.), *Educational measurement* (3rd ed., pp. 13-104). New York: American Council on Education and Macmillan.

Miller, H., & Williams, R. G. (1973). Constructing higher level multiple choice questions covering factual content. *Educational Technology, 13*, 39-42.

Miller, H., Williams, R. G., & Haladyna, T. M. (1978). *Beyond facts: Objective ways to measure thinking.* Englewood Cliffs, NJ: Educational Technology.

Miller, T., & Spray, J. A. (1993). Logistic discriminant function analysis for DIF identification of polytomously scored items. *Journal of Educational Measurement, 30*, 107-122.

Miller, W. G., Snowman, J., & O'Hara, T. (1979). Application of alternative statistical techniques to examine the hierarchical ordering in Bloom's taxonomy. *American Educational Research Journal, 16*, 241-248.

Millman, J. (1974). Sampling plans for domain-referenced tests. *Educational Technology, 14*, 17-21.

Millman, J., & Greene, J. (1989). The specification and development of tests of achievement and ability. In R. L. Linn (Ed.), *Educational measurement* (3rd ed., pp. 335-366). New York: American Council on Education and Macmillan.

Millman, J., & Westman, R. S. (1989). Computer-assisted writing of achievement test items: Toward a future technology. *Journal of Educational Measurement, 26*, 177-190.

Mislevy, R. J. (1993a). Foundations of a new test theory. In N. Frederiksen, R. J. Mislevy, & I. Bejar (Eds.) *Test theory for a new generation of tests*, pp. 19-39. Hillsdale, NJ: Lawrence Erlbaum Associates.

Mislevy, R. J. (1993b, April). *Test theory reconceived.* A revised version of a paper presented at the annual meeting of the National Council on Measurement in Education, Atlanta.

Mislevy, R. J., & Bock, R. D. (1990). *BILOG 3: Item analysis and test scoring with binary logistic models.* {Computer Software}. Chicago: Scientific Software.

Moss, P. A., Cole, N. S., & Khampalikit, C. (1982). A comparison of procedures to assess written language skills at grades 4, 7, and 10. *Journal of Educational Measurement, 19*, 37-48.

Muraki, E., Mislevy, R. J., & Bock, R. D. (1992). *BIMAIN.* {Computer Software}. Chicago, Scientific Software.

Muraki, E., & Bock, R. D. (1993). *PARSCALE: IRT based test scoring and item analysis for graded open-ended exercises and performance tests.* {Computer Software}. Chicago: Scientific Software.

National Commission on Educational Excellence (1983). *A nation at risk.* Washington, DC: U.S. Government Printing Office.

National Council of Teachers of Mathematics (1989). *Curriculum and evaluation standards for school mathematics.* Reston, VA: NCTM.

Nickerson, R. S. (1989). New directions in educational assessment. *Educational Researcher, 18*, 3-7.

Nishisato, S. (1980). *Analysis of categorical data: Dual scaling and its applications.* Toronto, Canada: University of Toronto.

Nitko, A. J. (1985). {Review of Roid and Haladyna's *A technology for test item writing*}. *Journal of Educational Measurement, 21,* 201-204.

Nitko, A. J. (1989). Designing tests that are integrated with instruction. In R. L. Linn (Ed.), *Educational measurement* (3rd ed., pp. 447-474). New York: American Council on Education and Macmillan.

Noggle, N. (1987). *Report on the match of standardized tests to the Arizona Essential Skills.* Tempe, AZ: College of Education School Personnel Evaluation and Learning Laboratory.

Nolen, S. B., Haladyna, T. M., & Haas, N. S. (1992). Uses and abuses of achievement test scores. *Educational Measurement: Issues and Practices, 11,* 915.

Norcini, J. J., Swanson, D. B., Grosso, L. J., & Webster, G. D. (undated). *A comparison of knowledge, synthesis, and clinical judgment multiple-choice questions in the assessment of physician competence.* Philadelphia: American Board of Internal Medicine.

Norris, S. P. (1990). Effects of eliciting verbal reports of thinking on critical thinking test performance. *Journal of Educational Measurement, 27,* 41-58.

Nunnally, J. C. (1967). *Psychometric theory.* New York: McGraw-Hill.

O'Neill, K. (1986, April). *The effect of stylistic changes on item performance.* Paper presented at the annual meeting of the American Educational Research Association, San Francisco.

Oosterhof, A. C., & Coats, P. K. (1984). Comparison of difficulties and reliabilities of quantitative word problems in completion and multiple-choice item formats. *Applied Psychological Measurement, 8,* 287-294.

Oosterhof, A. C., & Glasnapp, D. R. (1974). Comparative reliabilities and difficulties of the multiple-choice and true-false formats. *The Journal of Experimental Education, 42,* 62-64.

Osterlind, S. J. (1989). *Constructing test items.* Boston: Kluwer Academic Publishers.

Owen, D. (1985). *None of the above.* Boston: Houghton Mifflin.

Paris, S. G., Lawton, T. A., Turner, J. C., & Roth, J. L. (1991). A developmental perspective on standardized achievement testing. *Educational Researcher, 20,* 2-7.

Patterson, D. G. (1926). Do new and old type examinations measure different mental functions? *School and Society, 24,* 246-248.

Peterson, C. C., & Peterson, J. L. (1976). Linguistic determinants of the difficulty of true-false test items. *Educational and Psychological Measurement, 36,* 161-164.

Phillips, S. E., & Mehrens, W. A. (1987). Curricular differences and unidimensionality of achievement test data: An exploratory analysis. *Journal of Educational Measurement, 24,* 1-16.

Poe, N., Johnson, S., & Barkanic, G. (1992, April). *A reassessment of the effect of calculator use in the performance of students taking a test of mathematics applications.* Paper presented at the annual meeting of the National Council on Measurement in Education, San Francisco.

Popham, W. J. (1993). Appropriate expectations for content judgments regarding teacher licensure tests. *Applied Measurement in Education, 5*, 285-301.

Prawat, R. S. (1993). The value of ideas: Problems versus possibilities in learning. *Educational Researcher, 22*, 5-16.

Roberts, D. M. (1993). An empirical study on the nature of trick questions. *Journal of Educational Measurement, 30*, 331-344.

Roid, G. H., & Haladyna, T. M. (1978). The use of domains and item forms in the formative evaluation of instructional materials. *Educational and Psychological Measurement, 38*, 19-28.

Roid, G. H., & Haladyna, T. M. (1982). *Toward a technology of test-item writing.* New York: Academic Press.

Rosenbaum, P. R. (1988). Item bundles. *Psychometrika, 53*, 63-75.

Rovinelli, R. J., & Hambleton, R. K. (1977). On the use of content specialists in the assessment of criterion-referenced test item validity. *Dutch Journal of Educational Research, 2*, 49-60.

Royer, J. M., Cisero, C. A., & Carlo, M. S. (1993). Techniques and procedures for assessing cognitive skills. *Review of Educational Research, 63*, 201-243.

Ruch, G. M., & Charles, J. W. (1928). A comparison of five types of objective tests in elementary psychology. *Journal of Applied Psychology, 12*, 398-403.

Ruch, G. M., & Stoddard, G. D. (1925). Comparative reliabilities of objective examinations. *Journal of Educational Psychology, 12*, 89-103.

Ryan, K. E. (1993, April). *A comparison of the single right answer format and the multiple answer format with one correct answer: Is there a one right answer mentality?* Paper presented at the annual meeting of the National Council on Measurement in Education, Atlanta.

Samejima, F. (1979). *A new family of models for the multiple-choice item.* (Office of Naval Research Report 79-4). Knoxville, TN: University of Tennessee.

Sanders, N. M. (1966). *Classroom questions. What kinds?* New York: Harper & Row.

Sato, T. (1975). *The construction and interpretation of S-P tables.* Tokyo: Meiji Tosho.

Sato, T. (1980). *The S-P chart and the caution index.* Computer and Communications Systems Research Laboratories. Tokyo: Nippon Electronic Company Limited.

Sax, G., & Reiter, P. B. (undated). *Reliability and validity of two-option multiple-choice and comparably written true-false items.* Seattle: University of Washington.

Seddon, G. M. (1978). The properties of Bloom's taxonomy of educational objectives for the cognitive domain. *Review of Educational Research, 48*, 303-323.

Shahabi, S., & Yang, L. (1990, April). *A comparison between two variations of multiple-choice items and their effects on difficulty and discrimination values.* Paper presented at the annual meeting of the National Council on Measurement in Education, Boston.

Shapiro, M. M., Stutsky, M. H., & Watt, R. F. (1989). Minimizing unnecessary differences in occupational testing. *Valparaiso Law Review, 23*, 213-265.

Shavelson, R. J., Baxter, G. P., & Pine, J. (1992). Performance assessments: Political rhetoric and measurement reality. *Educational Researcher, 21*, 22-27.

Shea, J. A., Poniatowski, P. A., Day, S. C., Langdon, L. O., LaDuca, A., & Norcini, J. J. (1992). An adaption of item modeling for developing test-item banks. *Teaching and Learning in Medicine, 4,* 19-24.

Shepard, L. A. (1991). Psychometrician's beliefs about learning. *Educational Researcher, 20,* 2-9.

Shepard, L. A. (1993). The place of testing reform in educational reform—A reply to Cizek. *Educational Researcher, 22,* 10-13.

Sherman, S. W. (1976, April). *Multiple-choice test bias uncovered by the use of an "I don't know" alternative.* Paper presented at the annual meeting of the American Educational Research Association, Chicago.

Sireci, S. G., Thissen, D., & Wainer, H. (1991). On the reliability of testlet-based tests. *Journal of Educational Measurement, 28,* 237-247.

Sirotnik, K. (1980). Psychometric implication of the unit-of-analysis problem (with examples from the measurement of organizational climate). *Journal of Educational Measurement, 17,* 245-282.

Skakun, E. N., & Gartner, D. (1990, April). *The use of deadly, dangerous, and ordinary items on an emergency medical technicians-ambulance registration examination.* Paper presented at the annual meeting of the American Educational Research Association, Boston.

Slogoff, S., & Hughes, F. P. (1987). Validity of scoring "dangerous answers" on a written certification examination. *Journal of Medical Education, 62,* 625-631.

Smith, J. K., & Smith, M. R. (1984, April). *The influence of item format on measures of reading comprehension.* Paper presented at the annual meeting of the American Educational Research Association, New Orleans.

Smith, M. L. (1991). Put to the test: The effects of external testing on teachers. *Educational Researcher, 20,* 8-11.

Smith, R. (1986, April). *Developing vocabulary items to fit a polytomous scoring model.* Paper presented at the annual meeting of the American Educational Research Association, San Francisco.

Smith, R. M. (1993). *Item and person analysis with the Rasch Model (IPARM).* {A computer program and manual}. Chicago: MESA Press.

Smith, R. M., & Kramer, G. A. (1990, April). *An investigation of components influencing the difficulty of form-development items.* Paper presented at the annual meeting of the National Council on Measurement in Education, Boston.

Smith, R. M., Kramer, G. A., & Kubiak, A. T. (1990). Frequency of measurement disturbances in the Dental Admissions Test. *Journal of Dental Education, 54,* 314-318.

Snow, R. E. (1989). Toward assessment of cognitive and conative structures in learning. *Educational Researcher, 18,* 8-14.

Snow, R. E. (1993). Construct validity and constructed-response tests. In R. E. Bennett & W. C. Ward (Eds.), *Construction versus choice in cognitive measurement: Issues in constructed response, performance testing, and portfolio assessment* (pp. 45-60). Hillsdale, NJ: Lawrence Erlbaum Associates.

Snow, R. E., & Lohman, D. F. (1989). Implications of cognitive psychology for educational measurement. In R. L. Linn (Ed.), *Educational measurement* (3rd ed., 263-332). New York: American Council on Education and Macmillan.

Spady, W. G. (1977). Competency-based education: A bandwagon in search of a definition. *Educational Researcher, 6*, 9-14.

Statman, S. (1988). Ask a clear question and get a clear answer: An enquiry into the question/ answer and the sentence completion formats of multiple-choice items. *System, 16*, 367-376.

Sternberg, R. J. (1977). *Intelligence, information processing, and analogical reasoning: The componential analysis of human abilities.* Hillsdale, NJ: Lawrence Erlbaum Associates.

Sternberg, R. J. (1985). *Beyond IQ: A triarchic theory of human intelligence.* New York: Cambridge University Press.

Stiggins, R. J., Griswold, M. M., & Wikelund, K. R. (1989). Measuring thinking skills through classroom assessment. *Journal of Educational Measurement, 26*, 233-246.

Subhiyah, R. G., & Downing, S. M. (1993, April). *K-type and A-type items: IRT comparisons of psychometric characteristics in a certification examination.* Paper presented at the annual meeting of the National Council on Measurement in Education, Atlanta.

Swaminathan, H., & Rogers, J. (1990). Detecting differential item functioning using logistic regression procedures. *Journal of Educational Measurement, 27*, 361-370.

Sympson, J. B. (1983, August). *A new item response theory model for calibrating multiple-choice items.* Paper presented at the annual meeting of the Psychometric Society, Los Angeles.

Sympson, J. B. (1986, April). *Extracting information from wrong answers in computerized adaptive testing.* In *New Developments in Computerized Adaptive Testing.* Symposium conducted at the annual meeting of the American Psychological Association, Washington, DC.

Sympson, J. B. (1990). *POLY: A program for polychotomous item analysis and scoring.* {Computer Software}. San Diego: Navy Personnel Research and Development Center.

Tatsuoka, K. K. (1985). Rule space: An approach for dealing with misconceptions based on item response theory. *Journal of Educational Measurement, 20*, 345-354.

Tatsuoka, K. K. (1990). Toward an integration of item response theory and cognitive error diagnosis. In N. Frederiksen, R. Glaser, A. Lesgold, & M. G. Shafto (Eds.), *Diagnostic monitoring of skill and knowledge acquisition* (pp. 453-488). Hillsdale, NJ: Lawrence Erlbaum Associates.

Tatsuoka, K. K., & Linn, R. L. (1983). Indices for detecting unusual patterns: Links between two general approaches and potential applications. *Applied Psychological Measurement, 7*, 81-96.

Technical Staff (1933). *Manual of examination methods* (1st ed.). Chicago: The Board of Examinations of the University of Chicago.

Technical Staff (1937). *Manual of examination methods* (2nd ed.). Chicago: The Board of Examinations of the University of Chicago.

Terman, L. M., & Oden, M. (1959). *The gifted group at mid-life*. Sanford, CA: Sanford University Press.

Thiede, K. W., Klockars, A. J., & Hancock, G. R. (1991, April). *Recognition versus recall test formats: A correlational analysis*. Paper presented at the annual meeting of the National Council on Measurement in Education, Chicago.

Thissen, D. M. (1976). Information in wrong responses to the Raven Progressive Matrices. *Journal of Educational Measurement, 14*, 201-214.

Thissen, D. (1991). *MULTILOG. Version 6.0*. {Computer Program}. Chicago: Scientific Software.

Thissen, D. (1993). Repealing the rules that no longer apply to psychological measurement. In N. Frederiksen, R. J. Mislevy, & I. Bejar (Eds.), *Test theory for a new generation of tests* (pp. 79-97). Hillsdale, NJ: Lawrence Erlbaum Associates.

Thissen, D., & Steinberg, L. (1984). A response model for multiple-choice items. *Psychometrika, 49*, 501-519.

Thissen, D., & Steinberg, L. (1986). A taxonomy of item response models. *Psychometrika, 51*, 566-577.

Thissen, D., Steinberg, L., & Fitzpatrick, A. R. (1989). Multiple-choice models: The distractors are also part of the item. *Journal of Educational Measurement, 26*, 161-175.

Thissen, D., Steinberg, L., & Mooney, J. A. (1989). Trace lines for testlets: A use of multiple-categorical-response models. *Journal of Educational Measurement, 26*, 247-260.

Thorndike, R. L. (1967). The analysis and selection of test items. In S. Messick & D. Jackson (Eds.), *Problems in human assessment*. New York: McGraw-Hill.

Thorndike, R. L. (Ed.). (1970). *Educational measurement* (2nd ed.). Washington, DC: American Council on Education.

Thurstone, L. L. (1938). *Primary Mental Abilities*. Chicago: University of Chicago Press. (Reprinted in 1968 by the Psychometric Society).

Toch, T. (1991). *In the name of excellence: The struggle to reform the nation's schools, why it's failing, and what should be done*. New York: Oxford Press.

Traub, R. E. (1993). On the equivalence of traits assessed by multiple-choice and constructed-response tests. In R. E. Bennett & W. C. Ward (Eds.), *Construction versus choice in cognitive measurement: Issues in constructed response, performance testing, and portfolio assessment* (pp. 1-27). Hillsdale, NJ: Lawrence Erlbaum Associates.

Traub, R. E., & Fisher, C. W. (1977). On the equivalence of constructed response and multiple-choice tests. *Applied Psychological Measurement, 1*, 355-370.

Trevisan, M. S., Sax, G., & Michael, W. B. (1991). The effects of the number of options per item and student ability on test validity and reliability. *Educational and Psychological Measurement, 51*, 829-837.

Wainer, H. (1989). The future of item analysis. *Journal of Educational Measurement, 26*, 191-208.

Wainer, H. (1992). Measurement problems. *Journal of Educational Measurement, 30*, 1-22.

Wainer, H., & Braun, H. I. (Ed.). (1988). *Validity*. Hillsdale, NJ: Lawrence Erlbaum Associates.

Wainer, H., & Kiely, G. (1987). Item clusters and computerized adaptive testing: A case for testlets. *Journal of Educational Measurement, 24*, 185-202.

Wainer, H., & Thissen, D. (1993). Combining multiple-choice and constructed response test scores: Toward a Marxist theory of test construction. *Applied Measurement in Education, 6*, 103-118.

Wang, M. D., & Stanley, J. C. (1970). Differential weighting: A review of methods and empirical studies. *Review of Educational Research, 40, 663-705.*

Ward, W. C. (1982). A comparison of free response and multiple-choice forms of verbal aptitude tests. *Applied Psychological Measurement, 6*, 1-11.

Ward, W. C., Frederiksen, N., & Carlson, S. B. (1980). Construct validity of free-response and machine scorable forms of a test. *Journal of Educational Measurement, 17*, 11-29.

Washington, W. N., & Godfrey, R. R. (1974). The effectiveness of illustrated items. *Journal of Educational Measurement, 11*, 121-124.

Webb, L. C., & Heck, W. L. (1991, April). *The effect of stylistic editing on item performance.* Paper presented at the annual meeting of the National Council on Measurement in Education, Chicago.

Wesman, A. G. (1971). Writing the test item. In R. L. Thorndike (Ed.) *Educational Measurement* (2nd ed., pp. 99-111). Washington, DC: American Council on Education.

What Works. (1985). Washington, DC: United States Office of Education.

Wiggins, G. (1989). Teaching to the (authentic) test. *Educational Leadership, 76*, 41-47.

Williams, B. J., & Ebel, R. L. (1957). The effect of varying the number of alternatives per item on multiple-choice vocabulary test items. *The 14th Yearbook of the National Council on Measurement in Education* (pp. 63-65).

Williams, R. G. (1977). A behavior typology of educational objectives for the cognitive domain. *Educational Technology, 17*, 39-46.

Williams, R. G., & Haladyna, T. M. (1982). Logical Operations for Generating Intended Questions (LOGIQ): A typology for higher level thinking test items. In G. H. Roid & T. M. Haladyna, *A technology for test-item writing.* New York: Academic Press.

Wilson, D. T., Wood, R., & Gibbons, R. (1992). *TESTFACT: Test scoring, item analysis, and full information or MINRES item factor analysis.* {Computer Software}. Chicago: Scientific Software.

Wilson, M. R. (1989). Saltus: A psychometric model of discontinuity in cognitive development. *Psychological Bulletin, 105*, 276-289.

Winne, P. H. (1979). Experiments relating teachers' use of higher cognitive questions to student achievement. *Review of Educational Research, 49*, 13-50.

Woods, R. (1977). Multiple-choice: A state of the art report. *Evaluation in Education: International Progress, 1*, 191-280

Wright, B. D. (1977). Solving measurement problems with the Rasch model. *Journal of Educational Measurement, 14*, 97-116.

Wright, B. D., & Linacre, J. M. (1992). *A User's Guide to BIGSTEPS-Rasch-Model Item Analysis and Scaling.* {Computer Software}. Chicago: MESA Press.

Wright, B. D., & Stone, M. H. (1979). *Best test design*. Chicago: MESA Press.

Wright, B. D., & Masters, G. N. (1982). *Rating scale analysis*. Chicago: MESA Press.

Yeh, J. P., Herman, J. L., & Rudner, L. M. (1981). *Teachers and testing: A survey of test use*. Center for the Study of Evaluation, University of California, Los Angeles. (ERIC Document 218 336).

Yoon, B., Burstein, L., Gold, K., Chen, Z., & Kim, K. (1990, April). *Validating teachers' reports of content coverage: An example from secondary school mathematics*. Paper presented at the annual meeting of the American Educational Research Association, Boston.

Zoref, L., & Williams, P. (1980). A look at content bias in IQ tests. *Journal of Educational Measurement, 17*, 313-322.

AUTHOR INDEX

219

SUBJECT INDEX

A

ability 4, 185
abstract thinking 9, 89
achievement x, 3, 4-5, 185
all of the above option 78
answer justification 138-140
appropriateness measurement 167-168
Ascal 147
authentic assessment xi, 7, 32, 183

B

behaviorism 5, 183
Bigsteps 148
Bilog 148
Bimain 148
binary scoring 146, 189, 197

C

calculators 52-53, 55
classical test theory 145, 186
cognitive psychology 183-185
competence 5
concept 48, 92, 115
construct validation xii, 3, 8-14, 90, 122, 138, 163, 187
    formulation 9, 11, 15, 190

explication 9, 11, 13, 15-16
    validation 13-14, 16-17
constructed-response xii, 14, 21, 23-24, 52, 80, 91, 192
correct answer 24, 35, 36
criterion-referenced 176, 185
critical thinking xi, 23, 91, 187

D

dangerous answers 56
defining 94-100, 112-113
developmental field test 138
differential item functioning 161-163
distractor analysis and evaluation 81-83, 153-159, 194, 195
    frequency table 154-155, 156
    statistical methods 155-157
    trace line 17, 157

E

editing 63, 131
essay 22, 28, 29, 33
evaluating 101-103, 112-113
Excel 156
expert judges content 174
explication 9, 11-13, 15-16